John Overall, William Sancroft

Bishop Overall's Convocation book MDCVI

Concerning the government of God's Catholick church and the kingdoms of the whole world

John Overall, William Sancroft

Bishop Overall's Convocation book MDCVI

Concerning the government of God's Catholick church and the kingdoms of the whole world

ISBN/EAN: 9783337274436

Printed in Europe, USA, Canada, Australia, Japan

Cover: Foto ©Lupo / pixelio.de

More available books at **www.hansebooks.com**

Bishop OVERALL's
Convocation-Book,
M DC VI.

Concerning the

GOVERNMENT
OF
God's *CATHOLICK CHURCH*,
AND THE
KINGDOMS
OF THE
Whole WORLD.

LONDON,
Printed for *Walter Kettilby*, at the *Bishop's Head* in
St. *Paul's* Church-Yard, 1 6 9 0.

AN
Advertisement
TO THE
READER.

THat Convocation *in which the* Acts *and* Canons (*now Printed*) *pass'd, was first* call'd An. 1603. 1ᵐᵒ Jac. *and continued by* Adjournments *and* Prorogations *to* 1610.

The Three *following* Books *are publish'd from a Copy carefully and faithfully transcribed from the* Original MS. *which was* Bishop Overall's, *and drawn up by him; after whose Decease, it came into the Possession of* Dʳ John Cosin, *sometime*

A 3 *his*

To the READER.

his Secretary, and after Lord Bishop *of* Duresm, *who bequeathed it, with other his Books, both Printed and Manuscript, to the Publick Library, by him founded, at* Duresm, *for the use of that* Church, *where (it is suppos'd) it is yet to be seen.*

The First *of these Three Books was also heedfully compar'd, and in some casual defects, supply'd from another* MS. *which from the Attestation of Archbishop* Bancroft *(who there presided) at the end thereof, under his own hand, seems to have been the* Original, *that then pass'd the* Upper-House *of Convocation; And after his Decease, it came to his Successors the Archbishops of* Canterbury. *And among them, to Archbishop* Laud, *as appears under his own hand-writing, in the last Page of it. And is now, or was lately, in the Possession of* Dr Barlow, *the present Lord Bishop of* Lincoln.

In

To the READER.

In the First *and* Second *of these* Books, *there were several* Amendments *made by the* Upper-House *of Convocation; all placed at the end of Bishop* Overall's MS. *and according to such* Amendments, *inserted in their proper places, is the following Book Printed.*

Note,

Reverendus in Christo Pater D.D. Johannes Overall, Decanus quondam Paulinus, deinde Episcopus Coventrien= sis postremò Norvicensis.

[1]
Bishop OVERALL's
CONVOCATION-BOOK, 1606.
CONCERNING
The Government of God's Catholick Church, and the Kingdoms of the whole WORLD.

LIB. I. CAP. I.

Amongst those Attributes, and Names of God, which are common in the Scripture to all the blessed Trinity, are these, To be the *Creator, and Governour of the World, the Lord of lords, and King of kings,* which be there applied as well to the Son of God, our Lord *Jesus Christ,* the second Person in the sacred Trinity, as to God the Father, and God the Holy Ghost. Agreeably whereunto, and not otherwise, our chief purpose being to imitate the Scriptures, in setting out, and describing the Deity, and Dignity of our Saviour Christ, by his Almighty Power, and universal Government of all the World, as Heir of all things, and Head of his Church; we hold it fit to begin with his Divine Power of Creation: and thereupon in the sense aforesaid do affirm, That *He* in the beginning did create both Heaven and Earth; and that amongst the rest of the Creatures, which he then made, he Created our first Parents, *Adam* and *Eve,* from whose Loins Mankind is descended.

1 Tim. 6. 15.
Apocal. 19. 16.
Joh. 1. 2, 10.
Hebr. 1. 3, 10.
Coloss. 1. 16.
Prov. 8.

Placet eis.

B   CAN.

CANON I.

If any Man therefore shall affirm with any Pagan, Heretick, Atheist, or any other profane Persons, which know not, or believe not the Scriptures, either that Heaven and Earth had no beginning; or that the World was made by Angels, or the Devil; that the World was not otherwise made by Christ, than as he was an Instrument of God the Father for the making of it; or that he did not as God, create our said Parents, Adam and Eve; he doth greatly Erre.

Placet eis.

ii. p. in MS.

CAP. II.

TO him, that shall duly read the Scripture, it will be plain and evident, That the Son of God having created our first Parents, and purposing to multiply their Seed into many Generations, for the replenishing of the World with their Posterity, did give to *Adam* for his time, and to the rest of the Patriarchs, and chief Fathers successively before the Flood, Authority, Power and Dominion over their Children, and Offspring, to rule and govern them; Ordaining by the very Law of Nature, That their said Children and Offspring (begotten and brought up by them) should fear, reverence, honour, and obey them. Which power and Authority before the Flood, resting in the Patriarchs,

Patriarchs, and in the chief Fathers, becauſe it had a very large extent, not only for the Education of their ſaid Children and Off-ſpring, whilſt they were young; but likewiſe for the ordering, ruling, and governing of them afterwards, when they came to Mens Eſtate. And for that alſo it had no ſuperiour Authority, or power over, or above it on Earth, appearing in the Scriptures, although it be called either *Patriarchal, Regal,* or *Imperial,* and that we only term it *Poteſtas Patria*: yet, being well conſidered, how far it did reach, we may truly ſay, that it was in a ſort *Poteſtas Regia*; as now in a right and true conſtruction, *Poteſtas Regia* may juſtly be called *Poteſtas Patria*.

Placet.
iii. p. in MS.

CAN. II.

If any Man ſhall therefore affirm, that Men at the firſt, without all good Education, or Civility, ran up and down in Woods, and Fields, as Wild Creatures, reſting themſelves in Caves, and Dens, and acknowledging no ſuperiority one over another, until they were taught by Experience the neceſſity of Government; and that thereupon they choſe ſome among themſelves to order and rule the reſt, giving them power and authority ſo to do; and that conſequently all civil Power, Juriſdiction, and Authority was firſt derived from the people, and diſorder'd multitude; or either is originally ſtill in them, or elſe is deduced by their conſents naturally from them; and is not

B 2 God's

God's Ordinance originally descending from him, and depending upon him, he doth greatly Erre.

Placet eis.

iv. p. in MS.

CAP. III.

BY the sin of our first Parents, *Adam* and *Eve*, both they, and in them all their Posterity, being so fallen from God, as that they were not able by any natural power, or faculties in them to discharge their duties towards him, or rightly in any sort to know him, as they ought, unto Salvation, or duly serve his Divine Majesty; it pleased Almighty God in mercy (besides the Law of Nature left in them) to propound unto them another kind of Doctrine, than Nature could ever have taught them, *viz.* the Mystery of Salvation through our Lord and Saviour *Jesus Christ*; how the Son of God, who created them, when they were not, should in fullness of time take upon him their Nature, and reconcile to God again as many as should believe in him; the ground of which Doctrine God himself did lay down as the foundation of the Church of Christ, when he said, *that the seed of the Woman should break the Serpent's head.*

CAN. III.

If any Man therefore shall affirm, either that our first Parents after their Fall, or consequently any of their Posterity could serve, or please God truly by any natural Powers, or Faculties, that were left in them after

[5]

after the said Fall; or that the Mystery of Salvation through Jesus Christ, was not a secret, whereunto our corrupt Nature could not attain; or that our Saviour Christ is not the promised Seed that should break the Serpent's head; or that any can possibly be partakers of Everlasting Life without Faith in him, he doth greatly Erre.

Placet eis.

CAP. IV.

v. p. in MS.

AS the Son of God, having created Mankind, did ordain by the Law of Nature, and Light of Reason, that there should be some amongst them furnished with lawful Power, and civil Authority to rule and govern the rest, in things belonging to this natural Life, and civil Society, according to the true Rules both of Nature and Reason: So did he also, according to the supernatural Doctrine of the Gospel, not only ordain, that there should be some likewise in his Church, to rule and govern it; but also gave them another kind of Power, Superiority, and Authority, which is termed *Ecclesiastical*, both for the teaching, and instructing of his People in the Mysteries hid from Nature, concerning their Salvation through the Seed of the Woman; and for the better direction and government of them in the Service of God, touching their Duty towards God, and their Neighbours. The Institution of which Ecclesiastical Calling, and Authority, as also the Manner of the Worship of God, through the blessed Seed, from the Fall of our First Parents to the Flood, although besides their Sacrifices, Prayers, and Preachings, they be not expresly set down in the Scriptures; yet it is not

Gen. 4.
2 Pet. 2. 5.

to be doubted, but that, first, *Adam* for his time, and afterward the Heads of every Family of the Faithful, were not only civil Governours over their Kindred, but likewise had the Power and Execution of the Priestly Office; and that they were themselves instructed and taught from God, as they afterward did instruct, and teach such as were under them in the said Mysteries of Man's Restitution, through the promised Seed, by Faith, and in the right Worship and Service of the true God.

Placet eis.

v. in MS.

CAN. IV.

If therefore any Man shall affirm, that the Son of God having from the beginning a Church upon Earth, did leave them till the Flood without Priests, and Priestly Authority to govern and instruct them in those ways of their Salvation, and in the right manner of the Worship and service of God; or that they might teach them any other Doctrine in that behalf, than that, which they had received from God himself, he doth greatly Erre.

Placet eis.

CAP. V.

Gen. 5.
Gen. 9. 19.
Gen. 10. 32.

AS all Mankind, from the Creation of the World, till the Flood, descended from the Loins of *Adam*; so after the Flood, have they all descended from the three Sons of *Noah*, *Sem*, *Cham*, and *Japhet*.

CAN.

CAN. V.

AND therefore if any Man shall affirm, with any Pagan, or profane Atheist, either that there was not any such general Deluge; or that there is any Nation, or people in the World, that doth not descend from one of the said three Sons of Noah, he doth greatly Erre.

Placet eis.

CAP. VI.

vii. in MS.

NOAH lived after the Flood, 350. Years, and saw his Children's Children wonderfully multiplied; during which term of Years, he was the Patriarch, or chief Governour over them; ruling and ordering them by Virtue of that Superiority, Power, and Authority of the Sword of Justice, which was given unto him by Almighty God, and was also warranted by the Laws of Nature and Reason. Touching this Patriarchal, or, in effect, Regal Government of *Noah*, there is more expreſt in the Scriptures, than there was before the Flood, of the Power and Authority of *Adam*, or of any of the chief Fathers and Rulers that were descended from him. For now there is mention made by God himself of punishing Blood by Blood, which was done by the Sword of Justice, being the chief Ensign, and Warrant of Supream and Regal Authority. Also the Extent of this Right and Authority was so large, as that he lawfully distributed the whole World unto his said three Sons, and their Posterity. So that his said three

Gen. 9. 6.
Rom. 13. 4.
Epiph. in Anchor.
Luther.in Gen.
Perer. in Gen.
Func.Chron.
Sulpit Sever.

[8]

<small>Selnec. Georg.
Fabric & Nic.
Gibbons in
Gen.</small>

three Sons, after him, were by the Ordinance of God (the chief Authour of the said Distribution) made three great Princes; and also the Sons of those three great Princes (of whom about Seventy are named) were the Heads, and Governours of the Families and Nations that descended from them, according to their Tongues, in their several Countries.

CAN. VI.

<small>Placet.
vñ. in MS.</small>

If any Man shall therefore affirm, either that the civil Power, and Authority, which Noah had before the Flood, was by the Deluge determined; or that it was given unto him again by his Sons and Nephews; or that he received from them the Sword of his Sovereignty; or that the said Distribution did depend upon their consents, or received from them any such Authority, as without the same it could not lawfully have been made; or that this Power, Superiority, and Authority, and all the Parts thereof, which Noah's three Sons, and their Children had (as is before declared) did not proceed originally from God, or were not properly his Ordinances, but that they had the same from the People, their Off-spring, He doth greatly Err.

Placet eis.

CAP.

CAP. VII.

IT is also certain, that as the Civil Magistrates, and their Authority continued after the Flood for the government of Mankind according to the Laws of God and Nature, that thereby they might be kept in Order, touching their Duties both toward God and their Neighbours, agreeably to the said Laws, written afterward more fully by God himself in two Tables: so did the Priesthood and Authority Ecclesiastical also by the like Ordinance of God continue, especially amongst the Off-spring of *Sem*, both to govern them Ecclesiastically, and to instruct them in the Mysteries of their Salvation through the blessed Seed of the Woman, according to the Doctrine of the Gospel, which was from time to time in divers Manners delivered by the Son of God unto them. This Priestly Office, and Ecclesiastical Authority, was yet joyned, (as before the Flood) with the Office of the chief Fathers, and civil Governours. *Noah* himself was both a Prince and a Priest; he built Altars, offered Sacrifices, and taught the Church, after the Flood 350. Years, all that which he had learnt from his Fathers, concerning the Creation of the World, the Fall of Man, and of his Restitution by Christ, and generally, all that did concern necessarily, either civil Societies and Government, or Ecclesiastical Assemblies and Authority, not omitting the very Ceremonies. After *Noah*, the chief Fathers, *Sem*, *Abraham*, *Isaac*, and *Jacob* did execute that Office, God himself renewing unto them this Promise of Salvation through the blessed Seed; and not only confirming the same to *Abraham*, and his Posterity by the Sacrament of Circumcision; but likewise teaching and instructing them in that Heavenly Mystery, sometimes by his own Voice, and sometimes by Visions, and divers other ways, whereof the Scriptures make more

Placet.

ix. in MS.
Gen. 8. 20.
Gen. 9. 28.

Gen. 8. 20.

Gen. 17. 10.

plain

[10]

plain mention, than they do of the delivery of the same Evangelical Doctrine before the Flood.

CAN. VII.

Placet.
x. in MS.

If any Man shall therefore affirm, either that the Priestly Office, and Authority Ecclesiastical, which Noah had before the Flood, was by that Deluge determin'd, or that it was by the Election of his Off-spring confer'd again upon him; or that Sem, Abraham, Isaac and Jacob, were neither Priests, nor had any Ecclesiastical Authority, until they were chosen thereunto by their Children and Nephews; or that the Priesthood and Ecclesiastical Authority were not the Ordinances of God, for the governing and instructing of the Church, according to the Will and direction of God himself delivered and revealed unto them, as is aforesaid, he doth greatly Erre.

Placet eis.

CAP. VIII.

AS before the Flood *Cain* and his Posterity were opposite to the Posterity of *Seth*, and might therefore generally have been called the *Church Malignant*; so fell it out after the Flood in the Generations of *Japhet*, but especially of *Cham*, against the Posterity of *Sem*, in whose Lineage the true worship of God, through the blessed Seed was especially continued: and not that only,

[11]

only, but in like manner as the Children of *Seth* in Gen. 6.
proceſs of time provok't againſt them the wrath of
God by corrupting their ways, and following in their
Converſations the Generations of *Cain*, and were in Gen. 7.
that reſpect all of them, with the reſt of *Cain's* Off-
ſpring, juſtly puniſht and drown'd by the Flood, ſaving
eight Perſons (*Noah* and his Wife, *Sem*, *Cham* and *Japhet*, and their three Wives) ſo did the Poſterity, not
only of *Cham* and *Japhet*, as well before as after the
confuſion of Tongues, and the death of *Noah*, but like- Placet.
wiſe the Off-ſpring of *Sem* (who were called more effe- xi. in MS.
ctually to the knowledge of the Myſteries of Chriſt,
and right ſervice of the true God) leave the ways of
Noah and *Sem*, and gave juſt occaſion to Almighty God
(had he not bound himſelf by his Covenant to the contrary) to have drowned them all again. *Nimrod*, de- Gen. 10. 8.
ſcended of *Cham*, not contenting himſelf with the Patriarchal, or Regal mild Government, ordain'd of God
by the Laws of Reaſon and Nature, became a Tyrant,
and Lord of Confuſion; and by Hiſtories it is apparent, that within few Ages after the Death of *Noah*'s
Sons, great Barbariſm and confuſion fell among their
Generations, through their Pride and diſſoluteneſs, in
that they thought ſcorn to be govern'd, either Civilly
or Eccleſiaſtically, as God himſelf, by *Noah*, had ordain'd, or to be ruled otherwiſe than as they liſt themſelves: and touching the Service of God, and the Eccleſiaſtical Authority, they mingled with true Religion
many falſe worſhips, and choſe Prieſts among themſelves to ſerve God after their own Faſhions; or rather
they devis'd to themſelves many Gods, and found out
Prieſts accordingly, ſuch as were content to train them
up in thoſe kinds of Impiety. In *Chaldea* it ſelf, and
the places adjacent, the Children of *Sem* were all of Placet.
them almoſt grown to be Idolaters; inſomuch as God xii. p. in MS.
himſelf to keep a remnant more carefully, that ſhould
through the publick profeſſion of his name be partakers

C 2   of

of his Mercies in Christ, called *Abraham* with his Family from the habitation of his Fathers, to become a Stranger in the Land of *Canaan*.

CAN. VIII.

If therefore any Man shall affirm, That the said Posterity of Noah's Children did Well in altering either the manner or form of civil Government, which God had appointed, by bringing in of Tyranny or factious Popularity; or of the Ecclesiastical, by framing unto themselves a new kind of Priesthood and Worship after their own humours; or that it was lawful for such as then served God, upon any pretence to have imitated their Examples in either of those courses, he doth greatly Erre.

Placet eis.

CAP. IX.

Placet.
xiij. in MS.

IT is apparent in the Scriptures, That although God was not pleased, that the Issue of *Jacob*'s Children should by the Example of the Sons of *Noah*, grow up to become the heads of so many several Nations, but continuing together, should make one People and Nation to be ruled and governed by the same Laws and Magistrates: yet it seemed good to his Heavenly Wisdom, that in so great a People as should descend from *Jacob*'s Children, no one Tribe or Family should continue charg'd, both with the Civil (or Regal) and
Eccle-

Ecclesiastical Function; and therefore *Jacob* making way to the fulfilling of the will of God herein, did take just occasion, moved thereunto by the Spirit of God, to deprive his eldest Son *Reuben* of his Interest by Birthright in both those Prerogatives, to be disposed afterward by God unto other of his Brethren. Now after *Jacob*'s Death, the former thereof, *viz.* the Scepter, in process of time, fell to *Judah*, as *Jacob* before had Prophesied; and the other also, *viz.* the Priesthood, was afterwards given to *Levi* by God's Ordinance.

CAP. X.

After *Jacob*'s Death, till *Moses* was sent to deliver the Children of *Israel* out of *Egypt*, there is little in the Scriptures touching either the Civil or Ecclesiastical Government. It appeareth, that *Joseph* being a great Prince in *Ægypt*, by the King's Authority, was, whilst he lived, chief amongst his Brethren: but after his Death, through the Tyranny of the Kings of *Ægypt*, which God suffer'd to lie heavily upon them for many Years, the civil Authority, which any of the Tribes had, was very small; there was such jealousy of their number, (which daily encreast above all ordinary expectation) as it is not likely, that the Kings successively would suffer any great Authority to rest in them; howbeit we think, they had some, either the chief heads of the Tribes generally, or of the Tribe of *Ephraim* and *Reuben* (for it may be *Jacob*'s Prophecy of *Reuben*'s losing the Prerogatives of his Birthright, was not presently executed) which did in their civil affairs, appertaining to themselves, bear some chief sway amongst them. And touching the Priesthood, although the People were then generally much polluted with Idolatry, yet therein also they had some, most likely the first-born, who although they durst not there offer

Placet. xiv.

Sacri-

Sacrifices to God, as they should, in that servitude: yet some of them (we doubt not) instructed the people in matters concerning the Promises of the blessed Seed, and perform'd, as they might, the other Offices of their Priesthood, although many of the People, and of the Priests, as it seemeth, were then greatly polluted with Idolatry.

Josh. 24. 15.
Ezek. 20. 8.

CANONES IX, and X.

IX. If any Man therefore shall affirm, either that the uniting of the Children of Jacob into one Nation, or the severing of the Civil and Ecclesiastical Functions (the Prerogatives of Birthright) from Reuben the first-born, and dividing of them from one person was made by themselves;

Placet.
XV.

X. Or that their servitude in Ægypt was unjustly suffer'd to lie upon them so long by Almighty God; or that they being his Church, he left them destitute of such comforts of direction, and instruction, as were necessary, those times consider'd, for their Civil or Ecclesiastical Estate; or that the People took upon them the appointing of the heads of their Tribes and Families, or the choice of their civil Superiours, or of the Priests, or that the Example of those wicked Kings may be any lawful Warrant for any other King so to oppress the People, and Church of God, he doth greatly Erre.

Placet eis.
CAP.

CAP. XI.

When the time came that God in mercy was pleased to deliver the Children of *Israel* out of *Egypt*, and to place them in the Land which he had promised them, he raised up his Servants, *Moses* and *Joshua*, to take that charge upon them ; and accordingly *Moses* Deut. 23. 5. being made their Prince, or (as the Scripture speaks) *their King*, did not only by Gods Appointment and Assistance lead them, out of *Egypt*, but governed them, (being 600000 Men, on foot, besides Women and Children) forty years by his Authority in the Wilderness ; and *Joshua* likewise succeeding *Moses*, in the same Princely Power and Authority, did, after many difficulties, bring them into the Land of *Canaan*, and gave them lawful possession thereof. So that although formerly the Children of *Israel* were kept in such great Servitude and Bondage, whilst they were in *Ægypt*, as notwithstanding their number, they were no way able, like a free People, to lift up their Heads: yet now they are knit together in one Body, and set- Places. led, as a particular State, and free Nation, in their xvj. own Countrey, being rul'd and govern'd successively after a mild and temperate manner ; first by *Moses*, in the Wilderness, (as is aforesaid) and then by *Joshua*, in *Canaan*, whilst he lived.

CAN. XI.

If any Man therefore shall affirm, either that the Children of Israel were delivered out of Ægypt by their own strength, and not by God's special Direction, and mighty Power ; or that it had been lawful for

for them (not warranted by God) to have departed thence, as they did, (without Licence first obtained of King Pharaoh) or that Moses and Joshua were not called to that high Authority by God himself, but received the same from the People, as depending upon their choice; or that Dathan and Abiram (descended from Reuben) can be justified, in challenging of Moses, that he took too much upon him, in executing only that Authority which God hath given him, he doth greatly Erre.

Placet eis.

CAP. XII.

Exod. 28.
Levit. 8.
Num. 1, & 3.

Placet.
xvij.

AS Almighty God took order for the setling of his People in the Land of *Canaan*, and established a Princely Authority, to rule and govern them civilly; so was he no less careful of his Church. For however the Priesthood was disposed of before this time, yet now it is apparent in the Scriptures, that the same was after setled in the Tribe of *Levi*, and *Aaron* was made, by God's appointment, (for the better Government of the Church) the Chief and *High Priest*; the whole Priesthood being assigned to his Children, and their Off-spring, as well to succeed him in the said highest place; as also to execute the other inferiour Functions belonging to Priests; and the rest of the Tribe of *Levi* were to attend other Ecclesiastical Services.

CAN.

CAN. XII.

If any man therefore shall affirm, either that the Tribe of Levi was assigned by the People, to undertake the said Ecclesiastical Offices; or that Aaron and his Posterity were chosen by the People, to be their Priests; or that they were not chosen directly by God himself; or that the People had any lawful Interest, at any time afterward, either to chuse their Priests, or (they being appointed of God, as is aforesaid) to deprive them of their places; or that Corah, of the Tribe of Levi, can be justified in saying, That Aaron took too much upon him, thereby repining, either that Aaron was rather made High Priest, than he himself, or that the Priesthood was annexed to Aaron's Posterity, Whereas the rest of the Levites were to serve in inferiour places; he doth greatly Erre.

Placet eis.

CAP. XIII.

BEfore *Moses*'s Death, God had appointed *Joshua* Num. 6. 18. to succeed him, but in *Joshua*'s days he appointed none to follow him immediately: whereupon, after his Death, the *Israelites* were left without a Chief Head, or Prince to govern them. They had then remaining

maining the particular Officers and *Judges* appointed by *Moses*, at *Jethro*'s Council, in their several Tribes; as also the general Senate of *Seventy Elders*, ordained by God, upon *Moses*'s complaint, over all the Nation. Yet there fell very great Disorders and Confusions amongst them, for want of a chief Judge and Governour, whereby they might see their own Disabilities and Errors, and find, by experience, what it was to want a chief Governour; and furthermore be moved, when they were in distress, to fly unto God, and depend only upon him for the raising up of One, from time to time, to deliver and defend them: and it is apparent, that the People, shortly after *Joshua*'s time, falling most strangely into gross Idolatry, and being, from time to time, during the History of the *Judges*, very grievously afflicted by the bordering Nations, and such as dwelt amongst them, when they found themselves still unable to withstand their Enemies, using any great Force against them; then they had (for the most part) recourse to God by Prayer, who did, at such times, appoint one for their Prince, chief Captain and Ruler, to deliver them from their said Enemies; we say, *for the most part*, because sometimes they attempted some matters of Importance without seeking any chief Governour from God, as, at one time, the People of *Sichem* presumed to chuse them a Prince of their own, after *Gideon*'s Death, which turned both to his Ruine, and their Destruction. And it is here generally to be observed, that when there was the greatest liberty among the *Israelites*, during the time from *Joshua* to *Saul* (whatsoever the People thought of their own Courses) the Disorders and Idolatry, in those days, were ascribed, by the Holy Ghost, to the want of Judges, Chief Rulers or Kings, amongst them, who should have reformed those Enormities, not only in them, but likewise in the Priests themselves; if they did not their Duties, especially in suppressing of Idolatry, as they should have done. CAN.

Margin notes: Judg. 2. & Ch. 11. & 13. — Placet. xviij. — Judg. 5. — Chap. 17. 6, 12. & 19. 1. & 21. 25.

CAN. XIII.

If any Man therefore shall affirm, either that the Iſraelites fell not into many Evils and Diſorders, by being left deſtitute of a certain chief Governour after Joſhua's Death; or that When God raiſed up Judges to rule and govern them, the Peoples conſent was neceſſary thereunto; or that the ſaid Judges, being once appointed by God to thoſe places, received their Authority in that behalf from the People; or that the fact of the Sichemites may lawfully be imitated by any Chriſtian People, in ſo chuſing to themſelves a King or Judge, according to their own humours; or that the Want of Kings, Princes and Rulers in any Country, is not the Mother of diſorder and confuſion; he doth greatly Erre.

Placet eis.

CAP. XIV.

IT is manifeſt in the Scriptures, That *Moſes* (directed by the Spirit of God) did foreſee, that the time ſhould come, when the *Iſraelites* being quietly ſetled in the Land of *Canaan*, ſhould be govern'd by Kings after the manner of other Nations. And therefore Almighty God did ſet down by *Moſes*'s Pen, the Duty of all Kings, and the Rules whereby they ought

Deut. 17. 15, 16.

to

to govern. *Jacob* also (being illuminated by the same holy Spirit) did not only foretel, that it would come to pass, that the Tribe of *Judah* should bear the Scepter; and that the Kingdom, or Government of *Judah*, should be held by Succession, according to the manner of other Nations; but likewise, that the said Scepter or Government, should not be taken away from that Tribe until the coming of Christ. And it seemeth, that the People were not altogether ignorant of this foreseen alteration; when finding divers wants and confusions amongst them after the Death of one Judge, before God was pleased to appoint them another; they first offer'd rashly to *Gideon*, their Prince, that his Children and Off-spring should succeed him in that Government. And afterward, being weary of depending upon God's pleasure, and misliking the rule of *Samuel*'s Sons, they urged him undutifully and unseasonably, that they might *have a King to rule over them as other Nations had*: meaning thereby principally (as we suppose) that such their Kings might by Succession govern them; so as one being dead, they might still have another. We say, that they urged *Samuel* to this purpose undutifully and unseasonably; and that thereupon *Saul* was appointed to be their King: because otherwise, if they had expected God's good pleasure and time, and contented themselves with his care over them, in raising up (when he thought meet) their Judges to govern them; they should have found shortly after, that the Prophecy of *Jacob* should have been fulfilled, and that God would have given the Scepter of *Judah* into the hands of *David*, and of his Posterity according to their desire.

Placet. xix.

Gen. 49. 10.

Judg. 8. 22.

1 Sam. 8. 5.

Sam. 9. 17.

C A N.

CAN. XIV.

If any Man therefore shall affirm, either that the People of Israel did not grievously sin in being Weary of Gods immediate Election and appointment of their chief Governors; or that the peoples preposterous hast did any way prejudice the Dignity and Authority of Saul's Regal Power, or afterward of the Scepter of Judah; or that the People then had in themselves any Authority to set up a King over them (for then they would not have been so earnest with Samuel to make them a King) or that after David's advancement to that Kingdom, he was not as truly call'd thereunto by God himself, as Aaron was to the Priesthood; or that David's Posterity had not by God's Ordinance as rightful an Interest to succeed him in his said Kingdom, as either Aaron's Sons had to succeed him in the Priesthood, or Moses, Joshua, and the rest of the Judges, notwithstanding that God himself did chuse, and named them particularly, had in their Governments; or that the People then had any more Authority to have withstood either David, or any of his Posterity from being their King, than they had to have expelled either Moses or Joshua, or any of the rest.

Placet. xx.

reſt of the Judges, whom God by name did appoint to govern them; he doth greatly Erre.

Placet eis.

CAP. XV.

IT is manifeſt in the Scriptures, that the Kings in the Old Teſtament (notwithſtanding that they had their Kingdoms by Succeſſion) were as ſtrictly bound to the obſervation of God's Laws in their Government, as *Moſes*, *Joſhua*, or any other the Judges, or Princes, elected, named, and appointed by God himſelf. They knew well, as *Jethro* ſaid, that it was impoſſible for themſelves to hear and decide all the Cauſes and Controverſies that might happen in their Kingdoms: and by *Moſes*'s Example were not ignorant, that they might appoint and have Judges to govern under them, not only in every Tribe, but generally over all their Kingdom; and therefore they did therein accordingly follow the Example of *Moſes*, being approved by God himſelf: no ways either diminiſhing their Regal Authority, or purpoſing to puff up their Subjects with a conceit of any their own Intereſt in the Government, which they had not from, or under them; but thereby ordering their Kingdoms with ſuch a temperate and Fatherly Moderation, as was moſt agreeable for the Government of God's People.

Placet. xxi.

CAN. XV.

If any Man therefore ſhall affirm, either that the Kings in the Old Teſtament were not bound as ſtrictly to obſerve the Laws

Laws of God in their Governments, as were Moses, Joshua, and the rest of the Judges; or that they had any greater liberty to do what they list, than the others had; or that they had no Authority, by the Example of Moses, and of all the rest of their Predecessors in their Princely Government, to delegate and appoint such Judges and Governours under them, as the other Princes formerly under them had appointed; or that because the said Kings did imitate the said Princes, in appointing such Judges to assist them in the Government of their Kingdoms, therefore their Governments were to be judged rather Aristocratical than truly Monarchical; he doth greatly Erre.

Placet eis.

CAP. XVI.

WHen God first ordained civil Magistrates, and gave them Authority, his meaning was, that the People, whom they were to govern, should be subject unto them. From the beginning of the World, till *Moses*'s time, whilst the People of God, that profess'd his true Worship, were governed by that Authority, which was *Potestas Patria*, and in a sort *Regia* ; Placet their Children and Nephews were bound, by the Law xxij. of Nature, to honour, reverence and obey them. God having raised up *Moses* to deliver the Children of
Israel

Deut. 5. 27. *Ifrael* out of *Egypt*, and to govern them afterward, as their King or chief Ruler; they promiſed that they would hear him, and do thoſe things, which he, in the Name of God, ſhould command them. Being in *Num. 12. 10. Chap. 16. 32.* the Wilderneſs, his own Siſter *Miriam*, for uſing ſome undutiful ſpeeches againſt him, was ſtrucken by God with an exceeding great Leproſie; and ſo odious was the murmuring of *Korah*, *Dathan* and *Abiram*, and their Confederates, as the Lord cauſed the Earth to open, and to ſwallow ſome of them quick, and the Fire to conſume the reſt. *Joſhua* ſucceeding *Moſes*, the People profeſſed their Subjection and Obedience unto him, *Joſh. 1. 16,17, 18.* ſaying, *All that thou haſt commanded us, we will do; and whitherſoever thou ſendeſt us, we will go; as we obeyed Moſes in all things, ſo will we obey thee. Whoſoever ſhall rebel againſt thy Commandment, and will not obey thy Words, in all that thou doſt command him, let him be put to death.* During the Reign of all the Judges, though the People are noted for many great Enormities; yet we do not find, that they rebelled, or ſhewed any great diſobedience againſt them, whom God had ſet over them to rule them, except the particular murmuring and oppoſition of the *Ephramites*, againſt *Gideon* and *Jephtha*, at their firſt entrance, upon conceit they had been contemned; which oppoſition God puniſhed with a great overthrow of them. When the People had Kings, according to the manner of other Nations, to order and govern them; their ſubjection was rather encreaſ'd than diminiſhed, ac- *1 Sam. 8. 10.* cording to *Samuel*'s deſcription of the King's (Claim or) *manner of ruling*, which ſhould reign over them, To command, not only over the Perſons of his Subjects, but alſo over their Goods: which *manner of ruling* or dealing, by any King, without a juſt cauſe, as it was Tyranny; ſo to deny it, when the neceſſity of the King and State did require it, according to the Laws of the Kingdom, was a great neglect of preſer-
ving

ving the publick good, and a high degree of disobedience. Besides it is generally agreed upon, that Obedience to Kings and civil Magistrates is prescribed to all Subjects in the Fifth Commandment, where we are enjoyn'd to *honour our Parents*. Whereby it followeth, that subjection of Inferiours unto their Kings and Governours, is grounded upon the very Law of Nature; and consequently that the Sentences of Death, awarded by God himself, against such as shewed themselves disobedient and incorrigible to their Parents, or cursed them, or struck them, were likewise due unto those, who committed any such Offences against their Kings and Rulers, being the Heads and Fathers of their Commonwealths and Kingdoms; which is not only apparent by way of consequence, but likewise by Example, Practice and Precept; as, where *Shimei* is judged to die for cursing of *David*, the Lord's Anointed; where *David* himself, appointed by God to succeed King *Saul*, would not be induced, by any perswasions, to lay violent hands upon his Master the King; and where it is said, *Principi populi tui non maledices*; and again, *Ne maledicas Regi in corde tuo*: to which purpose more might be alledged.

Exo., *Place* xxiij
1 Kings 11. 9.
1 Sam. 24. 7.
Exod. 22. 28.
Eccles. 10. 20.

CAN. XVI.

𝕴𝖋 any 𝔐an therefore shall affirm, that it was lawful, in the 𝕺ld 𝕿estament, either for 𝕮hildren or 𝕹ephews, to have been disobedient to their 𝕱athers, being their chief 𝕲overnours, from the 𝕮reation till Moses's time, or afterward for the 𝕮hildren of Israel, either under Moses, Joshua, the 𝕵udges,

E

Judges, or their Kings, to have been disobedient to them in their lawful Commandments, or to have murmured, or rebelled against them; or that it was, in those times, more lawful unto Subjects, for any cause whatsoever, either to curse their Princes, Kings or civil Governours; or to bear Arms against them, or to depose them from their Kingdoms or Principalities, or to lay violent hands upon their Persons, than it was in the said times lawful upon any occasion, for Children, either to have cursed their Parents, or to have rebelled against them when they did reprove or correct them, or to have withdrawn themselves from their subjection, saying unto them, (they being private Men) We will be no more your Children, or you shall be no more our Fathers; or (bearing civil Authority over them) we will depose you from your Government over us, and will be no longer ruled by you; or to have offered any violence unto them, or to have beaten them, and much less to have murthered them; He doth greatly Erre.

Placet. XXIV.

Placet eis.

CAP.

CAP. XVII.

WHen God appointed Princes, Judges and Kings to Reign over his people, the manner usually was, that they had notice of it; thereby to conform themselves to obedience. *Moses* and *Aaron* acquainted the *Israelites* with God's pleasure for their deliverance out of *Egypt*, by their service, agreeably to his Promise formerly made to *Abraham*: and they chearfully, and with great thankfullness submitted themselves to be ruled by them. God having appointed *Joshua* to succeed *Moses*, the same was signified by *Moses* to the *Israelites*, and they willingly protested their obedience unto him. Likewise no sooner did the Lord assign Judges to defend and govern them, but presently they followed, and obeyed them. Upon the people's request, *Samuel* having anointed *Saul* for their King, when the same was made apparent to them, either by casting of Lots, or by answer from the Lord, they shouted when they saw him, and said, *God save the King*. King *David* being anointed by *Samuel* at God's appointment to succeed King *Saul*, and after *Saul*'s Death coming thereupon by God's direction to *Hebron*, the Tribe of *Judah* presently anointed him again for their King, and yielded themselves to be governed by him. Seven years after (all which time, King *David* had Wars with *Ishbosheth*, *Saul*'s Son) the rest of the Tribes came unto *David*, and acknowledged, that God had ordained him to be their Governour. King *David* growing old, and having appointed, by God's direction, his Son *Solomon* to be anointed King in his own Life time; when the people knew, that *Zadok* the Priest had so anointed him, they forthwith upon the blowing of the Trumpets, said all with one Voice, *God save King Solomon*. Afterwards also the like course was held upon the Death of every King, to make his Successor known

Exod. 4. 3.
Num. 27. 18
Deut. 13. 9.
1 Sam. 10. 24.
1 Sam. 16. 13.
Placet. xxv.
2 Sam. 2. 4.
2 Sam. 5. 1, &c.
1 Reg. 1. 34.
1 Chron. 29. 5.
1 Reg. 1. 39.

known to the people. Sometimes they were so addicted unto new Kings, as they expected no further Circumstance, but submitted themselves to their Government: and sometimes it was held fit for the young Princes to imitate King *David*'s Example, by kind usage, and loving words, to knit more firmly their Subjects hearts unto them.

1 Reg. 12. 7.

Placet eis.

CAN. XVII.

xx 2.

If any Man therefore shall affirm, either that the callings of Moses, **of** Aaron, **of** Joshua, **of the Judges, of** Saul, **of** David, **of** Solomon, **or of any other of the Kings of** Judah, **elected and named by God himself, or coming to their Kingdoms by Succession (according as** Jacob **by the Spirit of Prophecy had foretold) did receive any such virtue or strength from the people, their said notice, presence and applause, as that without the same the said callings of God, either by Name or by Succession had been insufficient; or that, if the people had Withstood any of them, so called by God, as is aforesaid, they had not thereby sinned, and unjustly opposed themselves against God; or, that the Kingdom of** Judah, **by God's Ordinance going by Succession, When one King was dead, his Heir was not in Right their King, (however by some** Athaliah **he might**

might be hindred from enjoying it) or, that the people were not bound without any further circumstance upon sufficient notice of their former King's Death, to have obey'd his Heir Apparent, as their lawful King; he doth greatly Erre.

Placet cis.

CAP. XVIII.

ALthough we doubt not, but that the Priests and Levites in the Old Testament, were reckon'd amongst the rest of such, as were subject to their Princes, Judges, and Kings; yet we have thought it fit to make the same more apparent by some particulars. *Aaron* the chief Priest, and the rest of the *Levites*, after that *Aaron* was possest of the high Priesthood, were at *Moses*'s direction all the time that he lived: and when he the said *Aaron* had in some sort forgotten his duty to *Moses*, in joining with his Sister undutifully against him; he found his offence therein, and did humbly submit himself in this sort to him; *Alas, my Lord, I beseech thee, lay not this sin upon us which we have foolishly committed.* It is likewise manifest in the Book of *Joshua*, that *Eleazer*, who succeeded *Aaron*, with the rest of the Priests and Levites under him, dispos'd of themselves, and of their service, as *Joshua* their Prince and Governour did command them. And how obedient and humble, both the Priests, and the Levites, and the Prophets themselves were, to their Kings, the Examples of *Zadok*, *Jehojadah*, *Azariah*, *Helchiah*, *Nathan*, and divers others do declare, they submitted themselves to their directions, and when they came into their presence, made Obeysance before them.

Placet. xxvii.

Num. 12. 11.

them upon their Faces to the ground. Likewise having Offices diftributed, and affigned feverally unto them by fundry Kings, they executed the fame in the fervice of the Temple accordingly. And as, while they did their duties, they were cherifhed; fo upon any notorious offence committed by them, they were cen-
1 Reg. 2. 26. 35. fur'd and punifhed. *Solomon* depofed *Abiathar* from the High Priefthood, and placed *Zadok* in his room.
2 Reg. 23. 5. And *Jofiah* likewife thruft all the Priefts from the Altar xxviii. of the Lord in *Hierufalem*, who had burnt Incenfe in the high places.

Placet eis.

CAN. XVIII.

If any Man therefore fhall affirm, either that the Priefts in the Old Teftament were not as rightly and properly fubjects to the civil Governours, as the reft of the people; or that when they any ways offended, they might not be punifhed as lawfully by them as any others; he doth greatly Erre.

Placet eis.

CAP. XIX.

AS we have faid of the people, that when the Kings of *Judah* were to fucceed one another, their Duty was to come together with joy and gladnefs to receive them for their Kings (as fent unto them as from God himfelf) and accordingly to fubmit themfelves unto their Authority and Government: fo at fuch times,

times, the Priests for the most part, besides their general duties, as Subjects, had some further service to be then by them perform'd: the parts of which service are all of them manifest in the advancement of King *Solomon* to the Royal Throne of his Father King *David*; where the Priests, by King *David*'s direction, did give thanks to God, and prayed for King *Solomon*; they offered the peoples Sacrifices of Praise and Thanksgiving to God for their new King; and *Zadok* the High Priest did himself anoint him. Howbeit this their service thus by them perform'd, did neither give to King *Solomon* any Right or Title to succeed his Father; nor to themselves any priviledge or exemption from their subjection and Obedience unto him. *Abiathar* the High Priest did anoint *Adoniah* to have succeeded King *David*; and no Duty (of likelyhood) was omitted which was to be done in such a solemn action: but thereby *Adoniah* received nothing but a badge of Treason against the King his Father, which he carried with him to his Grave; and *Zadok* the High Priest (notwithstanding that he had anointed King *Solomon*) was afterward as much subject, and as dutiful unto him, as he had been before unto his Father King *David*. Nay, the greater the services are of any persons to their Soveraigns, the greater is, and so ought to be, their subjection and obedience unto them.

1 Reg. 1. 33, &c.

1 Reg. 1. 7. *Placet eis.* xxix.

CAN. XIX.

IF any Man therefore shall affirm, either that Adoniah was ever lawfully King of the Israelites, because Abiathar the High Priest had anointed him; or that King Solomon received from Zadok, or from the holy Oyl, which he poured upon his head, any Interest

Interest to his Fathers Kingly Seat, which he had not before by the Ordinance of God, and his Fathers appointment; or that Abiathar might not justly have been condemn'd for a Traytor, in that he anointed Adoniah, as is aforesaid; the Right of the Kingdom being then in King David, and in him by God's appointment, to be disposed of, and bestow'd upon his younger Son Solomon; or, that it had not been a traiterous offence in Zadok, if being commanded thereupon by King David to anoint King Solomon, he should have refused so to have done; or, that either Zadok, or any other Priest, who afterward according to their duties, anointed the Kings of Judah, were thereby more exempted from their subjection and obedience unto them, than were the rest of the people by their joy and applause, when their Kings were newly advanced to their Kingdoms; he doth greatly Erre.

Placet.
XX.

Placet eis.

CAP. XX.

AS it is apparent in the Scriptures, that the *Iſraelites* generally, as well the Prieſts as the People, were equally bound, as Subjects, perſonally to honour, reverence, and obey their Kings: So is it there alſo as manifeſt, that the Authority of their Soveraigns over them,

them, did not only extend to civil Causes, but in like manner to Causes Ecclesiastical. For as it was then the duty of Parents, so by the Law of Nature, was it of good Kings and Civil Magistrates, to bring up their Children and Subjects, in the true service and worship of God; as having a care committed unto them, not only of their Bodies but likewise of their Souls. In which respect the chief charge that all Subjects and inferiour Persons, of what condition soever, should diligently observe the said Law of Nature (being the very same in substance that God, writing with his own Finger, gave unto *Moses*, and stiled by the name of his *Ten Commandments*) was principally imposed upon Kings and civil Rulers. "They were to provide, that their "Subjects had no other God but him, who made Hea‑ "ven and Earth; that they made to themselves no gra‑ *Plut.* "ven Images, nor bow'd down to them, nor worship'd xxix. "them; that they did carefully meet at certain times, "to serve, honour, and magnifie the Name of God; "and that they might not be negligent in the observing "of the rest of his Commandments. And albeit, through the sin of our first Parents, both Kings and Subjects were become unable so to perform these their Duties of Piety, as they should have done; and that there‑fore the Priesthood was not only to instruct them in the mysteries of their Salvation hid from Nature, but likewise to teach them, that Grace did not so evacuate the Law, but that still they were bound to obey it, with this addition or interpretation, That their Faith being grounded upon the blessed Seed of the Woman, if they endeavoured to do that which God had com‑manded them, that which either they did amiss, or omitted, should, upon their Repentance, be forgiven, and not imputed unto them. Yet this mystical and Heavenly Doctrine did no way release, or set at liber‑ty Kings and Princes from their Charge before‑men‑tioned; but rather laid a heavier burthen upon them,

F   to

to provide that their Subjects might be train'd up both in the Doctrine of Faith, and in such Obedience to God, as his said Commandments, so qualified by Grace, as is before-mentioned, did require.

CAN. XX.

Placet.
xxxij.

If any Man therefore shall affirm, either that Natural or Political Fathers (Kings and Princes) in the Old Testament, had not a charge laid upon them by God to bring up their Children and Subjects in his fear; or, that the Institution of the Priesthood did more prejudice the Authority of natural Fathers, or of Kings and Princes in that behalf, than Grace did abrogate the Commandment and the Obedience of the Law; or, that Natural Parents, Kings and Princes in those days, were not more strictly bound by the Doctrine of Grace, than they were before (in respect of God's great Mercy unto them) to provide, that their Children and Subjects were not suffer'd, either to have any false Gods among them, or to bow unto, or worship the likeness of any thing, which they had made to themselves, to blaspheme and take in vain the blessed name of God; or to profane his Sabbaths, or to neglect the observation of the rest of God's Commandments, by committing of Murther, Adultery, Theft, and such

such like Offences, to the displeasure of God, and disturbance of their Families, Principalities and Kingdoms; or that the Kings, Princes, or Governours of the Israelites, being instructed in the Mysteries of their Salvation, were not as much bound, by the Law of Grace, to bring up their Subjects in the true Doctrine, that was grounded upon the blessed Seed, as they were by the Law of Nature, that they should carefully observe the moral Precepts and Commandments of God; or, that being so far bound, they had not equal Authority to compel (as need should require) all their Subjects, of every Calling and Condition whatsoever, to keep and observe both the said Laws, as well of Grace, as of Nature; he doth greatly Erre.

Placet eis.

CAP. XXI.

ALthough it were sufficient to have shewed, that godly Kings and Rulers amongst the *Jews*, had Authority from God, as well in causes of true Religion, as in other of their temporal Affairs; yet, if they had never put the same in practice, some scruple, in the minds of the simpler sort, might thereby have risen, to the prejudice of it. But this point also is manifest in the Scriptures, and ought always, with due thankfulness for the same, to be remembered. It is true, that the Dignity of the Priests, in the Old Testament, but especially of the *High-Priest*, was very great and eminent: howbeit (the same notwithstanding) had it not been for godly Kings and Princes, Religion, among the *Jews*, after the first publick establishment of it, would not have continued, so long as it did, without very great and intolerable Corruptions. *Mo-*

Exod. 32. 4.
c. 21.

ses did blame *Aaron*, for yielding to the making and worshipping of Idols, and reformed the offence. And again, when *Aaron*, being consecrated *High-Priest*,

Lev. 10. 16, 17.

had, with his two Sons, *Eleazar* and *Ithamar*, done amiss, in burning the Sin-offering, which they should, by God's appointment, have eaten; and *Moses*, being angry with them, reproved them for it. In the days of the Judges, when the People fell to the worshipping

Judg. 2. 13.
& 10. 6.

of *Baalim* and *Ashtaroth*, the Scriptures are silent, what became of the Priests; but it is apparent, that,

Placer.
xxxiv.

during the lives of the Judges, the People were, by them, restrained, in some sort, from that Impiety,

Judg. 2. 18.
2 Chro. 19. 4, 8.
Cap. 17. 7, &c.

whereunto, still after their death, they greedily returned. When *Jehosaphat* came to his Kingdom, he found the People so destitute of Teachers, as that he was moved, in zeal, to send the Priests and many of the Levites through all the Cities of *Judah*, to teach and instruct them. *Ahaz*, the King of *Judah*, was a

2 Reg. 16. 3.
c. 11.

very great Idolater, delighting himself altogether in the Abominations of the Heathen; and *Uriah*, the High-Priest, was a fit Instrument for him; For what the one did wickedly command, the other, to the intolerable Profanation of God's true Worship, was ready to put the same in execution. In the days of *Ma-*

Chap. 23. 11.

nasses and *Ammon*, Groves were planted hard by the Temple; Horses were kept by the entrance of the House of the Lord, either to be offered (as 'tis thought) for Sacrifices to the Sun; or else to carry the Picture of it as an Idol to be worshipped: The Priests sundry of them served in high places, and many of the

the People burnt incense unto *Baal*, to the *Sun*, to the *Planets*, and to the *Host of Heaven*: all which abominations the godly King *Josiah* did abolish, reforming both the Priests and the People: and afterwards, when the Kings of *Judah* did altogether neglect their Duties in Church Causes, Religion decreased, and went to havock. Insomuch as the Scriptures rehearsing the causes of the Destruction of *Hierusalem*, do set down this, among the rest, for one, *viz. All the chief of the Priests had trespassed wonderfully, according to all the abominations of the Heathen, and polluted the house of the Lord, which he had sanctified.* Much more might be alledged to this purpose; as also to shew how King *David*, King *Solomon*, and King *Jehosaphat* distributed the *Levites* and *Priests* into their Orders, and prescribed certain Rules for them to observe in the manner of their Attendance and Service. But to the purpose in hand this is sufficient.

Placet. xxxv.

2 Chr. 35. 14.

1 Chron. 15.
2 Chron. 1o.

CAN. XXI.

If any Man therefore shall affirm, either that the godly Princes and Kings, in the Old Testament, did not practise their Authority in Causes Ecclesiastical; or that, in such their Practice of it, they did not that which they were bound to do; or that amongst the Jews the true Worship of God was not very much furthered, and continued by the godly Care and Endeavours of their Princes and Kings; or that the want of such godly Kings and Princes was not then an occasion, and an opportunity taken, both

Placet. xxxvj.

[38]

both by the Priests, and by the People, to follow their own fancies, and to run into many Disorders, false Worships, Idolatry, and sundry such Abominations; he doth greatly Erre.

Placet eis.

CAP. XXII.

What we have said, either of the Authority of Kings, or of the practice of it in Causes Ecclesiastical among the *Jews*; we would not have it extended so far, as if we imagined that in matters of Religion Kings might then lawfully command, and do what they list. In the separation of the Priesthood from the Regal Principality (the same having been formerly in one Person) they were then so, by God, distinguished, as in some things, appertaining to the Office of Kings, no Priest, as he was a Priest, had any Authority to intermeddle; as in some other things, appertaining to the Office of Priests, no King, as he was a King, might lawfully be an Actor: both of them having their bounds and limits appointed unto them by God, which, without Sin, they might not exceed. And therefore, as we greatly blame the High-Priest, *Uriah*, for obeying the wicked Command of King *Ahaz*, in building, by his direction, an Altar in the Temple, according to the Form of One that was in *Damascus*: so do we greatly commend the godly Zeal of *Azariah*, the High-Priest, and of Eighty other *Priests* that were with him, in withstanding (as far as lawfully they might) *Uzziah*, King of *Judah*, when, in the Pride of his Heart, he went into the Temple of the Lord, and would have burnt Incense upon the Altar

of

2 Reg. 16. 11.

2 Chr. 26. 17.

of Incense, which none might lawfully do but Priests. But it is to be observed, that they did not withstand the King by force, or Armies, but told him that it *did not appertain unto him, but to the Priests, to burn incense unto the Lord*; and therefore urged him to go forth of the Sanctuary. Howbeit the King, being angry with them, for the same, persisted (as it appeareth) in his former purpose; and having Incense in his hand, would have burnt it upon the Altar, if God himself had not struck him in the Forehead with a Leprosie, wherewith being terrified (as also with a great Earthquake then happening, as some learned Men have written from *Amos* 1. 1.) he was constrained, not only to desist from that rashness, and to depart hastily out of the Sanctuary; but likewise as a Leper, to dwell in a house apart (according to the Law) and *Jotham* his Son, as Viceroy, ruled his Father's house, and judged the People of the Land *Uzziah* himself, during his life, remaining King.

Placet. xxxvij.

2 Chr. 25. 21.

CAN. XXII.

If any Man therefore shall affirm, either that Uriah, the High-priest, was bound to have built the said Altar, because King Ahaz did command him; or that Azariah, and the other Priests did amiss, in reproving King Uzziah so plainly; or that they lawfully might have used any violence or force against the King's Person, either in hindering him from burning of Incense, or in thrusting him out of the Temple, or in compelling him to dwell apart in a house,

Placet. xxxviij.

as he did (though he was a Leper) if he had not, of himself, yielded to the observation of the Law in that behalf; or that he was deprived of his Kingdom, either by the said stroke of God, or by his dwelling in a house apart; or that any thing, which the Priests then did, might have been a lawful Warrant to any Priest afterward, in the Old Testament, either to have deposed, by sentence, any of their Kings from their Kingdoms, for the like offences, or to have used Arms, or repressed such their unlawful attempts, by forcible ways, though they had imagined the same might have tended to the preservation of Religion; or, that either before that time, or afterward, any Priest did resist by force of Arms, or depose any of the Kings, either of Israel or of Judah, from their Kingdoms, though the Kings of Israel, all of them, and fourteen of the Kings of Judah, were open and plain Idolaters; he doth greatly Erre.

Placet eis.

C A P.

CAP. XXIII.

WE have shewed before, that King *Solomon* did lawfully depose *Abiathar* from the Priesthood, and placed *Zadok* in his room; but that any Priests, in the Old Testament (as likewise we have before declared) did ever depose, from their Crowns, any of their Kings, how wicked soever, or had any Authority so to do, it can never be proved. Howbeit one Example of *Jehoiada*, the High-Priest, is fit to be considered. After the Death of *Ahaziah* King of *Judah*, his Mother *Athaliah* finding his Children to be very young, killed them all but the youngest, and reigned, by Usurpation, six Years over the Land. The said youngest Child, (whose Name was *Joash*) was secretly conveyed away by his Aunt *Jehoshabeth*, his Father's Sister, and the Wife of *Jehoiada* the High-Priest; who kept him so secretly in the Temple, as that *Athaliah* the Usurper could never hear of him. Now after the said six Years, that *Joash*, the true and natural Heir apparent to the Crown, had been so brought up; he, the said *Jehoiada*, being the King's Uncle, and the chief Head, or Prince of his Tribe, sent through *Judah*, for the *Levites* and chief Fathers both of *Judah*, and of *Benjamin*, to come unto him to *Hierusalem*: who accordingly repairing thither, and being made acquainted, by him, with the Preservation of their Prince, (as is aforesaid) and that it was the Lord's Will that he should reign over them; they altogether, by a Covenant, acknowledged their Allegiance unto him, as unto their lawful King; and so disposed of things, as presently after he was crowned and anointed: which dutiful Office of Subjects being performed, they apprehended the Usurper *Athaliah*, and slew her, as before it was, by the said States, resolved. In all the process of which Action nothing was done, either

2 Reg. 11. 2.

Placet. xxxix.

by

by *Jehoiada*, the High-Priest, or by the rest of the Princes and People of *Judah* and *Benjamin*, which God himself did not require at their hands; *Joash* their late King's Son, being then their only natural Lord and Sovereign, although *Athaliah* kept him for six years from the Possession of his Kingdom.

CAN. XXIII.

Placet.
xl.

IF any Man therefore shall affirm, either that Athaliah did Well, in murthering her Son's Children; or that Jehoiada and his Wife, did amiss, in preserving the Life of their King Joash; or that Athaliah was not a Tyrannical Usurper, (the right Heir of that Kingdom being alive) or that it was neither lawful for Jehoiada, and the rest of the Princes, Levites, and People, to have yielded their subjection unto their lawful King; nor, having so done, and their King being in Possession of his Crown, to have joyned together for the overthrowing of Athaliah the Usurper; or that Jehoiada, the High-Priest, was not bound, as he was a Priest, both to inform the Princes and People, of the Lord's Promise, that Joash should reign over them, and likewise to anoint him; or that this fact, either of the Princes, Priests or People, was to be held for a lawful Warrant, for any afterward, either Princes, Priests or People,

People to have deposed any of the Kings of Judah, Who by right of Succession came to their Crowns, or to have killed them for any respect whatsoever, and to have set another in their places, according to their own choice; or, that either this Example of Jehoiada, or any thing else in the Old Testament did give then unto the High-Priest any Authority to dispute, determine, or judge, whether the Children of the Kings of Judah should either be kept from the Crown, because their Fathers were Idolaters, or being in possession of it, should be deposed from it in that respect, or in any other respect whatsoever; he doth greatly Erre.

Placet eis.

CAP. XXIV.

ALmighty God foreseeing what Defects there would be sometimes in Kings and civil Magistrates, and sometimes not only in the inferiour Priests, but likewise in the High-Priests themselves; did still (as occasion required, and for the benefit of his Church) raise up, and send unto them his Prophets, Men indued by his holy Spirit with extraordinary Authority, Knowledge, Zeal and Courage; who neither fear'd King nor Priest, but told them plainly of their faults, denounced the Judgments of God against them for their Sins, and executed without respect of Persons such *Placet.* other parts of their duties, as God himself immediate- xli. ly gave them in Charge. Notwithstanding the Priests stood

[44]

stood much upon their Authority, and bragged, that the *Law should not perish from them*, flattering themselves and the people with lying words (as appeareth by the peoples Speeches, taught most likely by them) *The Temple of the Lord, the Temple of the Lord, This is the Temple of the Lord*; yet the Prophets told them plainly, "That they erred, that they were covetous, re-
"ceivers of Gifts, and false Dealers; that they had pol-
"luted the Temple of God; that the Law should pe-
"rish from them; that God himself had found their
"wickedness in his own House; that *Hierusalem* should
"be destroy'd; and that they themselves should be
"carried into Captivity. In respect of which, their faithful, bold, and plain dealing, according to God's Commandment, and particular directions, the Priests were for the most part greatly moved, and incensed against them. *Pashur*, the High-Priest, struck the Prophet *Jeremy* upon the Face, and afterward cast him into Prison; also his Death was conspir'd amongst the Priests; and the rest from time to time were little better treated by them. It is true, that there were in those times very many false Prophets; who pretending, that they likewise were sent from God, did greatly trouble that Church and State; but their falshood and lewdness, ought neither to have prejudiced the good Priests, nor the true Prophets.

_{Jer. 18. 18.}

_{Jer. 7. 4.}

_{Jer. 20. 2.}

CAN. XXIV.

If any Man therefore shall affirm, either that the Priests in the Old Testament, from the highest to the lowest, were not bound to have obey'd the directions which God himself delivered unto them by his Prophets; notwithstanding that now and then some

some of them were of the Tribe of Levi, and *Placet. xlii.* consequently in other Causes were subject unto them; or, that the Examples of the true Prophets were any lawful Warrant, either for any false Prophets, or for any other person or persons whatsoever, to have railed, libelled, threatned, or denounc'd the Judgments of God against any of the said Priests, according to their own malicious humours (God himself having never given them any such Warrant or foreknowledge to pronounce of such particular Judgments to come:) or, that because the High-Priest, and the rest of the Priests did amiss in the malicious prosecution of God's true Prophets, they might not therefore lawfully take order for the punishment of false Prophets, he doth greatly Erre.

Placet eis.

CAP. XXV.

IT is apparent likewise in the Scriptures, that as the godly Prophets in the Old Testament dealt with the Priests; so did they in like manner deal with their Kings; although otherwise they were their Subjects, and owed them as much duty as any other. *Nathan* the Prophet, by God's particular direction, spared not King *David* to tell him of his offences. No more did *Abijah*, *Jeroboam*; nor *Elias*, King *Ahab*: they denounced God's Judgments boldly against them, and 2 Sam. 12. 1 Reg. 14. 1 Reg. 18.

accordingly

accordingly they came to pass. Also the Lord, being not bound to those Laws which he prescribeth others to observe, commanded *Jehu*, a Subject, to be anointed King over *Israel*; of purpose to punish the sins of *Ahab* and *Jezabel*: and accordingly *Elizeus* the Prophet caused *Jehu* to be anointed, and God's Message to be delivered unto him; who presently upon the knowledge of God's will, and the submission of the Princes and Captains of *Israel* unto him, as to their lawful King, did put in execution the said Message by killing *Joram* (before that time his Soveraign, but then his Subject) and by destroying and rooting out the whole Posterity, Sons, Familiars, and Priests of *Ahab*. In like manner, *Samuel* (a Prophet, but the subject of King *Saul*) did not refuse, when God directly, and in express terms, bad him, both to tell his Master the King, That *the Lord had rent the Kingdom of Israel from him*, and to anoint King *David* to succeed him. We say, *to succeed him*, because we think, that God's purpose only was to cut off *Saul*'s Posterity from reigning after him; and not actually, while he lived, to deprive him of his Kingdom; but principally to provide that *David* might succeed him. Certain it is, that *David* lied not, when, notwithstanding that he himself was anointed to succeed King *Saul*; yet he call'd him his *Master*, and the *Lord's anointed*: also he prayed, that *God would keep him from laying his hands upon King Saul*; for that he was the *Lords anointed*. Likewise, when one of the Captains would have slain King *Saul*, he said, *destroy him not, for who can lay his hands upon the Lord's anointed, and be guiltless?* Furthermore, when the Messenger brought him news of *Saul*'s Death, *Was't thou not afraid* (quoth he) *to put forth thy hand to destroy the anointed of the Lord?* and commanding the said Messenger to be kill'd for his offence therein, *Thy blood* (saith *David*) *be upon thine own head, for thine own mouth hath witnessed against thee, saying, I have slain the Lord's anointed*. Besides,

sides, it is manifest, that the Tribes of *Israel* accounted *Saul* to be their lawful King, during his life. And al- so that they construed *Samuel*'s words to be meant on- ly of *David*'s Interest to succeed him after his Death: and *Samuel* himself (notwithstanding all that he had done was by God's Commandment) left the success thereof to the disposition of his Heavenly Providence; and afterward, both honoured *Saul* before the People, as his King; and likewise continued, whilst he lived, a dutiful Subject unto him.

Placet. xliv.

1 Sam. 15. 30, 31.

CAN. XXV.

If any Man therefore shall affirm, either that the Prophets were to blame for dealing so sharply with Kings and Princes, being their Soveraigns; as though God's express Commandments had not been sufficient to have authorized them so to have dealt; or, that the Example of God's Prophets in this behalf were a sufficient Warrant for any false Prophets, or other lewd Persons, to have railed and libelled against their Kings, or to have denounced such judgments against them, as they in malice either desired, or vainly imagined; or, that any Prophets, Priests, or other Persons, having no direct and express Command from God, might lawfully imitate the said facts, either of Samuel or of Elizeus, in anointing and designing Successors to Kings, which otherwise had no just interest, title and claim to their Kingdoms; or that it is lawful for any Captain or Subject, high or low whosoever, to bear Arms against their Sovereign, or to lay violent hands upon his Sacred Person, by the Example of Jehu, (notwithstanding that any Prophet, or Priest should incite them thereunto, by Unction, or any other means whatsoever; except first, that it might plainly appear, that there are now any such Prophets sent extraordinarily from God himself, with sufficient and special Authority in that behalf; and that every such Captain and Subject, so incited, might be assured, that God himself had, in express Words, and by Name, required and commanded him so to do;) He doth greatly Erre.

Placet. xlv.

Placet eis.

CAP. XXVI.

FUrthermore, that nothing may be omitted, concerning the Authority and Dignity of God's Prophets, in the Old Testament; the Words of the Lord to *Jeremy*, in that behalf, are, with due care and diligence, to be observed. *Behold* (saith the Lord) *I have set thee over the Nations, and over the Kingdoms, that thou mayst pluck up, and root out, and destroy, and throw down, and build, and plant.* Now for as much as it doth not appear in the Scriptures, that the Prophet *Jeremy* did, at any time, as a Warriour and great Emperour,

Jer. I. 10.

Emperour, dispose of Nations and Kingdoms, or plucked up, rooted out, destroyed, or threw down Kings; or that he built, or chose, or set up Kings, in the places of those that he had deposed or thrown down; the ancient Writers, do deliver the true sense and meaning of the said words, when they expound them in sort and effect, as followeth: *I have set thee over Nations and Kingdoms*, that is, I have imposed upon thee the Office of prophesying, not only against the people and Kingdom of *Judah*, but likewise against the Nations and Empires, viz. the *Ammonites*, the *Moabites*, the *Egyptians*, and the *Babylonians*, &c. *That thou mayst pluck up, root out, destroy, and throw down*; that is, that thou mayst pronounce that wicked Nations shall be pulled, or carried away out of their own Provinces; and that thou mayst prophesie, that they shall be destroyed, or killed and dispersed in divers places, or consumed. *That thou mayst build and plant*; that is, that thou mayst declare, that both the *Jews*, and other Nations, shall, after a just and due Castigation, be repaired and restored to their own proper Countries. So that the Prophet *Jeremy*, and the rest of the Prophets, in like manner, although they were chosen of God, to denounce to wicked Persons, Countries, Kingdoms and Nations, his deserved Judgments for their Sins; yet were they neither the Workers, nor the Authors of those Judgments. *Noah* denounced the Flood, but it cannot therefore be truly affirmed that *Noah* drowned the World. *Daniel* denounced *Nebuchadnezzar*'s fall, but it was not *Daniel* that took his heart and understanding from him, nor that made him to eat Grass like an Ox. *Samuel* denounced the Judgments of God against King *Saul*; but *Samuel* did not thrust him out of his Kingdom. And even so, although the Prophet *Jeremy* denounced the Bondage of *Babylon*, and many other Judgments of God, against the said Nations; yet it cannot be either truly said,

Places. xlvi.

Gen. 7. 1, &c.
2 Pet. 2. 5.
Dan. 4. 22.

that *Jeremy* delivered the whole Kingdom of *Judah* into Captivity, or that he overthrew, or deſtroyed any of the reſt: only he propheſied, as God did command him, and left the Executions of ſuch Judgments to the Times and Perſons, which the Lord had deſigned and appointed for that purpoſe.

CAN. XXVI.

Ezcet. xlvii.

If any Man therefore ſhall affirm, that the Prophet Jeremy had any Authority to depoſe Kings from their Kingdoms, for any cauſe whatſoever, and to beſtow them upon others, as he thought fit; or that, albeit the ſaid Words were ſpoken by the Lord to Jeremy, and that he, being otherwiſe an inferiour Prieſt, had no Authority, literally, ſo to caſt down and ſet up Kings, yet the High-prieſts, Men of greater Power and Dignity, might then have uſed Kings in that manner and ſort, according to their Deſerts (the benefit and preſervation of the Church ſo requiring): or that any of the High-prieſts (as deriving their Authority, either from the ſaid Words, ſpoken to Jeremy, or from any thing elſe, that is written in the Scriptures) either might, or ever did take upon them, to give this Neighbour Kingdom to one Man, and that remoter Kingdom to another Man; or to depoſe any of their own Kings, either

of

of Judah, or of Israel, from their Kingdoms, though many of them (as elsewhere we have said) were exceeding great Idolaters, and sundry ways stained with lamentable blots; he doth greatly Erre.

Placet eis.

CAP. XXVII.

THE History of *Jehu* before-mention'd, doth put us in mind, what is written of *Ahud*, one of the Judges of *Israel*. We have elsewhere shew'd, that from *Joshua*'s Death to the time of *Saul*, God himself, when his People were opprest by their bordering Neighbours, did still raise up unto them, Governours and Leaders, called *Judges*, without respect either of any Tribe, more one than another, or of the dignity of any Person, or of the Peoples pleasure, choice and consent first required; but simply, according to his own choice and wisdom: In which number the said *Ahud* was one; the manner of whose entrance into that charge, we could not (our course consider'd) pretermit with silence. The *Israelites* had been eighteen years in subjection to the *Moabites*; as they had been a little before, eight years to the *Aramites*. They knew that it was not lawful for them of themselves, and by their own Authority, to take Arms against the Kings, whose Subjects they were, though indeed they were Tyrants: and therefore they *cried unto the Lord for succour*. Who, in compassion of their servitude and miseries, appointed *Othoniel* to deliver them from the *Aramites*; and afterward *Ahud* from the *Moabites*. In the choice of which two Judges it is to be observ'd, that

Placet, xlviii.

Judg. 3. 9, 15.

the Scriptures do tell us, that *God raised them up* (and therefore 'tis most certain he did so) and also, that in such raising of them to their places he made them *Saviours to his People* (as the Scriptures speak) giving them thereby Authority to save and redeem the Israelites from the Tyrants that oppressed them: without both which Prerogatives it had been altogether unlawful for them to have done as they did. Besides, it appeareth in the Scriptures, that when the Lord did thus chuse out, and authorize the said Deliverers and Rulers, he did not only give them, by his holy Spirit, full assurance of their lawful Callings, but likewise did furnish them with such wisdom and courage, as was necessary for them in those kinds of Services. So as *Ahud* (at whom we principally aim) being thus both called and instructed from God, how he should begin his Peoples deliverance from the *Moabites*, by killing of *Eglon* their King, he framed his course accordingly; and preparing for himself a meet Weapon, took a fit Opportunity, and thereupon (as God had directed him) he, wholly resting upon the Lord's assistance, executed that Judgment upon the said King; and afterward so vanquished the *Moabites*, and subdued them under the hand of *Israel*, as the whole Land was at rest from the oppression of their Enemies *eighty years*. Besides, it is to be observ'd, that as God's appointing by Name and Election of *Moses*, *Joshua* and *Saul*, and after that the Kingdom was held by Succession; the very being of the King's Son, and the true Heir Apparent after his Father's Death, gave unto them all the actual Interest, Right and Possession (as Possession in those cases is to be expounded) of their several Governments, to do any act or acts, as well before as after any subsequent Formalities and Ceremonies: even so the said form of calling the Judges by God himself immediately, made them also Judges actually, and did give unto them a full and absolute Authority (independent upon any but upon

him

Placet.
xlix.

him that gave it them) to undertake any thing, that by God's direction appertain'd to their places. Again, there is one other Example of *Jehu* amongſt the Kings of *Iſrael*, which we have before touched, like unto this of *Ahud:* wherein it appeareth, that he the ſaid *Jehu* was of a Subject firſt made the King of *Iſrael*, before it was lawful for him to have killed *Joram*; As *Ahud*, a Subject, was firſt made the Judge, Prince and Ruler of the People, before he might have lawfully killed King *Eglon*. Both which Examples (being but in number two throughout the Hiſtories of all the Princes, Judges, and Kings, either of *Judah*, or *Iſrael*) do make it known unto us, That although the Lord both may, and is able to overthrow any Kings or Emperours, notwithſtanding any claim, right, title, or intereſt, which they can challenge to their Countries, Kingdoms or Empires; yet foreſeeing in his Heavenly Wiſdom, and Divine Providence, what miſchief private Men, under colour of theſe Examples, might otherwiſe have pretended, or attempted againſt their Soveraigns (as being either diſcontented of themſelves, or ſet into ſome fury by other Malitious Perſons) he did ſo order and diſpoſe of all things in the Execution of theſe ſuch his extraordinary Judgments, as that thereby it might plainly appear to any (that ſhould not willfully hoodwink himſelf) never to be lawful for any Perſon whatſoever, upon pretence of any Revelation, Inſpiration, or Commandment from his divine Majeſty, either to touch the Perſon of his Soveraign, or to bear Arms againſt him; except God ſhould firſt advance the ſaid Perſon from his private Eſtate, and make him a King, or an abſolute Prince, to ſucceed his late Maſter in his Kingdom, or Principality.

Placet. l.

Placet. li.

CAN.

CAN. XXVII.

If any Man therefore shall affirm, either that any godly, or dutiful Subject in the Old Testament, did ever (by the direction of God's Spirit) account this fact of Ahud to be a lawful Warrant for him to have murder'd the Kings, under whose subjection he lived, for any cause whatsoever; though he should have had never so many motions in his heart thereunto; or, that the High-Priest himself, or all the rest of the Priests (who then lived) join'd together with him, could have given Authority to any Person, born a Subject, to have so dealt with his Soveraign, though he had been never so wicked, and that such his Death, might have availed the Church (in their Opinions) never so greatly; or, that either the said High-Priest, and all his Consistory of Priests, might lawfully have encouraged any, who being born Subjects, should have pretended in their Zeal toward Religion, never so many Illuminations, Directions, or Commandments from God, to have laid violent hands upon their King the Lord's anointed, for their proceeding in that course; or, that any Person, born a Subject, and affirming by all the Arguments,

Placet. lii.

ments, which Wit or Learning could devise, that God had called him to murther the King, de facto, under whom he lived; yea though he should have first procured himself to be proclaimed, and anointed King, as Adonijah did, and should afterward have laid violent hands upon his Master; ought therefore to have been believed of any that feared God; except (which is impossible) he should first prove his Credit, in so affirming, to be equal with the Scriptures, and that Men were bound as strictly to believe him, in saying, that God called and stirred him up to the perpetrating of that fact, as we are bound to believe the Holy Ghost, (by whose Instinct the Scriptures were written) when he telleth us, that God raised up Ahud for a Saviour to his People; he doth greatly Erre.

Placet eis.

CAP. XXVIII.

Hitherto in the whole courfe of that mild and temperate *Monarchical* Government, which it pleafed God to eftablifh among his own People ; the duty of Inferiour Perfons and Subjects, of all forts, was ever Obedience. They neither took upon them to chufe their Governours, nor to bear Arms againft them. Howbeit it happened otherwife amongft fome other Nations.

Placit. lii.

Nations. *Nimrod*, not contenting himself with the portion, which, by *Noah*'s general direction, appertained unto him, could never have erected his Tyrannical Government, if a number of rebellious and discontented Persons had not cleaved unto him (as the factious *Sichemites* did to *Abimelech*) and made him their King. The *Romans*, having Kings, rebelled against them, and took the Government into their own hands; the execution whereof did trouble them exceedingly. Sometimes they committed it to many, and sometimes to fewer: their two *Annual Consuls* pleased them long, but at the last they thought it fit to have a *Dictator*; till, in the end, *Julius Cæsar* and *Augustus* reduced their Government again into a *Monarchy*. And as the *Romans* dealt with their Kings, so did the People, in some other Countries, with their Governours. Whereupon divers other kinds of Governments, termed according to their Temper, *Aristocratical, Political, Tyrannical, Oligarchical* or *Democratical*, &c. were afterwards setled in many places. The Inconveniencies of which Forms of Government being found (upon many occasions oftentimes) to be very great; the People have been driven, of necessity, in sundry Countries, to frame them again, as near as they could, to the *Monarchical* Government, either by electing to themselves, Kings, upon certain Conditions, to reign over them; or by appointment of Dukes or Princes to be the Managers of their chief Affairs, according as they themselves should direct them. Besides, as the said rebellious Humours of the People, declining from their Obedience, did, in many Countries, alter that temperate and fatherly Government, which *Noah* had prescribed unto his Off-spring, and which God himself established afterward amongst his own People: so did the ambitious and insatiable dispositions of sundry, no less elsewhere impeach the same; as by the beginning and progress of the four Monarchies, it is most apparent

Placit. liv.

apparent. In all which Abberrations from the said mild and temperate Government, before specified, Almighty God (who, for the Sins of any Nation or Country, altereth their Governments and Governors; transferreth, setteth up and bestoweth Kingdoms, as it seemeth best to his heavenly Wisdom) did ever, by his Foresight and Providence, so dispose both the Rebellion of Subjects, and the Malice and Greediness of encroaching Kings upon their Neighbours, as albeit such their attempts of all sorts, were, in themselves, very wicked and detestable in his sight; yet he (having the skill to bring Light out of Darkness, and to use wicked Instruments and Actions for a good purpose) did always frame and apply them to execute his own just Judgments. When the Sins of a Nation (but principally of his own People) were of that Nature, Height and Ripeness, as his Justice could not fitly be put in execution by any other, but by the wicked: for example, in the overthrowing of *Hierusalem* (God's own City) in burning of the Temple (that was the place of his Glory) and carrying his own People into Captivity, (though never so much by them deserved) no godly King could well have been employed; but such a One only as the King of *Babylon* was. In respect of which their Imployment, such wicked Instruments to execute God's just Judgments, are called sometimes his *Servants*, and the *Rods of his Wrath*; or, as *Attila* termed himself, the *Scourge of God*. And when, having attained their ungodly desires (whether ambitious Kings, by bringing any Countrey into their subjection; or disloyal Subjects, by their rebellious rising against their natural Sovereigns) they have established any of the said *degenerate Forms of Government* amongst their People; the Authority either so unjustly gotten, or wrung, by force, from the true, and lawful Possessor, being always God's Authority (and therefore receiving no impeachment by the wickedness of those that

Dan. 2.
Ecclus. 10. 4.

Placet.
lv.

Jerem. 27. 5.
Isaiah 10. 5.

that have it) is ever (when any such alterations are throughly setled) to be reverenced and obeyed, and the People of all sorts (as well of the Clergy, as of the Laity) are to be subject unto it, not only *for fear, but also for conscience sake*: the *Israelites* in *Egypt*, after *Joseph*'s death, being oppressed very tyrannically, many ways, did never rebel against any of those Kings, but submitted themselves to their Authority, though their Burthens were very intolerable, both in respect of the impossible works imposed upon them, and because also they might not offer Sacrifices to the Lord (a special part of God's Worship) without apparent danger of stoning to death. Besides, it may not be omitted, when God himself sent *Moses* to deliver them from that Servitude, he would not suffer him to carry them thence, till *Pharaoh*, their King, gave them licence to depart. Afterward also, when the *Jews*, being brought into subjection to the Kings of *Babylon*, did, by the instigation of false Prophets, rebel against them, they were, in that respect, greatly condemned by the Prophet *Jeremy*: and in their Captivity (which shortly after followed) they lived by the direction of the said Prophet, in great subjection and Obedience; they prayed not only for their Kings and for their Children, that they might live long, and prosper, but likewise for the State of their Government; the good success whereof they were bound to seek and regard, as well as any other of the King's dutiful Subjects. And thus they lived in *Babylon*, and other places of that Dominion, till the King gave them leave to depart; notwithstanding, in the mean time, they endured many Calamities, and were destitute, for many years, of the publick Service and Worship of God, which was tyed to the Temple, and might not elsewhere be practised or attempted.

CAN.

CAN. XXVIII.

If any Man therefore shall affirm, either that the Subjects, when they shake off the Yoke of their Obedience to their Sovereigns, and set up a Form of Government among themselves, after their own humours, do not therein very wickedly: or that it is lawful, for any bordering Kings, through Ambition and Malice, to invade their Neighbours: or that the Providence and Goodness of God, in using of Rebellions and Oppressions to execute his Justice against any King or Countrey, doth mitigate or qualifie the Offences of any such Rebels or oppressing Kings: or that, when any such new Forms of Government, begun by Rebellion, are after throughly setled, the Authority in them, is not of God: or that any, who live within the Territories of such new Governments, are not bound to be subject to God's Authority, which is there executed, but may rebel against the same: or that the Jews, either in Egypt or Babylon, might lawfully, for any cause, have taken Arms against any of those Kings, or have offered any violence to their Persons; He doth greatly Erre.

Placet cis.

CAP. XXIX.

Placet.
lviij.

Nehem. 9. 36.

Ezra 4. 20.

Nehem. 9.

Placet.
lix.

Ezra 2. 63.

Although the *Jews* upon their deliverance out of Captivity, and restitution to their own Country, received many favours from the *Persian* Kings, and had liberty given them to live in a sort according to their own Laws; yet they never recover'd their former Estate, but liv'd in great subjection and servitude under them, whilst that Monarchy endured. The Temple and City of *Hierusalem* were again built, but not with the magnificence which they had before. *Zorobabel* first, and then *Nehemiah*, were made successively by the said Kings, the Rulers and Governours of the *Jews* so restored, but with divers restraints. It was not forgotten, what mighty Kings had ruled in *Hierusalem*, and therefore the said Rulers were not permitted to govern any more in that Regal sort. They were still subject to the direction of those Kings, and paid unto them very large Tribute and Customs; insomuch, as when the Priests gave publick thanks unto God, for his restoring unto them the state which they had, they said thus withal unto him, as bewailing their condition, *Behold we are Servants this day in the Land which thou gavest our Fathers; it yieldeth much fruit unto the Kings, whom thou hast set over us, because of our sins; and they have dominion over our Bodies, and over our Cattel at our pleasure, and we are in great affliction.* The extraordinary favour which was shewed to any, was principally extended toward the Priests, over whom the said Kings had not so jealous an eye, as they had over the Princes, and the rest of the People. Howbeit (the same notwithstanding) they the said Priests were subject to their own immediate Princes, both in Temporal and Ecclesiastical Causes; as formerly the Priests had been to the Kings of *Judah* before the Captivity. "Their Governours forbad certain, who said
"they

"they were Priests, from eating of the most holy Nehem. 5. 12.
"things. *Nehemiah* ministred an Oath unto the Priests: 13. 15.
"he reform'd the abuses of the Sabbath, and prescrib'd 13. 13.
"Orders for the better observing thereof. He appoin-
"ted certain of the Priests to oversee the Tithes in the
"Treasury. He commanded the Levites to cleanse
"themselves, and to keep the Gates, and to sanctifie
"the Sabbath. *Eliasib*, the High-Priest, having defi-
"led the Temple, by letting *Tobias*, a Stranger, a
"Chamber in the Court of the House of God (where
"in afore times the Offerings, the Incense, the Vessels,
"and such other things, used in God's Service, had been
"kept,) *Nehemiah*, the Governour, was greatly offen- *Placet.*
"ded with it; and displacing the said *Tobias*, cast lx.
"forth all his stuff out of his said Chamber, and
"brought thither again the Vessels of the House of
"God, with the Meat-offerings and Incense.

CAN. XXIX.

If any Man therefore ſhall affirm, either that Almighty God kept not his promiſe to the Jews made in his name by the Prophet Jeremy, **as touching their deliverance by** Cyrus **out of their Captivity; becauſe they were not reſtor'd to any ſuch perfect liberty and Government, as they had before: or, that the ſaid Kings of** Persia, **continuing ſtill by God's appointment a ſupream Authority over the Jews ſo reſtor'd, might by them for any cauſe, or under any colour, have been defrauded of their Tributes, or reſiſted**

[62]

resisted by force of Arms, or otherwise impeach'd, either in their States or Persons: or, that Zorobabel and Nehemiah were not lawful Princes over the Jews, because they were placed in that Government without the Peoples Election: or, that they the said Princes, by dealing in Cases Ecclesiastical (as is aforesaid) did take more upon them, than by God's appointment appertain'd to their charge: or, that the Priests, both high and low, had not grievously sinned, if they had not submitted themselves in the said Ecclesiastical Causes, to the direction of those their civil Governours; he doth greatly Erre.

Placet.

Placet eis.

CAP. XXX.

THE *High-Priest* (as before we have said) in that mild and temperate Government, which God himself had Ordained, was the second Person in the Kingdom. Whereupon the same (after the Captivity) being turn'd, as it were, into a Dukedom, and (for ought that appeareth) the Princes after *Nehemiah*'s time growing poor, by reason of their payments to those Kings to whom they were Tributary; and receiving small assistance or countenance from them, because they were still jealous of them, whereas the Priests (it seemeth) being freed from all Tributes and Impositions, grew rich, and were no way suspected: it came to pass (the sins of the people so requiring)

that

that the *High-Priest* did easily oversway both their Princes and their People, and thereby attained very great Authority in that Principality. Only they stood in awe for the time of the Kings of *Persia*, to whose Obedience they were bound by an Oath, when they were made *High-Priests*: but otherwise, for ought we find, they had no great regard of any other Authority: which so advanced the dignity of the Priesthood, as afterward the practices of the High-Priest's Children, to succeed their Father in that high dignity, grew as troublesome to the People, as was their servitude to the *Persians*. For *Jesus*, the younger Brother of *John*, the second High-Priest after *Eliasib* (mentioned by *Nehemiah*) procured by corruption the favour of the chief Governour of the *Persians* in those Countries adjoining for his assistance, to deprive his Brother, that he himself might enjoy the High-Priesthood; whereof his elder Brother having some notice, did kill him in the Temple: which the said Governour took in so evil part, as he spoiled the said Temple, being (as he said) profaned with Blood; and laid an exceeding great Tribute in that respect upon the People, to indure for seven Years. But *John* the High-Priest continued in his place. After whose Death, his two Sons, *Jaddus* and *Manasses*, fell at great variance: the younger (to make himself strong against his elder Brother) Married contrary to the Law of God, with a Daughter of *Sanballat*, another Chief Ruler in *Samaria*, under the King of *Persia*. For which offence *Jaddus* (notwithstanding the Authority of *Sanballat*) remov'd him from the dignity of Priesthood: and thereupon, he the said *Manasses*, procured by *Sanballat*'s means, a Temple to be built in Mount *Garizin*, near *Samaria*, in form and magnificence like to that in *Hierusalem*, where he flourished; and whither all the lewd persons of *Judah* had daily recourse. Upon which occasion much trouble arose afterwards betwixt the *Samaritans*, and the *Jews*. The said *Jaddus* lived

Placet. lxii.

Nehem. 13. 28.

Jos. Antiq. l. 11. c. 8.

Placet. lxiii.

till

till the Monarchy of the *Grecians* began; who, when *Alexander* (having overthrown *Darius* the King of the *Persians*) sent unto him, that he should assist him in his Wars, and become Tributary to the *Macedonians*, as he had been to the *Persians*; return'd for his Answer, that he might not yield thereunto, because he had taken an Oath for his true Allegiance to *Darius*, which he might not lawfully violate whilst *Darius* lived, being by flight escaped, when his Army was discomfited.

_{Jof. *ibid.*}

We have here cited, and shall hereafter cite some things out of the Books of the *Maccabees*, and other ancient Historiographers, of purpose to continue the manner of the Government of the *Jews*, in what case they stood from time to time, after the days of *Nehemiah*: not meaning thereby to attribute any *Canonical* Authority unto them, nor to establish any point of Doctrine out of them, but only to proportion and measure the regiment and actions of that people, by the rules and analogy of the holy Scriptures.

CAN. XXX.

_{*Placet.* lxiv.}

If any Man therefore shall affirm, contrary to the grounds and truths of the said holy Scriptures, either that, albeit Kings of Persia **had authorized some succeeding Princes, as they did** Zorobabel **and** Nehemiah **(and Whether they did so or no, is not certain;) yet the High Priests might afterward have lawfully born the sway, that they did, and not been subject unto them, as their Predecessors had been to** Zorobabel **and** Nehemiah**; or, that if** Nehemiah **continued**

nued alive in that Government, till Jaddus's time (as it is probable he did) he might not lawfully, being authorized as before, (though he were old) have reform'd any abuse in the Priests, both high and low: or, that they were not bound in Conscience to have obey'd him therein: or, that the Jews might lawfully have rebelled for any cause against the Persians, during their Government over them: or, that Jaddus, the High-Priest did amiss in binding his Allegiance to King Darius by an Oath: or, that he had not sinned, if he had refused (being thereunto required) so to have sworn: or, that having so sworn, he might lawfully have born Arms himself against Darius, or have sollicited others, Whether Aliens or Jews, thereunto; he doth greatly Erre.

Placet eis.

CAP. XXXI.

Alexander, by God's Providence, having vanquished the *Persians*, the *Jews* (amongst many other Nations) became his Subjects. He dealt favourably with them, released them of some Payments, granted them liberty, to live according to their own Laws, and left their Government, in every point, as he found it: their Duties, ordinary Tributes, and some of their Royal Prerogatives, always reserved to the *Macedonians*, as they had been before to the *Persians*; but this

Placet. lxv.

their

their tolerable Eftate endured not long. For, upon *Alexander's* death, his chief Captains confpiring together, made fuch a fcambling Divifion of the Empire, amongft themfelves, as they could; every one almoft, notwithftanding, feeking how he might fupprefs the reft, and attain the whole alone to himfelf. So as, thereupon, the *Jews* were as free from the *Macedonians,* as any other of their bordering Neighbours; none of the faid Captains having any lawful Intereft, or Title, to *Judah.* But that which turned to the benefit of fome others, brought a great detriment (for want of Ability) unto them: for one of the faid Captains having gotten to himfelf a very ftrong Kingdom, in *Syria,* and another of them in *Egypt,* the *Jews* dwelling betwixt them both, were miferably, on every fide, vexed by them. Sometimes the *Egyptians,* by Oppreffion and Force, brought them under their Subjection, and impofed great Tributes upon them: and fometimes the *Syrians,* growing mightier than the *Egyptians,* did likewife very greatly afflict them; efpecially in the Reign of *Antiochus Epiphanes,* whofe Invafion and Government was moft unjuft and Tyrannical. "He fhed innocent Blood on every fide of the Sanctua-"ry, fpoiled the Temple, erecting in it the Abomina-"tion of the Gentiles, and caufed it to be named the "Temple of *Jupiter Olympius.* The Books of the "Law, by his Commandment, were cut in pieces and "burnt; and they, with whom they were found, "were put to death. A general Commandment was, "by him, publifhed, that they fhould offer no more "Sacrifices, nor circumcife their Children, nor exe-"cute any other parts of their own Law in the Service "of God, but wholly to conform themfelves therein "to the manner of the *Gentiles.* Whereupon the People, by heaps, forfook the Lord, and offered Sacrifices to Idols; and fuch as refufed fo to do (chufing rather to obey God than Man) were moft cruelly flain and murthered,

Placet. lxvi.

1 Macc. 1. 37.

2 Macc. 6.2,4.

thered, by thousands; until *Mattathias*, moved with the monstrous Cruelty and Tyranny of the said *Antiochus*, made open Resistance; the Government of that Tyrant being not then, either generally received by submission, or setled by continuance. It is not pertinent to our purpose, to intermeddle with sundry Questions, which might here arise. Only we observe, that *Mattathias* undertook that charge; that he commended the same afterwards to his Sons, and that it continued in them and their Posterity, until both they and their whole Countrey were vanquished by the *Romans*.

Placet. lxvii.

CAN. XXXI.

If any Man therefore shall affirm, either that the Jews, generally, both Priests and People, were not the Subjects of Alexander, after his Authority was setled amongst them, as they had been before the Subjects of the Kings of Babylon and Persia: or that they might lawfully have born Arms against him; or that they were not all bound to pray for the long life and prosperity, both of Alexander and his Empire, as they had been bound before, to pray for the life and prosperity of the other said Kings and their Kingdoms, whilst they lived under their subjection: or consequently that they might lawfully, upon any occasion whatsoever, have offered violence and destruction, either to their Persons or to their Kingdoms, for the long continuance

K 2 and

and prosperity whereof, they were bound to pray: or that, after the Jews were delivered from their servitude under the Kings of Syria, and the Government over them was settled in Mattathias's Posterity, it was lawful for the People, upon any occasion, to have rebelled against them, or to have offered violence to their persons; he doth greatly Erre.

Placet eis.

CAP. XXXII.

THE afflictions, which the *Jews* endured, whilst the Government of the *Grecians* lasted, were much the more grievous unto them, by reason of the great disorders which were then amongst their Priests. For whereas they should have been a stay and a comfort unto them in their greater miseries; their negligence one way, and their ambition another way (in striving about the High Priesthood) did so distract them into parts taking, as that thereby great effusion of blood did oftentimes ensue: shortly after *Jaddus*'s time, this was the general report, which, for their Wickedness, was given out of them, The *Priests were now no more diligent about the Altar, but despised the Temple, and regarded not the Sacrifices. They did not set by the honour of their Fathers, but liked of the glory of the Gentiles most of all. The Temple was full of dissoluteness and gluttony of the Gentiles; which dallied with Harlots, and had to do with Women within the circuit of holy places; and brought in such things as were not lawful. The Altar also was full of such things, as were abominable, and forbidden by*

[69]

the Law; and two or three of the High Priests applauded thereunto. *Simon*, the High-Priest, leaving three Sons behind him, *Onias*, *Jason*, and *Menelaus*, was not long dead, but *Jason* for three hundred and sixty Talents of Silver, procured such assistance of *Antiochus* King of *Syria*, as he thrust his elder Brother *Onias* out of the High-Priesthood; and not long after had the same measure repay'd unto him again, by his younger Brother *Menelaus*; who upon some cunning information, and for six hundred and sixty Talents, got the place himself. Whereupon *Jason* assembled Forces, drove *Menelaus* into a Castle, slew the Citizens without Mercy, and in the end being repulsed, died abroad as an exile. *Menelaus* afterward caused his Eldest Brother, *Onias*, to be Murder'd; because he blamed him for stealing certain Vessels of Gold out of the Temple. Next *Menelaus* succeeded *Alcimus*, whereas *Onias*, the Son of *Onias* before-mentioned, should in right have had that dignity. Of all which, four Persons, eminent in their time, these things are left for Records unto Posterity. *Jason* to get *Antiochus*'s good will for the High-Priesthood, promised him, besides his great Bribe, to set up a School of Gentilism; likewise to build a Brothel-House by the Temple; and that the People of *Hierusalem* should be named *Antiochians*, after the Kings Name. He drew his Kinsmen to the Custom of the Gentiles, and sent to *Tyrus* three hundred Drachms of Silver for a Sacrifice to *Hercules*. *Menelaus* also took the like course, or rather a worse; for besides, that he conform'd himself wholly in effect to the manners of the *Grecians*; it is further thus written of him; *Antiochus* went into the most holy Temple, having Menelaus, *that Traytor to the Laws, and to his own Country, to be his Guide*. He thrust himself into the Kings Army against *Judas Maccabæus*, and the City of *Hierusalem*; hoping thereupon to have attain'd that Government. But *Lysias* the King's Lieutenant, crossed his purpose therein, and inform'd

Jos. Ant. l. 12. c. 6.

2 Macc. 5. 5.

2 Macc. 4. 34.

Places.
lxx.

2 Macc. 5. 15.
2 Macc. 13. 3.

inform'd the King, that he the said *Menelaus* had been the cause of all the mischiefs which had ensued the Wars with the *Jews*; as being the Man who perswaded his Father *Antiochus Epiphanes*, to compel them to forsake the Laws of their Fathers; adding thereunto, that whilst *Menelaus* lived, the *Jews* would never be quiet. Whereupon the King commanding him to be put to Death, he was smother'd in Ashes; because he had *committed many sins by the Altar, whose fire and ashes were holy*. *Alcimus*, the High-Priest, next succeeding, was no sooner in his place, but he took upon him to be the Captain of all the ungodly Men of *Israel*, and solicited King *Demetrius* to make War against *Judas Maccabæus*; complaining, that he had killed all the King's Friends. The King thus instigated sent an Army against *Hierusalem*, with one *Bacchides* and *Alcimus*; who, pretending that they came in Peace, and being thereupon trusted by the *Maccabees* themselves (because he was a Priest of the Seed of *Aaron*) did traiterously notwithstanding, and treacherously, Murder sundry of the *Jews*, and held the Government of that Country, till *Judas Maccabæus* put him to flight. Howbeit, accusing the *Maccabees* again of wicked things, he urged afterward the said King to send a new Army against them, and was himself, as it seemeth, in the Host, when *Judas Maccabæus* was slain. Besides, it is also reported of him, how he commanded that the Walls of the Inner-Court of the Sanctuary should be destroy'd, and how he pulled down the Monuments of the Prophets, and how in that his so wicked and profane an attempt, he was stricken with the Palsey, and died with great torment. Now concerning *Onias*, (who if he had been of lawful Age, and might have had his right, ought to have been High-Priest before both his Uncles, *Jason* and *Menelaus*) when he perceiv'd that *Alcimus* had gotten that place, and saw no probability how he might get it from him, he fled into *Egypt*, and there procured a Temple

Temple to be built, like unto that in *Hierufalem*; whereof he was made the principal Ruler. So greedy was he of the High-Priefthood, that feeing he might not be High-Prieft in *Hierufalem*, he would needs be a High-Prieft in *Egypt* againft God's Command. But perhaps the High-Priefthood amongft the *Jews* was better beftow'd afterwards. Indeed now it came into the hands of the *Maccabees*: but how they ufed it there is little mention. It is probable, that being fo diftracted as they were, and fo continually in a manner vexed with Wars, they had no time to execute that office in fuch fort, as otherwife divers of them no doubt would have done. But it cannot be denied, that fome of that rank were greatly puffed up with that Authority, and did thereby much forget themfelves, and the holy Duties appertaining to the High-Priefthood. Elfe would not *Ariftobulus* have fo unnaturally famifhed his own Mother, nor have fuffer'd the cruel Murther of his Innocent Brother *Antigonus*; nor would *Alexander*, fucceeding *Ariftobulus*, have committed the like Murther upon his younger Brother; nor would afterward, the two Sons of the faid *Alexander* (viz. *Hircanus* and *Ariftobulus*) have grown through their ambitious defires to fuch mortal hatred. For *Ariftobulus* thrufting his eldeft Brother *Hircanus* from the High Priefthood, and he the faid *Hircanus* continuing ftill his claim, they never ceafed their Hoftility, till *Pompey* having fubdued them both, brought both them and the whole Country under the fubjection of the *Romans*. We omit what great fums of money they beftowed on either fide, to procure *Pompey's* favour; to whom they had committed the deciding of their Caufes; and alfo how *Hircanus* affifted *Pompey* in his attempt againft *Hierufalem*, partly in hope thereby to get the High Priefthood, and partly in malice againft his Brother; who, as long as he could, defended that City; the Iffue of all which ftrife was this, *Pompey* fubdued the City; flew twelve thoufand

Places. lxxiii.

Places. lxxiv.

thousand Men; *Aristobulus* is put from the High Priesthood; the civil Government is separated again from the High-Priesthood; the High Priesthood is bestowed upon *Hircanus* for his Service, and the civil Government thenceforth translated to strangers; the Temple was spoiled, and *Hierusalem* was made Tributary to the People of *Rome*. Of all which Calamities falling in this sort upon the *Jews*, the dissention betwixt *Hircanus* and *Aristobulus*, was held in those days to have been the cause; to the great blemish of their credits, professing themselves to be God's High-Priests. Besides, while *Jason, Menelaus, Alcimus*, and the *Maccabees* were busied in their said Un-Priestly Contentions, and *Greekish* profanations, divers Sects of Religion arose, and encreased among the Jews; especially, that of the *Pharisees*, a crafty and an arrogant kind of Men, seditiously bent against their Kings, and impugners without fear of their Authority. In which course they were the rather animated, because they found through their Hypocrisy, that Women were generally addicted to them, and that the People did so admire them, as they believed in effect whatsoever they told them against any, although it were never so false, or maliciously devised by them. And thus Religion went in those days, when the Priests had gotten the Reins into their own hands, although we doubt not but that there were some few, notwithstanding, both of the Priests, and of the People, who disliking of all their said hypocritical, ambitious, profane, and wicked Practices (cover'd sometimes with a pretence of Zeal, and sometimes with the glorious name of the High Priesthood) did truly from their hearts, both fear and serve the Lord.

Jos. ant. l. 17. c. 13.
Placet. lxxv.
Jos. ant. l. 13. c. 23.

CAN.

CAN. XXXII.

If any Man therefore (because in the Law of God there was great obedience to the High-Prieſt, preſcribed and required; or, that it is ſaid by the Prophet, That the Prieſts Lips ſhould preſerve knowledge, and that the People ſhould ſeek the law of his mouth: Whereas the meaning of the Holy Ghoſt in thoſe and ſuch like places, only is, that the High-Prieſts were to be obeyed, when they commanded that which was not repugnant to the law of God; and that the Lips of the Prieſts ought to preſerve knowledge) ſhall affirm, either that it was not wickedly done by their Prieſts, to thruſt the People into many imminent dangers, for the maintenance of their lewd quarrels and factions: or, that they did not grievouſly offend God, when they forſook his true Worſhip, and brought heatheniſh and profane Sacrifices into his Temple: or, that the People were bound to obey, when they requir'd them to conform themſelves to the Idolatrous Worſhip of the Heathen: or, that it was lawful for any of the ſaid High-Prieſts, by injury, bribery, or cruelty, to ſeek the High Prieſthood: or, that the Prieſts and People, that joined with them, did not

Placet. lxxxvi.

L wickedly,

Wickedly, Who assisted Pompey **to invade** Hierusalem, **and to bring their own Countrey in Bondage to the** Romans: **or that any such** Pharisaical **Sects, (never ordained by God) were lawfully then permitted, to seduce the simpler sort of the People, leading them into Factions and Dislike of their Superiours; He doth greatly Erre.**

Placet eis.

---

lxxvii.

CAP. XXXIII.

THE *Jews* being subdued by the *Romans*, and brought under their subjection, about sixty years before the coming of Christ, were used by them very kindly, and with great respect. They had liberty granted them, to live according to their own Laws; so as they paid their Tributes, and framed their Behaviour to Quietness and Obedience. *Hircanus*, the High-Priest, placed by *Pompey*, lived long after, in great Authority. But nothing would satisfie them; till, in the end, it came to pass, that as the Ambition and Strife, betwixt *Hircanus* and *Aristobulus*, brought *Pompey* upon them; so now their own Wickedness, and rebellious Hearts, were the cause of their greater Servitude, Afflictions and Miseries. The remnant of the *Maccabees* (*Aristobulus* and his two Sons, *Alexander* and *Antigonus*) would never desist from their rebellious Attempts, until they were all cut off. *Antipater*, the first Governour, or *Procurator*, appointed by the *Romans*, was poysoned by one *Maticus*, hoping thereby, that *Hircanus*, the High-Priest, might have got a more absolute Authority, and have been the chief Governour.

Jos. de bel. Jud. lib. 6. c. 11.

Jos. Ant. l. 14. c. 18, 19.

Placet. lxxviij.

vernour. *Alexander*, the Son of *Aristobulus*, had been Jof. ib. c. 10.
before very troublsome, and carried many after him to
their destruction; but *Antigonus*, his Brother, did far
exceed him; who, by the help of the *Parthians*, rose
up against *Herod*, the Successour of *Antipater*, and taking that Government upon him, cut off *Hircanus*,
his Uncle's Ears, that thereby he might be unable af- Jof. ib. c. 13;
terward to bear any more, to his prejudice, the Office
of the High-Priest. But shortly after he was subdued, and put to death; and his Father, before him, was
poisoned by *Pompey*'s Followers. Howbeit, no sooner
were these *Maccabees* thus suppressed, but divers other
rebellious Persons, thrust forward the People into Arms,
under pretence of their Love they bare to their Countrey, and to the ancient Liberties thereof. In which
their wicked Fury, sometimes they were content to
follow this Man, as their King; and sometimes that
Man; such as were, one *Simon*, one *Athrogus*, and *Manahe-* Jof. ib. l. 17.
mus; all of them very lewd and base Companions: and c. 12.
at some other time every Rebellious Rout or Compa- Id. de bel. l.2.
ny would needs have a King of their own; where- Placet.
by, in every corner of that Commonwealth, there was lxxix.
a Petty King, who still led the People, by heaps, to the Jof. Ant. l. 15.
slaughter, and perished themselves with them. Also c. 1, 2.
there were some amongst them, who finding no good
success, by having of such Kings, did run into a contrary course, affirming it to be unlawful for the *Jews*
to acknowledge any Man, but God himself, to be
their King; and that they ought rather to suffer death, Id. de bel. l.2.
than to call any Man Lord. The sum is, That, notwith- c.7.& l.6.c.12.
standing any great Distractions, Dissention, or bloody
Combats amongst themselves, (which were very many and strange) their Hearts were so hardened in Rebellion against the *Romans* and their Governours, as they
refused, either to pay them any more Tribute, or to
pray for them; but standing upon their Walls, when
they were besieged, *Cæsari, & Patri ejus maledicebant*.

There was never (we think) so obstinate and desperate a People; for, in their greatest extremities, and when they saw nothing but imminent Death, destruction of the Temple, and the extirpation of their whole Nation, no reasonable Conditions or Perswasions could move them. *Titus* himself made a notable Oration unto them, and commanded *Josephus* to deliver his Mind at another time more amply, if it had been possible to have reclaimed them: which Duty, so imposed upon him, *Josephus* performed very eloquently. He told them," that tho' the *Romans* had dealt
" sometimes very hardly with them, yet their Rebelli-
" on was ever the cause of it; that albeit Men might
" lawfully fight in defence of their Countrey, when it
" was invaded by any; yet being subdued, and a new
" Government settled amongst them, it was not law-
" ful, by Rebellion, under pretence of Liberty, to cast
" off that Yoke; that their Fore-fathers being in Bon-
" dage, under the Kings of *Ægypt* and *Babylon*, and di-
" vers times in many other distresses, did never, of
" themselves, by force of Arms, seek their Liberty, or
" Deliverance; but ever expected the Lord's leisure,
" who always, in due time, had compassion upon
" them; and that although they were then in the
" greatest distress, that ever People were, and could
" expect nothing but utter Ruine and Desolation; yet
" if then they would submit themselves, they might
" be received to Mercy. For (saith he) the *Romans*
" ask but their ordinary Tribute, which your Fore-fa-
" thers paid unto their Predecessours: and if yet they
" may obtain the same, they will neither destroy your
" City, nor touch your Sanctuary; but grant unto you
" freely, your Families, your Possessions, and the Pra-
" ctice of your Sacred Laws. But all these Offers they refused. Howbeit the compassion of *Titus* towards them still continuing, he again (when they saw their Destruction more apparently) required the said *Jo-*
sephus

sephus to deliver his Mind, to the same effect, to their chief Captain, that he had done before to the People: which he accomplished (but in the hearing again of the People) very throughly; and in the end (finding them obstinate) *I my self deserve blame*, saith he, *quia hæc, adversus fata, suadeo; Deique sententiâ condemnatos servare contendo.* Whereupon, shortly after, *Titus* (protesting how loth he was thereunto) assailed them with all his Forces, which slew an infinite number of them, burnt the Temple, and destroyed the City. Since which time, they that then escaped, and the rest of all the Race of the *Jews*, have been dispersed far and near, and lived like a cursed Generation, in all Slavery and Servitude. So that, although we doubt not, but that this heavy Judgment of God fell upon them, principally for the hardness of their hearts, in that they did not only refuse to hear the Voice of our Saviour Christ, but likewise most malitiously, unjustly, and shamefully put him to death: yet the immediate, and apparent cause of it, was their never-before-heard-of-like obstinate Rebellion.

Placet. lxxxii.

CAN. XXXIII.

If any Man therefore shall affirm, either that Aristobulus, the Father, or either of his two Sons (Alexander or Antigonus) having all of them submitted themselves to the Government of the Romans, did not sin, when afterward they rebelled against them: or that Maticus did not very wickedly in poisoning of Antipater, because he thought thereby the better to strengthen Hircanus in his High-Priesthood: or that the People ought not

not to detest all such seditious Persons, as under pretence of Liberty and Religion, shall sollicite them to Rebellion: or, that the Jews were not bound, both to have paid their Tribute, and to have prayed for Cæsar without dissimulation, sincerely and truly, notwithstanding any pretence of Tyranny, which they had willfully drawn upon their own heads, or of any cause whatsoever: or, that such as cursed Cæsar (their chief Governour) did not thereby deserve any corporal punishment, which is due to be inflicted upon such Traytors: or, that the Rebellion against any King, absolute Prince, or Civil Magistrate, for any cause whatsoever, is not a sin very detestable in the sight of God, and therefore by all that fear the Lord to be eschewed, because it ever tendeth to mischief, and sometimes to the overthrow of the Kingdom, Principality, and Country, where it is raised; He doth greatly Erre.

Placet. lxxxiii.

Placet eis.

CAP. XXXIV.

WE have spoken in the former Chapter of the Rebellion of the *Jews*, against their civil Governours, and the success thereof. We made no mention, either of the Priests, or of any of those Sects of Religion,

Religion, which then bare sway amongst them. Indeed it is likely, that if they had done their Duties, the People upon their Repentance, might have regained God's Favour, and prevented that utter desolation: but it happen'd otherwise, two factious Persons (*Judas* and *Matthias*) the best learned Men of the *Jews*, and the most skilful Interpreters of the Laws of their Country, growing into great favour with the People, because of their said skill, and for that they took great pains in teaching of their Children, professing that they would refuse none that had any desire to be virtuously brought up; and did thereupon draw unto them many Disciples; and the rather, for that they pretended themselves to be *propugnatores pietatis*. The Issue of which godly pretence was, that having thereby got a number to follow them, they stirred them up to Sedition against the civil Magistrate, under colour, that in contempt of their Laws he had made some Innovation. But they were presently vanquished; *Matthias* and divers others were put to death; and the High-Priest himself (as having his part in that sedition) was deprived from that Dignity. When *Herod* upon occasion caused his Subjects to bind themselves by an Oath, *quòd non decessuri essent à fide, & officio*; the *Pharisees* refused to take that Oath: whom he forbare at that time, because he favour'd greatly one *Pollio*, a chief Man of that Sect. But about fifteen years after, when it was again thought fit to have the like Oath ministred, and that all the whole Nation of the *Jews* did accordingly take the same, and thereby bound their Faith and Allegiance, both to *Herod* and unto *Cæsar*, saving the *Pharisees* (being then in number six thousand) who would not yet be induced to take it; they were censured and fined for their offence; and divers of them thereupon entring into some traiterous Courses and Conspiracies, with sundry Courtiers, against their Prince, they were (as they deserv'd) put in like manner to death.   Not

Jos. ant. l. 17. c. 18.

Placet. lxxxiv.

Jos. ib. l. 15. c. 13.

Jos. ib. l. 17. c. 13.

[80]

<small>Placet.
lxxxv.
Ibid. l. 18. c. 1, 2.
Id. de bell.
Jud. l. 2. c. 7.
Id. antiq. Jud. l. 18. c. 1.
Id. de bell.
Jud. l 2. c. 7.</small>

Not long after another Sect sprung up, whereof the chief heads were *Judas Gaulonites*, *Sadoc* a *Pharisee*, *Judas Galilæus*, and one *Simon of Galilee*, who profest themselves to be *propugnatores libertatis publicæ*. These men were so far from moving the people to obedience, as they stirred them up (as much as they could possibly) to Rebellion, telling them, that to undergo any Impositions or Taxes, was manifest acknowledgment of their servitude; and that it was a shame for them to pay Tribute to the *Romans*, or *Dominos post Deum ferre mortales*: by which means they perturbed the

<small>Id. antiq. l. 12. c. 1.
Id de bell. l. 2. c. 17.</small>

whole Nation, and filled every place with their Robberies and Slaughters; under pretence indeed of defending their Countries, *sed reverâ privatorum lucrorum studio*. Also it was *Eleazarus*, the Son of *Ananias*, the High-Priest, who would not suffer the inferiour Priests to offer Sacrifices and Prayers, (as formerly had been accustomed) for the long life and prosperity of the Emperour; nor could be drawn by any perswasion from his obstinacy therein, but proceeded from evil to worse; and so excited the people to Arms, as his rebellious course therein was held to be the Seminary, and mat-

<small>Placet.
lxxxvi.</small>

ter of *those* Roman Wars, which overthrew that Nation. It is true, that the High-Priests were not themselves so busie as the inferiour Priests that lived under them. For the *Romans* suspecting (of likelihood) that if the Priesthood should have been held by Succession,

<small>Id. antiq. l. 18.
c. 3. & l. 20. c. 8.</small>

and for term of Life, by the chief Persons of *Aaron*'s Posterity, the same might have grown dangerous unto their Government; did thereupon take order, that the Princes and Presidents which ruled in that Country, should have the appointing of such, as should be High Priests, to be chosen by them out of *Aaron*'s Kindred; and that they should also have Authority to alter, and change them from time to time, as they found occasion. Whereby the High Priesthood came to be but an annual Dignity; and sometimes it was not held so long:

which

which caused them for the most part to keep themselves from entring into any actual Rebellion against their Governours; though otherwise they were in effect as hollow-hearted unto them as any other of the Priests. For albeit in their hatred and malice against Christ, they could say, *We have no King but Cæsar*; and tell *Pilate* flatly, that if he delivered Christ, *he was not Cæsar's Friend:* yet what their private opinions were, doth plainly appear, by their sending of the *Pharisees* unto Christ with their entangling Questions; to know of him, Whether it were lawful to give Tribute unto *Cæsar* or not: supposing if he were not a Dissembler, (as they themselves were) that he would deny it to be lawful, and so should incur the danger thereunto appertaining; or if he answer'd that it was lawful, he might thereby bring upon him the hatred of the People; whom they suffer'd (for ought that we find to the contrary) to be brought up in the rebellious Doctrine of some of the *Pharisees*, and to hold it unlawful to pay Tribute unto *Cæsar*. Besides, what a false, ignorant, and wicked Generation they were, is manifest by the whole course which they held with our Saviour Christ. It being agreeable to the just Judgment of God, that the most impious Hypocrites, who then lived, should be the chief Actors in the Crucifying of Christ; which was the most horrible fact that ever was committed.

Joh. 19. 15, 12.
Placet. lxxxvii.

Matth. 22. 17.
Mark 12. 14.
Luk. 20. 22.

CAN. XXXIV.

If any Man therefore shall affirm, either that because the civil Magistrate had made some Innovation, which they liked not, or for any other respect, the said Judas and Matthias**, might lawfully move the People**

Placet. lxxxviii.

[82]

People to Rebellion, though otherwise they taught Mens Children never so diligently: or, that the Pharisees in refusing to swear their Allegiance and Faith to Cæsar, by an Oath, did not thereby shew themselves to be traiterously affected toward him: or, that it was not a seditious Doctrine to be detested of all good Subjects, which Judas Gaulonites, and his Fellows, deliver'd to the People, in teaching them to refuse all Taxations imposed by the Romans, their lawful Magistrates; and rather to rebel than to pay any tribute unto them: or, that they did not very grievously sin (both the High-Priest's Son and the rest) who either refused to offer Sacrifice, or to pray for Cæsar: or, that the High-Priests then were not a wicked Brood, degenerated far from their first Institution; or, that they did not greatly offend God, in permitting the People to be infected by their inferiour Priests, and other religious Persons, with any of the said false positions, and traiterous conceits: or, that they (the said High-Priests) did not most grosly erre in all those points, and particulars, wherein they opposed themselves against the Person and Doctrine of our Saviour Christ; He doth greatly

Placet,   Erre.   Placet eis.

CAP.

CAP. XXXV.

WE have followed thus far that mild and moderate Form of civil Government, which God himself established, and preserved in the Lines of *Seth* and *Sem*, until through the obstinate Rebellion, from time to time, of the *Jews*, the Fame and the Authority thereof were first greatly diminished, and afterward taken wholly away from them. But it is further to be considered, that as, in the first Chapter, we have shewed the Creation of all the World, to be ascribed to the Son of God, the second Person in the Trinity: so is the Government of it, in the same sense, attributed to him. *The Earth is the Lord's, and all that therein is; the round World, and all that dwell therein.* Whereupon he was called ordinarily, in the Old Testament, *Dominator, Dominus,* the *Lord of Hosts,* the *God* and *Possessour* of *Heaven* and *Earth.* So as he being the universal Lord, and Ruler over all the World, the whole World was his Universal Kingdom: in the Government whereof he ever used the Ministry of civil Magistrates, as well in other Countries, as amongst his own peculiar People of *Israel*, without any desert of theirs, but as in his Heavenly Providente he thought it most convenient. *I have made* (saith he) *the Earth, the Man, and the Beasts that are upon the ground, and have given it to whom it pleaseth me*: and again, the Prophet *Daniel* telleth us, that *God changeth the times and seasons, that he hath power, and beareth rule over the Kingdoms of men;* that *he taketh away Kings, and setteth up Kings:* and that it *was the God of Heaven, who gave unto Nebuchadnezzar so great a Kingdom, Power, Strength and Glory, as then he had, to rule, with Majesty and Honour, a very great Empire.* In respect whereof, although Kings and Princes might have been satisfied with the Titles of Lieutenants or Vicegerents in Earth, to the Son of God; yet

yet he did communicate and impart so much of his Power, Authority, and Dignity unto them, as he was content to stile them with his own Name: *I have said, You are gods, and the Children of the most High*. Howbeit, for all their said Dignity and Greatness, he did not leave them at liberty to do what they list, but held himself the Helm of every Kingdom, and used their Services in such sort, as were they good or bad, and their designments holy or wicked, he ever made them the Executioners of his own just Judgments, Will and good Pleasure; according as he was minded, either to bless or to punish any Kingdom, People or Countrey. In regard of which his Might, Providence, and Wisdom, whereby he ruleth them after that sort, he is called the *Lord of lords*, the *King of Glory*, and the *God of gods*; that is, of Kings, Princes, Judges and Rulers of the Earth. And it may not here be omitted (which indeed ariseth of the Premisses) that the Son of God, in disposing of the Government, under him, of the Earth, did not appoint any one man to be the sole Monarch of the world; as from whom all other Kingdoms, Governments, Kings and Princes should receive their Directions, and unto whom they should be subject. It is true, that *Adam*, whilst he lived, was the chief Governour under the Son of God, over all his own Off-spring; and that *Noah* likewise, during his Life, had the like Authority. But when, after the Flood, the Issue of *Sem*, *Cham*, and *Japhet* grew to a great People, their Father, *Noah*, did not commit, to any one of them, the Government of the rest, and of all of their Posterity; but divided the whole World amongst them three: and from them, no one sole Monarch or Monarchy, but many Kings, Principalities, Kingdoms and Governments, by God's Providence, have descended. It is more than probable, that if the Son of God had been pleased to have committed to any one Man, a Government of so large an extent, he would

would have trufted his Servant, King *David*, with it, being a Man according to his own Heart. But the Kingdom of *Ifrael*, wherein *David* reigned, was bounded within the ftrait Limits affigned to the Twelve Tribes. And fuch other Kings, as fwerved, after that time, from *David*'s mild and temperate Government, and took upon them the Titles of Monarchies, having enlarged their Kingdoms by Injury and Oppreffion of their Neighbours; were, in their Pride and Greedinefs, but the Scourges and Rods of God's Indignation, and had their fatal Ends accordingly. So as where the Prophet *Daniel*, fpeaking of the Kingdom of *Nebuchadnezzar*, calleth him *King of kings*, and faith, that *he was the Ruler over all places, wherein the Children of Men dwelt*; and *Cyrus*, the King of *Perfia*, affirmeth, that the *Lord God of Heaven had given him all the Kingdoms of the Earth:* For as much as it is apparent, both by the Scriptures, and other Hiftories, that neither of them both had the Tenth part of the World under their Jurifdiction; and that there were very many Kings, who had Abfolute Government in their Kingdoms, and were no ways fubject unto them; the faid places, of neceffity, muft receive this Expofition, That either they are to be underftood *Hyperbolically*, whereby, to exprefs the Greatnefs of a thing, it is faid to be bigger than it was; or by a *Synecdoche*, which ufeth the whole fometimes for a part; or according to the ufual Phrafe of the Scriptures, where *All* are often taken for *Many*: or elfe both *Daniel* and *Cyrus* fpake after the manner of the *Chaldæans* and *Perfians*, who, to extoll the Greatnefs of their Kings, and the better to pleafe them, did, peradventure, fo enlarge and amplifie the Style.

Places.
xciij.
Dan. 2. 37, 38.
Ezra 1. 2.

Places.

C A N.

CAN. XXXV.

If any Man therefore shall affirm, either that the Son of God (according to the Doctrine of the Old Testament) was not the Governour of all the World: or that he did not appoint under him divers Kings, Princes and civil Magistrates, to Rule and Govern in the Kingdoms, and Places assigned unto them: or that having so appointed them, he did not himself direct, uphold, and rule them by his Omnipotence, according to his Divine Wisdom; and might not, in that respect, be truly called The Lord of lords, and The God of gods: or that all the World, and the particular Kingdoms, and civil kinds of Government in the World were not in respect of the Son of God, as he is the Governour of the World, and the Lord of lords, and God of gods, one Kingdom, Principality or Government (thereby to impeach the mild and temperate Government, which he had established amongst the Jews:) or that he ever committed the Government of all the World, after Adam and Noah's times, to any One Man, to be the Sole and Visible Monarch of it: or that the said Kingdom of Christ, as he was the Lord of lords, and God of gods,

gods, **and so govern'd the whole World, was otherwise visible upon the Earth, than** per partes, viz. **by the particular Kingdoms, and kinds of civil Government, or perhaps by some Representation; He doth greatly Erre.**

Placet.

Placet eis.

CAP. XXXVI.   xcv.

AS there hath been from the beginning one Universal Kingdom throughout all the World, whereof the Son of God was ever the sole (though invisible) Monarch, as we have shewed in the former Chapter: So it is generally agreed upon among all Christians, That from the Creation of Mankind, during the times aforesaid, there hath always been One Universal or *Catholick Church*: which began in *Adam,* and afterward (as his Posterity multiplied, both before and after the Flood) was dispersed over the face of the whole Earth; and whereof the Son of God likewise was always the head and sole (though invisible) Monarch. The foundation of which Church was ever one and the same Rock, to wit *Christ Jesus*, the promised *Seed of the Woman, that should break the Serpents head*: and as many Persons, Families, Societies, and Companies, as truly believed in that blessed Seed, without exception of any sort, or distinction of People, were the true Members and parts of the *Catholick Church*. For the death of our Saviour Christ, which long after did actually ensue; was virtually, through Faith, as effectual to all Believers before his Passion, as it hath been since. In respect whereof the Holy Ghost did not only affirm, That *Jesus Christ was the same,* (that is, the *Wisdom, Righte-*

Placet, xcvi.

ousness,

ousness, *Sanctification*, and *Redemption* of those that believ'd in him) *yesterday*, (that is, before and after the Law) *as to day* (that is, now in the time of the New Testament:) but likewise, that he was the *Lamb slain from the beginning of the World:* because his Death and Passion, being ever as present in the view and sight of God the Father (before whom *a thousand years are but as one day*;) the same was typically represented by Sacrifices and effectual Sacraments; and the merits thereof have from the beginning been communicated to all Believers. So that although in imitation of the Scriptures, we have spoken hitherto but of one particular Church, and of the Succession of it in the Lines of *Seth* and *Sem:* yet there have been other particular Churches in all Ages, which were built upon the said Rock and promised Seed. *Cain* offer'd his Sacrifice to God as well as *Abel*; though it was not for his sins accepted: and it is not to be doubted, but that every chief Family of his Posterity had their Priest and publick worship of God; albeit mingled with some such Superstition and Idolatry, as offended God, and made them less acceptable in his sight. For as of the Posterity of *Seth* many perished; so we are to judge on the other side, that many of *Cain*'s Line died in God's favour: except we should think, against the rules of Charity, that the Curse which fell upon *Cain*, killing his Brother *Abel*, did cause his Off-spring to become as brute Beasts: whereas having *Adam* their Grandfather, it is more than probable he did better instruct them, and prevail'd at least with some of them. Likewise after the Flood, all *Noah*'s Off-spring, being one Church under him, and grounded upon Christ the true Foundation of it, although afterward, when they were setled in their several Countries, allotted unto them, they swerved greatly from that Purity in Religion which *Noah* had taught them; yet they had still their Priests, their Sacrifices, and some outward worship of God amongst them.

Placet.
xcvii.

them. Besides, hitherto all the World being as one People, if there were then any visible Churches at all upon the Earth; it cannot be truly said, that the calling of *Abraham* out of *Chaldæa*, and the Erecting of the true worship of God in his Family, did make them to be in worse case than they were before. If Churches before, they so continued after, though Superstitious and Idolatrous Churches. Again, it is generally held, that God did not therefore distinguish the *Jews* from other Nations and People, and settle his publick worship amongst them; as purposing thereby, that his *Catholick Church*, in their times, should only consist of them and of their Nations; and such other Proselytes as would be circumcised, and join themselves unto them: but much more, because by that means the truth and certainty of all the Promises and Prophecies concerning the coming of the *Messias*, might be faithfully and diligently observ'd, and kept in one Nation, and visible known place and People. For it is plain in the Scriptures, that after the said distinction, many of the *Gentiles* served God, and believed in Christ, and were thereby made the true Members of the *Catholick Church*; though they were not circumcis'd, nor had any medling with, or dependency upon the *Jews*. Some are particularly named; as *Job*, *Jethro*, *Rahab*, the *Ninevites*, the Widow of *Sarepta*, *Naaman*, *Cornelius*, and some others: by whom we are not only to judge of their Families and Governments, that they were so many particular Churches: but likewise, that in every Country, and People, many such godly Men from time to time might have been found; who with their Families, and peradventure Subjects, were so to be held and esteemed of. We will not enter into the discussing of these places, how far they may be extended. *Without Faith it is impossible to please God. For he that cometh to God, must believe that God is, and that he is a rewarder of them that seek him.* *In the word was life, and the*

Placet. xcviii.

Placet. xcix.

Heb. 11.5.

John 1.4.

<small>Rom. 3. 29, 30.</small> the life was the light of men. Is God, the God only of the
<small>John 10. 16.</small> Jews, and not of the Gentiles also? Yes, of the Gentiles
also: for it is one God, who doth justify Circumcision by
Faith, and the uncircumcised through Faith. I have other
<small>Placet.</small> sheep, which are not of this fold. Only we do further
<small>c.</small>
observe, that it was lawful for any of the Gentiles to
come into the outward Court of the Temple, to bring
their Sacrifices unto the Lord, and there to offer up
their Prayers likewise unto him: that accordingly they
did often resort to the Temple for Devotion sake, there
to worship God: as by the Examples of the *Eunuch* of
<small>Acts 8. 27.</small> *Ethiopia*, and of certain *Grecians*, that are mentioned
<small>John 12. 20.</small>
in the Scriptures: and that many of them were so addicted to the true service of God, as the Prophet *Hag-
gai* calleth our Saviour Christ, *Desiderium Gentium*. So
that the *Catholick Church*, consisting from the beginning
till *Abraham*'s time, of such only as were afterward
for distinction sake called *Gentiles*; although God was
then pleased to bestow his Mercies more plentifully upon that one particular Church of the Jews, deduced
<small>Placet</small> from *Abraham*, than upon any other, or indeed upon
<small>ci.</small> all the rest, for the principal Causes before-specified;
yet they were not utterly so rejected, or cast out of
God's favour, but that many of them did continue as
dutiful Children in the Lap and Bosom of the said *Catholick Church*. Of which *Catholick Church*, it is true,
that *Adam* and *Noah*, for their times, were (under
Christ) the chief Governours. Howbeit afterward
the Posterity of *Noah* being mightily encreased, when
thereupon he distributed the whole World among his
three Sons, and their Issue; he did not appoint any
one of them to be the Ruler of the said *Catholick Church*;
but left the Government of every particular Family or
Church unto their chief Heads, Princes and Priests
and of the whole to the Son of God, and sole Monarch'
of it; who only was able to undertake such a charge.
Neither do we read, that *Aaron*, or any of the *High-
Priests*,

Priests, took upon them at any time to extend their Jurisdiction beyond the bounds and limits of the twelve Tribes; or so much as once dream'd, that the whole World was their Diocess: that which they had being indeed more than they well ordered.

CAN. XXXVI.

If any Man therefore shall affirm, either that during the continuance of the Old Testament, the Merits of Christ's Death actually to come, were not sufficient to save all true Believers: or, that there was then no Catholick Church: or, that at any time there was any other Rock but Jesus Christ, the blessed Seed upon Whom the Catholick Church was then built: or, that many of the Gentiles were not always (for ought that is known to the contrary) true Members of the Catholick Church: or that Christ himself was not the sole Head or Monarch all that while of the Whole Catholick Church: or, that the said Catholick Church, after the Members of it were dispersed into all the places of the World, was otherwise visible than per partes: or, that Noah did appoint any Man to be the visible Head of the said Catholick Church: or, that the High-Priest among the Jews, had any more Authority over the Catholick Church of God, than David had over the Universal Kingdom

[92]

God: oꝛ, that the ſaid High-Prieſt had not greatly ſinn'd, if he had taken upon him, oꝛ uſurped any ſuch infinite Authoꝛity; He doth greatly Erre.

Placet eis.

The ſaid XXXVI. *Chapters, with the Conſtitutions made upon them, have paſſed with one Conſent, both the Convocation-Houſes, and ſo are approved.*

* Sc. Dr. *Richard Bancroft* Archbiſhop of *Canterbury*.

* R. Cant.

The ſaid XXXVI. *Chapters, with the Conſtitutions made upon them, have been diligently read, and deliberately examin'd; and thereupon have likewiſe paſſed, with one Conſent, in the Convocation-Houſe of the Province of* York.

† Sc. Dr. *Thornborough* Biſhop of *Briſtol*, and ▇▇ of *York*; which Archbiſhoprick was then Vacant. He was afterwards, Biſhop of *Worceſter*.

† Jo. Briſtol *præſes Convocat*. Eborac.

LIB.

LIB. II.

CAP. I.

IN pursuing our intended course, through the Old Testament, and until the Destruction of *Jerusalem*, we over-slipped and passed by the fulness of that time, wherein the Son of God, (the Maker and Governour of all the World) our Lord and Saviour, *Jesus Christ*, was conceived by the Holy Ghost, and born of the Virgin *Mary*. So as now we are to return back, and prosecute our said course, as we find the true Grounds thereof are laid down, confirmed and practised in the New Testament. At our entrance into which course, we confess our selves to be indeed greatly astonished, considering the strange Impediments, and mighty Stumbling-blocks, which, through long Practice, and incredible Ambition, are cast in our way [in that we find the Estate of that Church (which would rule over all) to be degenerated, in our days, as far, in effect, from her primary and Apostolical Institution and Rules; as we have shewed before, the Estate of the *Jewish* Church to have swerved, through the like Pride and Ambition, from that excellent Condition, wherein she was first established, and afterward preserved and beautified by *Moses*, and King *David*, with the rest of his most worthy and godly Successours.] For except we should condemn the Old Testament (as many ancient Hereticks have done) and thereupon overthrow all, which hitherto we have built; and not that only, but should furthermore, either approve of their gross Impiety, who read the

Aug. de Hæres. cap. 46.

O   Scriptures

Scriptures of the New Testament, as if they were falsified and corrupted, and by receiving and rejecting as much of them as they list, do prefer before them (as not containing in them all necessary Truth for Man's Salvation) certain obscure, and Apocryphal Writings; Or, should our selves impiously imagine, that the New Testament (as now we have it) was but a rough Draught, and a fit Project compiled, for the time, by the Apostles, to be afterward better ordered, polished, and supplied with certain humane Traditions and Doctrines, by some of their Successours: We can see no Authentical Ground, nor sufficient Warrant, in those Writings, which ought to be the true Rule of every Christian Man's Conscience (as not being there to be found) for any Apostolical Priest or Bishop either to pretend, that all the particular Churches, in the World, are under his Government; or to tell the Subjects of any Christian King, opposite in some points, unto him, That they are no longer bound to obey him their said King, but until they shall be able, by force of Arms, or by some secret Practice, to subdue him; or to challenge to himself an Absolute and Universal Authority and Power over all Kings and Kingdoms in the World, to bestow them, in some cases, (under pretence of Religion) when he shall think the same to be most available, for the strengthning and upholding of such his pretended Universal Power and Dominion. To the Proof whereof, before we address our selves; because the same doth much depend upon the admirable Humiliation of the Son of God, in taking our Nature upon him, and performing the Work of our Salvation, in such a manner, as he did: We have thought it our Duties (left otherwise we might be mistaken, either through Weakness, Simplicity or Malice) first, briefly to observe (notwithstanding our Saviour's said Humiliation) the most wonderful Dignity, Preheminency and Royalty of his Person.

It

It is many ways apparent, that the mean Estate and Condition of our Saviour Christ, here upon Earth, was one especial Motive, both to the *Jews* and *Gentiles*, why, in their carnal Judgments, he was, to the one sort a Scandal, and to the other a Scorn; as if he had been a Man out of his Wits, and preached he knew not what. In which respect, partly not only the People of the *Jews*, the Priests of all sorts, the *Scribes* and *Pharisees*, with the rest of their Hypocritical Orders; but likewise the civil Governours, as well *Romans* as *Jews*, did utterly despise him, hate him, deride him, beat him, and put him to death. Since which time sundry sorts of Hereticks have stumbled at the same stone, labouring, by all the means they could, to impeach and dishonour the Person of Christ, in regard of the mean shew of his humane Nature, notwithstanding the many Arguments which they might have found in the Scriptures, (had not their Hearts been hardned) of his Divinity. On the other side, we are not ignorant, how the Bishop of *Rome*, and his Adherents, supposing it would too much impeach their Credits, and worldly Reputations; if they should be too much pressed to deduce the principal strength of their Estates and Callings, from the said mean Condition of our Saviour Christ, whilst he lived in this World; do thereupon attribute sundry Virtues, Powers, and Branches of Authority unto his humane Nature, which do not, in Truth, belong properly unto it, but are rather appertaining to his Person, being both God and Man; as hoping thereby to get some fair Pretences and Colours for the upholding of their usurped Greatness, and pretended uncontroulable Sovereignty. For the avoiding therefore of these Extremities, and because such as deny the Pope's Supremacy, are most falsly charged, by sundry passionate, and inconsiderate Persons, to be Men, that believe no one Article of the Christian Faith: We have thought it meet, to make it known, to all the Christian World, how detestable, to the Church of *England*, all such false Doctrine is, as doth any way, not only impeach the Sacred Person of our Saviour Christ, but likewise the other two Persons of the Blessed Trinity, God the Father, and God the Holy Ghost; in that the dishonouring of One of them, is the dishonouring of them all Three.

We do therefore, for our selves, and in the Name of all the rest of the Church of *England*, acknowledge and profess, from the bottom of our hearts, the Truth of all that is written in the Sacred Scriptures; and consequently, and in more particular manner, whatsoever is written in the same, that doth appertain to the most Holy and Blessed Trinity. Out of the Doctrine of which Sacred Writings, because the Apostles and Churches of God, (moved thereunto, by sundry sorts of Hereticks) have, long since, most faithfully and learnedly deduced, into certain Summaries, rightly termed *Creeds*, all those Points of true Doctrine, which do concern God the Father, God the Son, and God the Holy Ghost, and are necessarily to be believed, under pain of condemnation: We do resolutely embrace, and stedfastly believe, all and every one the Articles of the *Apostles Creed*; and all and every one the Articles of the other *Creeds*, made, by sundry Councils, for the further Declaration of the Christian Faith, and Apostolick Creed, as of the *Nicene Creed*, made, by the Council of *Nice*, against *Arius*, who denied the Divinity of the Son of God; and of the next *Creed*, made in the first Council of *Constantinople*, ratifying, and further declaring the *Nicene Creed* against *Eudoxius* the *Arian*, and *Macedonius*, who denied the Holy Ghost to be God; and of the *Creed*, made in the first Council of *Ephesus*, against *Nestorius*, who taught that the two Natures in Christ, were not united together personally, but that the Word, which did take our Nature upon him, for our Redem-

Redemption, did only assist Christ, our Saviour, as one Friend may assist another; and of the *Creed* made in the Council of *Chalcedon* against *Eutyches*, who did confound the two Natures of Christ. Against any of which Articles whosoever doth oppose himself, and doth willfully continue in such his Opposition; we hold and judge them to be worthily subject to all those Censures, and Anathematisms, which the several Constitutions and Canons of the said Councils have justly laid upon them.

Also with the same Resolution and Faith beforementioned, we receive and believe all and every one the several Points and Articles of the *Athanasian* Creed, made a little after the *Council* of *Nice*, against such blasphemous Opinions, as in those times were either directly or indirectly, published in Corners, and spread here and there to the seducing of many. According to some Articles of the which Creed, that do more nearly concern our Course; We stedfastly believe and confess, " That our Lord, *Jesus Christ*, " the Son of God, is both God and Man: God of the " substance of the Father, begotten before all Worlds; " and Man, of the substance of his Mother, born in the " World: perfect God, and perfect Man, of a reason- " able Soul, and humane flesh subsisting: Equal to the " Father, as touching his Godhead; and inferiour to " the Father, as touching his Manhood: who although " he be both God and Man; yet he is not two, but " One Christ: One, not by Conversion of the God- " head into Flesh; but by taking of the Manhood into " God: One altogether, not by Confusion of substance, " but by Unity of Person. In respect of which Personal Union of the two Natures of our Saviour Christ, without confusion or mixture of either of them, thus described in the said Creed; whatsoever is affirmed in the Scriptures, as well of the one Nature as of the other, the same is also truly to be affirmed *de toto Composito*,

that

that is, of his most sacred Person being both God and Man; the Essential Properties of them both remaining notwithstanding distinguished.

For as the said personal or hypostatical Union of the said two Natures, doth not make the one Nature to be the other; the divine Nature to be the humane Nature, or the humane Nature to be the Divine Nature: so doth it not make the Essential Proprieties of the one Nature to be the Essential Proprieties of the other Nature; but as well the Proprieties and actions as the Natures themselves do remain distinguished, though united in one Person; both of them concurring together, the Deity in working that which appertaineth to the Deity, and the Humanity executing those Essential Proprieties and actions which do belong unto the Humanity. For Example, the Divine Nature appear'd in Christ by Miracles, when his humane Nature was subject to many opprobries and injuries. In that our Saviour Christ did satisfie 5000. Persons with 5. loaves, did give Water of Life to the Woman of *Samaria*, did walk upon the Sea dry-foot, did by his Commandment calm the Winds; he shewed thereby some effects and works of his Divine Nature: because they were (as one well saith) *verbi propria, non carnis*, the Proprieties of the Word, and not of the Flesh. Again, in that Christ brake Bread, this was an Office of his humane Nature, but in that he multiplied it, the same did appertain to his Divine Nature. In that he cried out, *Lazarus come forth*, that was the office of his humane Nature; but in that he quickned him, and raised him from Death, that did belong unto his Divine Nature. In that he said, *Thy sins are forgiven thee*, that was an office of his humane Nature; but in that such sins were indeed remitted, the same did appertain to his Divine Nature. In that our Saviour Christ died, the same did proceed from the Flesh; but in that by his Death he did expiate our Sins, that did proceed from the Spirit.

rit. In that he was Buried, did proceed from the Flesh; but in that he did raise himself from the dead, that was he Office of his Divinity. In that he gave Bread to his Apostles in his last Supper, he did it as Man; but in that he made them partakers of his blessed Body, he did the same as he was God. In that now being in Heaven, he doth possess that Kingdom in the name and behalf of his Elect, that doth appertain to his humane Nature; but that he doth now remain with us, and dwell in our hearts, that is an Office of his Divine Nature. In that he maketh Intercession for us, that doth belong to his humane Nature; but in that he doth justifie us, regenerate us, work in us both to will and to perform, in that he ruleth us and leadeth us in the way of his Commandments; all these Offices do appertain unto his Divinity. Lastly, In that he shall come in the Clouds, and say unto one sort of Persons, *Come ye blessed*, and unto the other sort, *Depart ye Cursed*; he shall do the same according to his humane Nature: but in that he shall judge every Man according to his knowledge of all Mens hearts, their cogitations, desires and works, that he shall do as God.

Neverthelefs any thing by us thus affirmed notwithstanding, Christ himself is not divided, though the Proprieties and actions of his two Natures, are in this sort to be distinguished: as God himself is not divided, although the three Persons in Trinity are rightly held to be indeed distinguished: and yet all the said actions and proprieties of the two Natures of Christ, distinguished, as we have expressed they are, are notwithstanding very truly to be affirm'd of his sacred Person. The reason whereof, hath been before touched, and it is this; because seeing that both the Natures are joined together in the Person of the Son, by an *Hypostatical*, and consequently a true and essential Union; so as Christ is thereby both true God, in regard of his Divine Nature, and true Man, in respect

of

of his humane Nature: Whatsoever is the Propriety of the Divine Nature, and of the humane Nature, the same is wholly, and altogether in Christ, and is necessarily therefore to be affirmed of him, both essentially and properly. In respect whereof, we say, that Christ was dead, and that he could not die; that he is both finite and infinite; eternal and temporal; in every place, and yet circumscribed in one place. For, of necessity, whatsoever are the Properties of the humane Nature, the same are truly and properly to be affirmed *de vero homine*: and whatsoever are the Proprieties of the Divine Nature, the same are likewise to be affirmed *de vero Deo*; Christ being (out of all Controversie amongst the Children of God) *& verus homo, & verus Deus*. And thus we have, after a sort, both briefly and truly set down the Force and Efficacy of the Hypostatical Union of the two Natures of Christ, being distinguished, but no ways confounded; as the same, together with the true Doctrine of all other necessary Articles, concerning the Blessed Trinity, doth, by the Scriptures, most truly expounded in the Creeds abovementioned, many ways very notably appear.

To this purpose much more might have here been added by us; if (our Course considered) we had thought it necessary. Only we have thought it fit, furthermore to profess, and make it thereby known to all Men; that there are some other *Creeds*, made by other Councils and particular Bishops, like to *Athanasius*, and other worthy Persons: as *Irenæus*'s Creed, *Tertullian*'s Creed (as we may so term it) *Damasus*'s Creed, the Creed ascribed to St. *Ambrose*, and to St. *Augustine*, *Te Deum laudamus*, &c. the Creed of the first Council of *Toledo*, St. *Jerome*'s Creed, the Creed ascribed to *Leo*, which was approved by the Council of *Chalcedon*, and the Creed of the sixth Council of *Constantinople*, against the *Monothelites*, holding that in Christ, both God and Man, there was but One Will: all of them tending to
the

the setting forth the Orthodoxal and true Doctrine of One God in Trinity, and Trinity in Unity; not confounding the Persons, nor dividing the Substance; and of One Christ, true God and true Man, not confounding his Natures, nor dividing his Person. Which Creeds we do receive, embrace, and reverence in such sorts, as they have been received, embraced and reverenced hitherto, by all the particular Churches of the Christian World; in as much, as they agree both with the Scriptures, with the Apostles Creed, with the four Creeds mentioned of the four first general Councils, and with the *Athanasian Creed*; which contain in them that Faith, which was then, and so still ought to be accounted the true, Catholick Faith: nothing, in effect, being contained in all the Creeds before, by us specified, which may not be deduced, by necessary consequence, out of the said *Athanasian Creed*; and the Conclusion of which Creed is, in these words, expressed; *This is the Catholick Faith, which except a Man believe faithfully, he cannot be saved.* To which Conclusion, that, in sense, is very consonant, wherewith *Damasus* doth end his Creed, in these words; *Read these things, believe them, retain them: to this Faith submit thy Soul, and thou shalt obtain Life and Reward from Christ.*

In which Creeds, containing the Catholick Faith, in those days, or in any of the rest, we have thought it good, here to remember, that there is not any one Article, to warrant or prove those new Articles, which were coined long after the making of any of the said Creeds, by the Bishops of *Rome*, and are added to the *Nicene* Creed, by *Pius IV.* in the professing of the *Roman* Faith: especially that New Article of the *Pope's Supremacy*, which is still so stifly maintained and urged upon many, under pain of the loss of their Souls, viz. that it is altogether necessary for them, if they will be saved, to be obedient to the Bishop of *Rome*. Which New Article, being but an extravagant Conclusion;

P made

made by a very strange Man, and built upon as strange Collections out of the Scriptures; We leave it for a novelty unto all the Articles of the ancient Catholick Faith: and will now addrefs our felves to profecute the fame courfe and points in the New Teftament, which we held in the Old.

CAP. II.

IT is a certain rule in Divinity, that *Grace doth not deftroy Nature.* The Doctrine of the Seed of the Woman, that was foretold fhould break the Serpents head, did not abolifh the Moral Law. The Ceremonies in the Old Teftament, which fhadowed and fignified the mercies of God in Chrift, had no power to extinguifh the Laws, firft imprinted in mens hearts; and afterward ingraven in Tables of ftone by the Finger of God. The Prophets foretelling the coming of Chrift, and the merits of his Paffion, did likewife reprove all fins and offences committed againft the Ten Commandments. Chrift teftifieth of himfelf, that he came *not to deftroy the Law and the Prophets, but to fullfil them.* By his Death he hath delivered us from the Curfe of the Law; but not from the obedience of it. And St. *Paul* faith, that the Apoftles did not *make the Law of none effect through Faith*; *but they did thereby eftablifh the Law.* For that Faith doth only apprehend Chrift truly to Salvation, which worketh by Charity; that is, which purgeth the Confcience from dead works, to ferve the living God; and bringeth forth by the Spirit, Obedience to the Precepts and Laws of God.

It hath been fhewed by us at large in the former Book, that although the Son of God having made the World, did by his mighty Power and divine Providence, retain, as it were, in his own hands, the general Rule and Government of it: yet for a more vifible benefit

Matth. 5. 17.

Rom. 3. 13.

benefit and comfort to Mankind, he did divide and distribute the same into divers Countries, Principalities, and Kingdoms: and ordaining civil Magistracy, did not only appoint Soveraign Princes and Kings as his Deputies and Lieutenants upon Earth, to rule and govern under him, such Countries and Kingdoms as he had allotted unto them; but did likewise tie Mankind by one of the Moral Laws ingraven in their hearts, that they should honour them, serve them, and be obedient unto them. Which particular Commandment was no more abolished by the Incarnation of our Saviour Christ, than were all the rest. Nay it was in truth of such force and publick note, as that our Saviour having most willingly subjected himself to the obedience of the whole Law, did very carefully, upon every occasion, shew himself most observant of this one Law amongst the rest. For in the whole course of his Life here upon Earth, we find not any alteration that he made in the Civil State where he was conversant: which he must of necessity have done, if his coming into the World had any way impeached the Authority of the civil Magistrates. It is expresly recorded of him, that he lived in subjection to his Parents; Luc. 11. 51. herein fullfilling the said *Fifth Commandment*, which containeth as well the subjection due to Authority Civil as Paternal. He was *made of the Seed of* David *according to the flesh*, as the Apostle speaketh; and so had (no Rom. 1. 3. doubt) according to his Manhood, great natural compassion of those Miseries and Afflictions, which the *Jews* at that very time endur'd under the *Romans*. Howbeit as knowing the duties of their Allegiance, he neither moved, nor any way encouraged them to take Arms against the Emperour; nor filled their heads with shifts and distinctions, how Subjects in this Case and that Case, were superiour to their Soveraigns; nor did any way approve of those rebellious courses in them, whereunto they were of their own dispositions very

greatly

greatly addicted. He was so far from these exorbitant and bad Humours; as still he shewed, when there was cause, his great detestation of them. He did himself *very willingly* pay Tribute when it was demanded; and upon fit Occasion, gave all the *Jews* this following Rule, that they, living under *Cæsar*, were *bound to pay unto him those things that were his*; meaning such Obedience, Custom, Tributes, Tolls, Taxation and Payments, as, by the Laws, both Divine and Imperial, were due unto *Cæsar*. And certainly if ever it had, and might have been lawful for private Men, in respect of their own Zeal, to have used Force against Authority; it seemeth to us, that it might have been born with in the Apostles, upon some such Accidents, as then fell out. *Judas* had betrayed their Master, and thereupon a Multitude was sent, with a publick Officer, to apprehend him. Which the Apostles perceiving, conferred together, as it seemeth, how to make Resistance, and said, in their Zeal, *Master, shall we smite them with the sword?* But *Peter* seeing (of likelyhood) the Haste, Violence, and Fury that was used, by the said Multitude, did, upon the sudden, pluck out his Sword, and without any expectation, what Christ would answer to the said Question, smiting one of the Company, did cut off his Ear. Now if we shall consult, with Flesh and Blood, who would not approve this Fact of St. *Peter?* But our Saviour Christ, being void of any Heat or Passion, and only respecting the Will of God, and the due Observation of the said particular Law; did utterly condemn, in St. *Peter*, that violent and unlawful Attempt: because he, being but a private Man, had nothing to do with the Temporal Sword, which belonged to the Civil Magistrate; and much less should have used it against Authority. And therefore, as well to let St. *Peter* see his Offence, as also to leave a Caution, for the bridling, from thence forwards, of all future rash Zeal; in such a Case, he

Luc. 22. 49.

justified

justified the Law of God, and did leave the same, for a Rule, to all Posterity, saying, *All that take the Sword, shall perish with the Sword*: meaning all private Persons, that shall, at any time, abuse, after that sort, the civil Sword, which doth in no wise appertain unto them.

Besides, it is manifest, that our Saviour Christ, if, as he was God, he had been disposed, was able to have defended himself against all the World. Nay, as he was Man, he might, by Prayer to his Father, have procured sufficient Assistance against the Force of all his Enemies; had he not well known that Course to have been repugnant to the Obedience, which he had undertaken, of the said Commandment, and no way agreeable to the Vocation and Work which he had in hand: and therefore persisting in his Reproof of St. *Peter*, *Thinkest thou* (faith he unto him) *that I cannot now pray to my Father, and he will give me more than Twelve Legions of Angels?* but it is ever apparent, in all the Proceedings of our Saviour Christ, whilst he lived in this World, that he never liked, in any, the Resistance of Civil Authority by Force; or approved of any inconsiderate and rash Zeal, bent against Magistrates, or any other Persons; but was always ready to blame and check the same, as he did, when he found it in two other of his Apostles, who, to revenge an Injury offered to their Master, sought to have had it punished from Heaven. For when the *Samaritans* refused (upon conference and direction, we doubt not, of those that were in Authority over them) to give Christ entertainment, and lodging in one of their Cities; *James* and *John* were so moved therewith, as they would needs have licence of him, to command that Fire should come down from Heaven, as *Elias* did; shewing thereby, that in their Heat (if they had been able) they would have had them all destroyed. But our Saviour Christ, disliking such fiery and rash Zeal,

Luc. 9. 54, 55.

Zeal, rebuked them, and said, *You know not of what spirit you are :* that is, in effect, as if he should have said, You may pretend *Elias*'s Fact, but you are far from *Elias*'s Spirit. He only executed the Judgment of God, as, by the Spirit, he was extraordinarily directed; whereas Ye have received no such direction, but are only in your Passion and Heat stirred up to Revenge.

The Conclusion hereof is, That Christ, our Lord, all the time he remained here upon Earth, did not only, in his own Person, shew himself obedient to civil Authority, according to the said fifth Commandment; but did likewise utterly condemn, in others, (upon every occasion offered to him, throughout the Four Evangelists) all inconsiderate Zeal, and Opposition, against Temporal Magistracy. Insomuch as concerning his own said Obedience, when he was apprehended (notwithstanding *Peter's* Sword) he submitted himself to the publick Officer, that was then sent for him: and likewise being afterward carried to *Pilate*, (the Civil Magistrate, at that time, under the Emperour) and before him falsly charged, by his malicious Adversaries, with Treason; he behaved himself in such dutiful manner, as was fit and convenient for him, that truly had professed subjection, and did in no sort seek to decline his Power and Authority; either by alledging that he was not the Emperour's Subject, or that *Pilate* was not his competent Judge, or by using any other Tergiversation or Evasion: but acknowledged, very freely, his said Authority to be lawful, and yielding himself thereunto, did confess that it *was given him from above.*

John 19. 11.

CAN.

CAN. I.

AND therefore if any Man shall affirm, under colour of any thing that is in the Scriptures, either that the Doctrine of Grace in the New Testament doth more abolish the rules of Nature, or Moral Law of God, than it did in the Old; or that through Faith the said Law was not rather established than in any sort impeached; or, that because as many as believe are redeemed, and made free from the Curse of the Law, they are therefore exempted, and free from the obedience of the Law; or, that by the Incarnation of our Saviour Christ, obedience to the Fifth Commandment, touching honour due to Parents and Princes, was in any sort impeached, the rest of the Law being established; or, that our Saviour Christ having undertaken the fullfilling of the whole Law (as far forth, at the least, as ever Mankind was bound to have fullfilled it) came short in this one Law, by exempting himself from any obedience due to the civil Magistrate; or, that he, having tied himself according to the said Commandment, as well to the obedience of the civil Magistrate, as the obedience which
was

was due to his Parents, did not, whilst he lived in the World, fulfil the Law wholly concerning them both; or, that he did any way, or at any time encourage the Jews, or any other, directly or indirectly, to Rebel, for any cause whatsoever, against the Roman Emperour, or any of his subordinate Magistrates; or, that he did not very willingly, both himself pay Tribute to Cæsar, and also advise the Jews so to do; or, that when he willed the Jews to pay Tribute to Cæsar, including therein their duty of obedience unto him, he did not therein deal plainly and sincerely, but meant secretly that they should be bound no longer to be obedient unto him, but until by force they should be able to resist him; or, that he did not utterly and truly condemn all devices, Conferences and resolutions whatsoever, either in his own Apostles, or in any other Persons, for the using of force against civil Authority; or, that it is, or can be more lawful for any private Persons, either of St. Peter's calling, or of any other Profession, to draw their Swords against Authority, though in their rash Zeal they should hold it lawful so to do, for the preservation of Religion, than it was for St. Peter for the preservation of his Masters Life; or, that

that by Christ's words above-mentioned, all Subjects of what sort soever, without exception, ought not by the Law of God, to perish with the Sword that take, and use the Sword for any cause against Kings and Soveraign Princes, under whom they were born, or under whose Jurisdiction they do inhabit; or, that seeing our Saviour Christ would not have the Samaritans to be destroyed with Fire from Heaven, although they were at that time divided in Religion from the Jews, and refused to receive him in Person, it is not to be ascribed to the Spirit of Satan for any private Men to attempt by Gunpowder, and Fire from Hell, to blow up and destroy their Soveraigns, and the whole State of the Country where they were born and bred, because in their conceits they refused some part of Christ's Doctrine and Government; or, that Christ did not well, and as the said Fifth Commandment did require, in submitting himself as he did to Authority, although he was first sent for with Swords and Staves, as if he had been a Thief; and then afterward carried to Pilate, and by him (albeit he found no evil in him) condemned to Death; or, that by any Doctrine or Example, which Christ ever taught, Matt. 26. 55.

taught, or hath left upon good Record, it can be proved lawful to any Subjects, for any cause of what nature soever, to decline either the Authority and Jurisdiction of their Soveraign Princes, or of any their lawful Deputies and inferiour Magistrates ruling under them; He doth greatly Erre.

CAP. III.

'TIS many ways very plain and evident, that the *Jews* did expound all those places of the Prophets, which do notably set forth the spiritual Kingdom of our Saviour Christ, to be meant of a temporal Kingdom, which he should erect upon the Earth. And upon that false ground they did imagine, that when their expected *Messiah* should come into the World, he was to advance them unto a glorious Estate here upon Earth, and to reign in the midst of them as a most mighty and temporal Monarch. Which erroneous conceit, when *Herod* heard of the Birth of Christ, made him to fear lest the new-born Babe should deprive him of his Kingdom, and induced him thereupon to seek his destruction. Thence also did proceed, that when the People were so much moved with admiration of one of Christs Miracles, as that they used these words, *This is of a truth the Prophet which should come into the World*; they presently devised how they should make him their King. But Christ perceiving their drift, prevented their purpose by departing from them; as well observing and knowing, that their erroneous imagination of him. Nay the better sort of those that followed Christ, were not free from this erroneous cogitation;

John 6. 14, 15.

as

as it appeareth by the Petition, that the Mother of *Ze-*   Matth. 20. 21.
bedee's Children, made unto Christ, saying, *Grant that*   Mar.10.35,41.
these my two Sons may sit, the one at thy right hand, and the
other at thy left hand, in thy Kingdom. It seemeth, by
St. *Mark*, that her said two Sons, *James* and *John*, did
join with their Mother, and made likewise the same
Petition themselves, unto Christ, in their own Names.
And it is plain, that the rest of the Apostles, having
aspiring Minds to have been great Men in the World,
(as dreaming of a Temporal Kingdom, that Christ
was in time, to establish amongst them) when they
heard this Suit, did begin, as the Evangelists testifie,
to disdain at *James* and *John*, for seeking, in that sort,
to prefer themselves before them; some of them perhaps thinking themselves more worthy of those two
great Dignities, than either of them were. But our
Saviour Christ, finding these carnal Imaginations amongst them, did throughly reprove them, for those
their vain conceits; and did make it well known unto
them, how far they over-shot themselves, when they
supposed that he should become a Temporal King; or
that they themselves should be honoured by him with
Temporal Principalities. Which Course also our Saviour Christ held, when (as St. *Luke* saith) *There arose a*   Luc. 22. 24.
strife amongst the Apostles, which of them should be the
greatest. For then, they persisting in their former Errour, he did again renew his Reproof (if this were a
several contention from the former) saying unto
them, *The Kings of the Gentiles reign over them, and*
they that bear rule over them, are called Benefactors, (as
using to reward their Servants with great and extraordinary worldly Preferments;) or as St. *Matthew* re-   Mat.20.25,26.
cordeth Christ's Words, (whether upon this, or the
former Occasion mentioned, it is not greatly material,
because they are all one in sense) *Ye know that the Lords*
of the Gentiles have Dominion over them, and they that are
great, exercise authority over them: but (saith Christ) *it*

Q 2   *shall*

shall not be so among you. But whosoever will be great among you, let him be your servant; even as the Son of Man came not to be served, but to serve: or as St. *Luke* hath Chrift's words, *Ye shall not be so:* that is, Ye shall not live as Kings upon the Earth, nor have such worldly Estates, as that thereby ye might have occasion to vaunt in the World, what great Benefactors you have been, in advancing your Followers, to this, or that Dukedom, according as great Kings and Monarchs are accuftomed to deal with their Servants, and principal Subjects: but let the greateft amongft you be as the leaft, and the chiefeft as he that ferveth. *For who is greater? he that sitteth at the table, or he that serveth? Is not he that sitteth at the table? and I am among you as he that serveth.* By which words of our Saviour, it is very manifeft, how far he was from challenging to himfelf any worldly Kingdom; and how much his Apoftles were deceived, in apprehending what great Men they should become, by being his Followers and Difciples.

To this purpofe much more might be here alledged by us: as alfo, it would not be forgotten, what we have before obferved in the former Chapter, tending to the fame effect; in as much as Chrift having made himfelf fubject to the Obedience of the Fifth Commandment, which tied him as well to be a Subject unto the Emperour, under whom he was born, as to the obedience of his Parents; did thereby fhew himfelf to be no temporal Monarch. Howbeit, all this notwithftanding, there are fome fo much addicted in thefe days unto the faid erroneous opinion of the *Jews*; as for the advancement of the glory of the Bifhop of *Rome*, they will needs have Chrift to have been here upon the Earth a Temporal King; Affirming, "that upon his " Nativity all the Kings in the World loft their Regal " Power and Authority, all their Kingdoms being de- " volved unto him; and that they could no longer
" poffefs

"possess them by any Right, Interest, or Title, until
"they had again resum'd them from him, as he was
"Man, and forsaken their ancient Tenures, whereby
"they had held them of him, as he was God. Insomuch as some of them say in effect, that neither *Augustus Cæsar*, nor *Tiberius*, his Successor, were lawful Emperours, from the time of Christ's Birth for above the space of thirty years, until our Saviour had required the *Jews* to pay Tribute to *Cæsar*: as if in so doing *Tiberius* had again received thereby his former right to the Empire; and that thereupon he was from that time forward to hold it of Christ, as he was Man. In which erroneous conceits these Men proceed further than ever the *Jews*, or the Apostles in their weakness did. For the *Jews* never imagin'd of their *Messiah*, that when he came into the World he should abolish all civil Government amongst the Gentiles, and be a temporal King to Rule all Nations; or that as many Soveraign Kings and Princes, as should from that time forward desire to rule their Subjects by any lawful Power and Authority, must receive and hold the same from (the said *Jews*) their temporal Kings: but did restrain their conceits within more narrow bounds, thinking, that their *Messiah* should not have such intermedling with the Gentiles, but only restore the Kingdom of *Israel*, which had for a long time been miserably shaken, and rent in pieces, and live in that Country amongst them in a much more glorious form and state, than any of their Kings before him had done. And yet notwithstanding, these the said Persons, having inconsiderately so far overrun the *Jews* in their Follies, are possessed nevertheless with some Imaginations (no doubt) that because the Pope doth either applaud, or wink at their proceedings, they may in time make it probable to the simpler sort (who when force is to be used, do bear the greatest sway) that as all Emperours and Kings, forsooth, held their Kingdoms from Christ, as he then

was,

was, and still is Man; so ought they now in these days to hold them of the Pope, in that (if Men might safely believe them) our Saviour Christ did (as they say) after his Ascension, bestow all such Worldly Dominions upon St. *Peter*, and consequently upon his Successors, the Bishops of *Rome*; and that now all Worldly Principalities are theirs, and must be held of them, as they were before of Christ after his Incarnation, by as many Kings and Princes as desire to hold their Kingdoms by any right title.

But these are Men not to be feared; For to say the truth of them, they are all of them in effect, either but gross and unlearned Canonists, or else but new upstart and sottish *Nerians*, and of great affinity with the Canonists; who meaning (as it seemeth) to outstrip the *Jesuits*, do labour as much to make the Pope a Temporal Monarch, as the Jesuits have done for his pretended Spiritual Soveraignty: whose endeavours are altogether (as we suppose) to be contemned; in that both the sorts of them, as well Canonists as *Nerians*, are more voluminous in their Writings than substantial; filling them principally with very idle and ridiculous Canons and Decrees of the Pope's own making; and having no true feeling, or sense of Divinity, do handle the Scriptures, when they have leisure to come unto them, with so foul and unwashed hands, as that their Master either is, or ought to be ashamed of them, in that he permitteth their so absurd Books to come abroad into the World.

Besides, it will not a little hinder their credit (if it make them not a scorn to all Posterity) even amongst such Men as have otherwise made themselves Vassals to the See of *Rome*; because the said *Jesuits*, and some others, not to have been despis'd for their learning, whilst they had strived to advance the Pope's Supremacy in Causes Ecclesiastical, have themselves (in a manner) broken the Neck of his fondly-conceited temporal Monarchy.

narchy. "Some of the chiefest among them affirming
"very peremptorily, That our Saviour Christ, as
"Man, was never a temporal King upon Earth; nor
"ever had any such temporal Authority, or Govern-
"ment, as doth appertain unto Kings and Soveraign
"Princes. We will set down some words of one that
is of especial Authority amongst them; not because
we intend to ground any thing upon them, but for that
they are true, and may perhaps be of more force than
ours are like to be with some kind of People; the recti-
fying of whose hearts in the truth we tender as much
as we do our own. "Christ (saith he) did not take
"Kingdoms from them whose they were; for Christ
"came not to destroy those things that were well set-
"led, but to make them better. Therefore when a
"King is become a Christian, he doth not lose his
"Earthly Kingdom, but procureth a new Interest to
"a Kingdom that is Eternal. Otherwise the benefit of
"Christ should be hurtful to Kings, and Grace should
"destroy Nature. And again; Christ, as he was Man,
"whilst he lived upon the Earth, neither did, nor
"would receive any Temporal Dominion. And again,
"I say, that Christ was always, as the Son of God, a
"King and Lord of all Creatures, in such sort as his
"Father is: but this Eternal and Divine Kingdom
"doth not abollish the Dominions of Men. Again; I
"affirm not (saith he) that Christ, as he was Man,
"could not, though he would, and had thought it ex-
"pedient for him, have received Regal Authority:
"but yet I say, that he would not, and therefore that
"he did not receive, nor had, not only the Execution of
"any Lordship or Regality, but neither the Authority
"or Power of any Temporal Kingdom. Again, Christ,
"as he was Man, had no Temporal Kingdom, neither
"by Inheritance nor by Election, nor by Conquest,
"nor by any special Gift of God: and therefore he con-
"cludeth, that Christ had no Temporal Kingdom at
"all;

Bellarm. de sum. Pontif.l.5.

"all; becaufe every fuch Kingdom is gotten by one of
"the faid four means. Again, faith he, Chrift never ufed,
"in this World, any Regal Power: He came to mini-
"fter, and not to be miniftred unto; to be judged,
"and not to judge. And again; Regal Authority
"was neither neceffary nor profitable to Chrift; but
"plainly idle and unprofitable. For the End of his
"coming into the World, was the Redemption of
"Mankind: but to this end Temporal Power was not
"neceffary, but only Spiritual. Laftly, All the pla-
"ces of Scripture almoft, (faith he) where is a Trea-
"ty of the Kingdom of Chrift, ought neceffarily to
"be underftood of his Spiritual and Eternal Kingdom:
"and therefore it cannot be deduced out of the Scri-
"ptures, that Chrift had any Temporal Kingdom.
So as, in this Man's Judgment, neither St. *Peter*, for
his time, nor fince, any of his Succeffours, did ever
receive any Temporal Kingdoms from Chrift, (he
himfelf being never poffeft of any, as he was Man)
either to retain, in their own hands, or to commit the
Execution of them, as in their Right, to other Kings
and Temporal Monarchs.

But to omit the further profecution of this *Loyolift*'s
faid Pofitions, delivered truly in this point, more at
large, and proved by fundry Arguments in his Book,
quoted by us: becaufe he is a Man (though he be a
Cardinal, and of great Eftimation with his own Society) whofe Credit feemeth to decay, efpecially with
the faid Canonifts, and others of that like Crew. For
if the reft fhall hereafter proceed with him, as One of
them hath already done (by perverting the whole
drift of his Difputation, in that behalf, very childifh-
ly and grofly) he will be driven, e'er it be long, to
range himfelf in the Troops of fome, who are falfly
fuppofed Hereticks; in that the faid grave Canonift is
fo couragious, as he dareth to adventure the pronouncing of a Curfe, of the greateft nature, againft him,

by

by name, even *Anathema sit*, and therefore We will clear our hands of him, and drawing to an end, in this matter, leave the Conclusion of it unto Christ himself; who knew his own Estate, when he lived here in the World, as well as any Canonist, either by Birth of *Padua*, *Naples*, or *Rome*, or of any other City or Countrey whatsoever.

It is true that our Saviour Christ, as soon as he was born, was a Spiritual King, not only over the *Jews*, but also over all Nations. And therefore, when at the time of his Arraignment, before *Pilate*, though in scorn the *Jews* termed him King, and that indeed he could not truly have denied it; yet he did not equivocate therein, but confessed unto them, what manner of King he was. For *Pilate* saying unto him, *Art thou the King of the Jews?* and telling him that *the Jews and High-Priests had delivered him into his hands*; *Jesus* answered thus, *My kingdom is not of this World: if my kingdom were of this World, my Servants would surely fight, that I should not be delivered to the Jews: but now is my kingdom not from hence.* As if he should have said, I am no Temporal King, nor have any Temporal Kingdom, in this World: for if I had, my Subjects (no doubt) would never have suffered me to come to this distress: or if it had been my hap, so to have been dishonoured, as now I am; they would (out of all doubt) have fought on my behalf, as all dutiful Subjects are bound to do, when the Persons of their Sovereigns shall be in any danger. But my Kingdom is of another Nature: it is no Temporal Kingdom; either of this World, (that is, such a Kingdom, as those who are Temporal Kings do possess) or from hence, that is, my Kingdom requireth no worldly Assistance; the World hath given me no Subjects, neither have I any worldly Estate or Possessions; so as it might be affirmed truly, either of me or of my Kingdom, that

John 18.36.

either for the Dignity of my Perſon, or the ſtrengthning of my Government, I have any thing hence, that is, from the World.

CAN. II.

AND therefore if any Man ſhall affirm, under colour of any thing, that is in the Scriptures, either that the Jews did not erre, in conceiving that their Meſſiah, when He came into the World, ſhould as a Temporal Monarch, reign amongſt them; or that the Apoſtles themſelves were not ſomewhat tainted with ſuch like imaginations; or, that Chriſt's Anſwers to his ſaid Apoſtles, did not ſufficiently ſhew unto them, that he came not into the World, to erect for himſelf a temporal Kingdom, and that therefore they were not to expect from him ſuch worldly preferments, as they had dreamed of; or that the Son of God, in that he was made Man, did by his bleſſed Nativity deprive all the Civil Magiſtrates, in the World, of that Power and Authority, which he had formerly given unto them, as he was God; or that Chriſt, as he was Man, was, by his birth, made a Temporal King over all the World; or that all Temporal Princes, and Sovereign

vereign Kings, were thenceforth bound to hold their several Countries, and Kingdoms no more under Christ, as he was God; but as being Man, he was become a Temporal Monarch over all Nations; or that the Emperour Tiberius, who then reigned, did govern the Empire for the space of above fifteen Years, without any lawful Authority, until our Saviour Christ willed the Jews to give unto Cæsar those things that are Cæsar's; or that Christ having willingly undertaken, for our sakes, the fulfilling of all the Law, (and consequently of the Fifth Commandment) did not hold it to be a part of his Office to obey the Emperour, upon whom he had, as he was God, bestowed such lawful Authority, as did appertain unto his Government; or that either Christ's fact, in paying of Tribute, or his words, in willing the Jews to give unto Cæsar those things that were Cæsar's, did then import that neither Obedience, Tribute, Custom, nor any other Duty of Subjection, did, until that time, belong to the Emperour, as being thitherto, by Christ's Birth, deprived of all his Regal Authority; or that it is not a great Impiety, in any Political Respect What-

Whatsoever, for any **Man, to maintain, When Christ saith, his** Kingdom is not of this World, **that it was a Worldly and Temporal Kingdom; or when Christ saith, his** Kingdom was not from hence, **that it was, notwithstanding, as a Worldly Kingdom, from hence, as having all other Kings and Princes here in the World, as Vassals, in that respect, and subject unto it; He doth greatly Erre.**

CAP.

CAP. IV.

The sum of the Chapter following.

That our Saviour Christ in working our Salvation, whilst he lived upon the Earth, conformed himself wholly, and his obedience unto the Ecclesiastical Government, and Laws of the Church then in force; inveighed not with any bitterness against the High-Priests, though they were his Enemies, and in many points faulty; but had ever a great respect of them, in regard of their Authority; made no new Laws when he expounded the old; erected no particular Congregations, or Churches apart from the Congregations and particular Churches of the Jews; but did together with his Apostles and Disciples, join with the Church of the Jews in their publick worship and service of God; omitting no one circumstance, Ceremony, or duty, undertaken voluntarily by him, which he did not very throughly perform, even with the loss of his Life.

AS our Saviour Christ, whilst he lived in the World, did no way disturb the civil state, but upon every fit occasion did submit himself unto it: So may it be truly said of him concerning the State Ecclesiastical, formerly by God himself established, and remaining still among the *Jews* (though in a very corrupt manner) that he did in every thing, thereunto by the Law of God appertaining, conform himself unto it, while it lasted: I say, while it lasted; because upon his Death there was a great alteration. According to the Ecclesiastical Laws, then (whilst he lived) in force, he was first Circumcised, and so made himself *subject to the fullfilling of the whole Law.* Then (as the Law did likewise require) he was brought by his Mother to *Jerusalem,* to be presented to the Lord, and to

Levit. 12:3.

have

have an Oblation (suitable to their poor Estate) of a
pair of Turtle-Doves, or two Pigeons, offered to God
with the price of Redemption for him, in that he was
a Manchild, and the first-born. There were no kind
of solemn Feasts appointed by the Law, which he honoured not with his presence according to the Law.
Nay he was pleased to be present at the Feast of the
Dedication of the Temple, which was instituted by *Judas Maccabæus*, and his Brethren: as well to teach all
Posterity, by his Example, what godly Magistrates
may ordain in such kind of Causes; as also how things
so ordain'd, ought to be observed. And as he was Circumcised, so did he celebrate and observe the chief
Feasts of the *Passover* : omitting nothing, which either on the behalf of the *Jews*, or for our sakes, he had
undertaken to perform. And although the Priests in
those days were very far out of square, and that our
Saviour Christ had very just cause in that respect to
have reprov'd them sharply, as other Prophets had
often dealt with their Predecessors: yet he did so much
regard them, by reason of their Authority, unless he
should otherwise have seem'd to have contemned both
them and it; as he did rather choose to let them understand their offences by Parables, than by any rough reprehension: still upholding them in their credits and
authority, as by the Law of God in that behalf it was
provided. When amongst many other his wonderful
great Miracles, he had healed certain Lepers, he bad
them go *show themselves to their Priests*; because they
were appointed Judges by the Law to discern the cu-
ring of that Disease, before the Parties (though indeed
healed of it) might intermingle themselves with the
rest of the People; and did further require them to
offer for their cleansing those things, which Moses *had commanded in testimonium illis*; that is, that so the said
Priests might plainly see, both that he was a Keeper of
the Law, and also, that he had healed them, and so be
driven

Exod.13. 13.
Num.18.15.

Deut. 16.
Joh. 10. 22,23.

Matth. 21.16.
---25. 28.

Matth. 8.4.

Mark 1.44.

Luke 5. 14.
---17. 14.

driven to repent them of their incredulity, or at the least prevented thereby from slandering either him, as a Breaker of the Law, or that which he had done for them, as if he had not throughly healed them. Neither is it any way repugnant hereunto, that when our Saviour Christ found chopping and changing, by buying and selling in the Temple, he made a Scourge of *John 2.15.* small Cords, and drave them thence with the Sheep, Oxen, Doves, and Money-Bags; forbidding them to *make his Fathers House an House of Merchandise.* For he did not thereby, in any sort, prejudice the Authority of the Priests (who should chiefly have prevented such gross abuses, and traffick in the Temple) as if he had done the same, either as a chief Priest, or a Temporal King (according to some Mens fond imaginations) by any Pontifical, or Regal Authority: but his fact therein (howsoever it might shew the negligence of the said Priests) did only proceed from his Divine Zeal, as he was a Prophet, and could not endure such an abominable profanation of God's House: many Prophets before him having done matters very lawfully of greater moment, through the like divine and extraordinary Zeal in them, without any impeachment of any Power, either Regal or Pontifical. Howbeit, that our Saviour Christ was oftentimes very vehement against the *Scribes* and *Pharisees,* it is plain and manifest, when joining them both together, he termed them *serpents,* the *Matth. 23.* *Generation of Vipers,* and denounceth against them in one Chapter eight Woes, concluding thus, *How should you escape the damnation of Hell?* The reason, that these Curses and hard censures were jointly laid upon them, was because they themselves were joined together in all kinds of Impiety and Malice against Christ; and were neither of them, especially the *Pharisees,* any Plants of God's Plantation. For whilst not only the *High-Priests* were still in Faction and Fury one against another, as well for the getting, as the keeping that

high

high preferment; and that many of the inferiour Priests were either siding amongst themselves for one Party or other, or else more idle and negligent in discharging of their duties than they ought to have been; these two Sects thrust themselves into the Church, and through their Hypocrisy so prevail'd with the People in short time, as the Priests afterward either could not, or would not be rid of them: because on the one side they thought it in vain to strive with them, they were so backed; and on the other side they found them so diligent in discharging of those duties, which did appertain to themselves, and withal so careful to uphold the state and authority of the Priesthood. "By means "whereof they grew very shortly into so great estima- "tion, that (as one writeth of the *Pharisees*) whatso- "ever did appertain to publick and solemn Prayers, "and to the worship of God, it was done according to "their interpretations, and as they prescribed. And the *Scribes* being likewise Doctors, and Expounders of the Law, and concurring still with the interpretations, and prescriptions of the *Pharisees*, came not by that policy in their credits and reputation had of them, far short behind them. The distinction between them may well be exprest by comparing the *Pharisees* unto the *Divines* amongst our Adversaries, who take upon them to search out more throughly the mysteries of the Scriptures; and the Scribes to their *Canonists*, who in respect of their said Divines, are but Novices in God's word, and Applauders to the Pope's Decrees, as the *Scribes* were, being compar'd to the *Pharisees*, in that they held it for a principal part of their office, to uphold and maintain, as much as they could, the Traditions of the *Pharisees*, and did only take upon them to deal with the bark and literal sense of *Moses*'s Law, leaving the more profound knowledge and mystical Interpretation of them unto the said *Pharisees*. But the Issue of the labours of both these Hypocritical Sects was

Jos. Antiq. l.18.c.2.

such,

such, as being blinded with their own devices, they became to be the specialiest Enemies that Christ found upon the Earth, and opposed themselves most against him. And yet notwithstanding, because he found them in so great Authority, and perceived how the knowledge of the Law, which ought to have been received from the lips of the Priests, did then depend upon the lips of the *Scribes* and *Pharisees*, he did neither blame them for it, nor impugn the said Authority. Insomuch as the multitude being many ways factious, and (though very ignorant) were become great Questionists, touching the Points of the Law; he referred them, with a very good Caution, to the *Scribes* and *Pharisees*, to be instructed by them, saying, *The Scribes and Pharisees sit in Moses's seat: all therefore whatsoever they bid you observe and do, that observe and do; but after their works do not, for they say, and do not.* Whereby it appeareth, how respectful our Saviour Christ was for the free passage and observation of *Moses*'s Law; in that he was content that the *Scribes* and *Pharisees* (notwithstanding he knew their Hypocrisie and Corruption, and how they had come by that Authority, which they then enjoyed) should yet instruct the People under them; so as the People did beware of their wicked Conversation, and approved no resolutions, that they might receive from them, which were not first proved unto them out of the Laws of *Moses*, and were fit to proceed from his Seat.

Touching which last point of *Moses*'s Law, and how nothing ought to have been taught out of *Moses*'s Seat, but that, which *Moses*, by the direction of the Holy Ghost, had prescribed; for as much as our Saviour Christ did well see, and understand how the *Scribes* and *Pharisees*, had, by their false Interpretations and Glosses, perverted and corrupted the true sense and meaning of divers of *Moses*'s Laws, he was greatly moved therewith, and did take great pains to refute the said false glosses,

glosses and interpretations, and to restore to the Laws mention'd their true sense and original meaning. Wherein, although by his strict Exposition of those Laws he might seem *(*to some not well advis'd*)* to have so extended and enlarged the meaning of them, as if he had thereby prescribed some new points or laws of greater perfection than were originally contain'd in the true meaning of the old; yet we cannot find, how either the said points may otherwise be termed new, than as Gold first purified and fined, after it hath either in time grown rusty, or been by false mixtures cunningly corrupted, may be called new gold, when it is again purged from the said false mixtures and refin'd; Or how the observation of them can bring with it to Men any greater perfection in the New Testament, than God himself did expect of his Servants in the Old Testament, by their observing of the said Laws (so expounded by Christ) in their ancient sense and meaning, which they first had, when by his appointment *Moses* did give them unto them. For if in proper Speech he had made any new Laws, coming only to fullfil the old, as himself in a true sense affirmed, the *Jews* might have had some good colour to have blamed him; in that, during the continuance of their Ecclesiastical Government, if any new Laws had been then to have been made touching the worship of God, the Authority in that behalf was limited by God himself unto their own Church-Governours. Again, considering that the Son of God in taking our nature upon him, did so make himself of no reputation, as being (of his own goodness towards Mankind) a Servant to his Father, he became (to do his will) *obedient unto the death, even the death of the Cross*; It cannot well be imagined by any, that have any true understanding of the Scriptures, that the Son of God, having so debased himself (as is aforesaid) did ever think in that his so admirable humiliation, of any Rules, or new Laws of
greater

greater perfection than he had before required and prescribed unto his true Servants and Children, as he was God in Majesty and Glory, without any such Exinanition, as the Apostle speaketh of. The obedience and duty which Almighty God ever did, or ever will require of his Servants, was, and is always to proceed, as well from their hearts, as from any other external actions. Insomuch, as if it fell out (as it may at sometimes) that they cannot perform their said duties, in respect of some impediments that will hold them from Christ: In that Case, be it riches, they are to leave them; their Eyes, their Hands, or their Feet, they are to cut them off; Nay be it their Blood, their Hearts, and Lives, they are rather, than to forsake their God, and his Christ, to yield them all in this World, with what ignominy soever, to the end they may receive them again with glory in the Kingdom of Heaven: Than which great obedience and perfection, what can be imagin'd greater? Or who is there in the World, that truly professeth Religion, who in that Case is exempted from it? Certainly, we think, none, of what Estate and Condition soever they be; but do rather hold, that as they, who shall yield up their Lives under pretence of any extraordinary perfection (saving in the Case above-expressed) are far from that which they make shew of, but are rather to be accounted desperate; so are they, in our Judgments, to be reckoned Men of very extraordinary humours, and most ignorant Persons, if not such counterfeit Hypocrites, as were the *Scribes* and *Pharisees* in professing extraordinary austerity of Life, that they might be the better esteem'd amongst Men, who shall without any necessity, either pull out their Eyes, or cut off their Feet and Hands, or forsake their Riches and Worldly Estates, as blessings of God not compatible, but repugnant to that perfection which God doth require at any Man's hands.

It

It is not our purpose to profecute all thofe particulars mention'd in the Evangelifts, wherein our Saviour Chrift fhew'd his Obedience: there being in effect nothing that he did, which was not either figur'd in the Law, or foretold by the Prophets, that he fhould perform. The time of his Incarnation, with the manner of it; his Entertainment in the World; his diligence in Preaching; his whipping, blows, and fcorns offer'd unto him; the Wounds of his hands, feet and fide; the beginning and progrefs of his Spiritual Kingdom; the feveral duties appertaining to him, as he was a Prophet, and likewife as he was our High-Prieft, the Inftitution of Baptifm, and of Chrift's laft Supper; his Righteoufnefs and Mercy; his Death, with the manner of it; his Refurrection and Afcenfion, with a number of other points; they were all forefeen, figur'd, and defcribed by the Holy Ghoft in the Scriptures; and were accordingly, with admirable Patience, Humility, Obedience, Courage, Zeal and Alacrity executed, undergone, and accomplifhed by him in fuch manner and fort, with the obfervation of all neceffary circumftances, and by fuch degrees, as from the beginning were limited and thought fit for fo great a work. For all things could not be done together by him, and at once. Although after his Baptifm he Preached moft diligently, wrought ftrange Wonders, and did chufe, to affift him, his Twelve Apoftles, and Seventy Difciples, who did likewife preach, baptize, and wrought Miracles in his Name: yet neither he, nor they did collect any particular Church or Churches, apart from the Synagogues of the *Jews*; but held Society and Communion with them, in all things, that did belong to the outward Service and Worfhip of God: becaufe, until his Paffion, as well the Ceremonies of the Law, as the *Aaronical* Priefthood, together with the Authority, thereunto appertaining, were all of them in force; and therefore it was not lawful, whilft the Old Church did ftand, stand, to have erected a New. Moreover it is not to be doubted, but that as before Christ's Incarnation there were many faithful and godly Persons, that believed in Christ, to come, and by that their Faith were saved: so there were many such Believers, after his Incarnation, who were likewise the Children of God, though they were ignorant (for a time) that Christ, when he was come, was the *Messiah*, whom they expected: none of the *Jews* so believing, being in state of Damnation, until after they had seen Christ, heard him preach, been present at his Miracles, or at the least had received full instruction of them all from his Apostles and Disciples, they did notwithstanding reject him. In which respect, the true Believers amongst the *Jews*, in those days, might not well have been distinguished into several, and different Congregations, or particular Churches, without many great and apparent Inconveniencies, but this Point is yet plainer, in that the *Jews*, who believed, at that time, that Christ, whom they saw, and heard, was the true *Messiah*; were, notwithstanding, subject to the Obedience of those Ceremonial and Levitical Laws, which did concern them every one in his Calling, which doth appear by the Examples of Christ himself and his Apostles: who, although they were baptized, did not sever themselves from the manner of Worshipping of God in those times. Insomuch as first they did celebrate together the Feast of the *Passover*, before our Saviour Christ made them Partakers of his last Supper. Neither is it to be questioned, but that many, who did believe in Christ, (their and our Saviour) then amongst them, had new born Children, before his Passion, which were as well circumcised as baptized. For then, as Circumcision was not repugnant to Baptism, no more was Baptism any Impediment to Circumcision; being both of them so united together, and qualified, as they could not well be sever'd, during the Continuance of the Levitical Law, and Priesthood. We

We grant, that upon our Saviour Chrift's Birth, and further proceedings in the execution of his Office, not only the Jewifh Ceremonies, but in like fort their Priefthood began both of them to fhake, and did, after a fort, draw near to their End: but until our Saviour Chrift faid upon the Crofs, *It is finifhed*, and that the *vail was rent in twain, from the top to the bottom*, they neither of them had utterly loft their *Levitical* Natures, Power and Authority, And therefore it muft be held, that although, by the preaching of our Saviour and of his Apoftles, many Mens hearts were drawn to believe that Chrift was the *Meffiah*, whom they expected, and that they were thereby made actually Partakers of many of thofe Mercies, which, by Figures, and Sacrifices had been formerly fet out unto them; as alfo, that in regard thereof, they might be termed, in a right, good fenfe, the beginning of a New Church: yet did they, neither in refpect of their Faith and Baptifm, make any Separation, but were only the better part of the old Church: nor might they, in regard of either of them, have lawfully exempted themfelves from the Government of it. Which is further manifeft by the words of our Saviour Chrift himfelf, when he faith thus; *If thy Brother trefpafs againft thee, go, and tell him his fault between thee and him alone. If he hear thee, thou haft won thy Brother. But if he hear thee not, take yet with thee one or two, that, by the mouth of two or three Witneffes, every word may be confirmed. But if he will not vouchfafe to hear them, tell it unto the Church.* For by the Church, in this place, the Ecclefiaftical Courts eftablifh'd amongft the *Jews*, at that time, muft (as we think) be underftood, there being then no other Courts, of that Nature, amongft them, which had any Authority to punifh any fuch obftinate Perfons, as Chrift there fpeaketh of. So as our Saviour Chrift did here refer the Parties, offended by fome of their Brethren, to the faid Ecclefiaftical Courts; in the fame refpect and fenfe, and

John 19. 30.
Matth. 27. 51.

Matth. 18. 15.

and no otherwife, than he fent the Lepers (whom he had healed) to the Priefts, according to the Law; or when he referred the multitude to the *Scribes* and *Pharifees*, to be inftructed by them, becaufe they *fate in Mofes's Chair*. Befides whatfoever is fpoken by the Evangelifts, of the *Church that fhould be built upon a Rock fo ftrongly, as that the Gates of Hell fhould not be able to prevail againft it*; or of the Power and Authority *to bind and loofe*, by Cenfures, or otherwife: that is no way to be applied to the faid Church or *Sanhedrim*, mentioned by St. *Matthew*, or to any particular Affembly of Chriftians, either before the Paffion of Chrift, or afterwards; but was only fpoken and delivered, by way of Prophecy, of the *Catholick Church*, which, after the Refurrection and Afcenfion of our Saviour Chrift, fhould be eftablifhed in the World, in a more confpicuous and univerfal fort, than formerly it had been. And yet we do not deny, but that Chrift, in the faid words, *Tell the Church*, meaning the *Jews* Courts, or *Sanhedrims*, might very well infinuate; in that he called not thofe Courts by their own Names, but termed them the *Church*, that, in fuch cafes as there are by him mentioned, the Chriftians, in time to come, fhould accordingly repair unto their Ecclefiaftical Courts, to be eftablifhed among them throughout the Chriftian World, for Reformation of Offenders, and Satisfaction in Points of Religion; as the *Jews* of all forts (whether Believers or not) were bound, until the Death of Chrift, to repair to their *Priefts* and *Sanhedrims*, if either they meant to be truly inftructed in the Laws, or to have fuch manner of Offences lawfully punifhed by thofe kind of Cenfures, that Chrift, in the faid place, fpeaketh of.

But what fhould we infift fo much upon this point, to prove that all the *Jews*, that either believed in Chrift, or did reject him, were bound (before the Paffion of our Saviour Chrift) to be obedient to the Ecclefiaftical Governours,

Governours, established, by God himself, in that visible Church: considering how careful our Saviour Christ was, upon every occasion offered, for the preservation of their Authority, whilst it was to endure, and with what Humility he did submit himself unto it? For being sent for by them, he was content, at that time, to go unto them, and to be examined by them; when he had found them many ways before to be his mortal Enemies: and knew how at that present, they were plotting to take away his Life, by corrupting of *Judas* to betray him into their hands, and by suborning of false Witnesses to accuse him: as also, how, after they had examined him, they would use him most despitefully and scornfully, spit in his Face, and buffet him, beat him with Rods, carry him bound as a Malefactour, and deliver him to *Pilate* the Civil Magistrate; Likewise how they themselves would be his Accusers; how they would practise with the People to prefer *Barabbas*'s liberty (being a Murtherer) before his, and to cry out with them, to *Pilate*, *Let him be crucified, Let him be crucified*; *Crucify him, Crucify him*; their Outrage and Fury being so bent against him, as that they themselves would have put him to death, if by the Laws of the *Romans* (whereunto they were then subject) they might have been permitted so to have done.

CAN. III.

AND therefore if any Man shall affirm, under colour of any thing that is in the Scriptures; either that our Saviour Christ whilst he lived upon the Earth, was not obedient to the State Ecclesiastical, as he was to the Temporal: or, that all Christians

Christians by his Example, are not bound to be as well obedient to their Church-Governours, as they are to their civil Magistrates: or, that Christian Kings have not now as full Authority to appoint some Festival Days of publick thanksgiving to God, in remembrance of some great and extraordinary mercies of his, shew'd unto them upon those days, as Judas Maccabæus had to ordain the Feast of the Dedication of the Temple to be yearly celebrated: or that, where any such Festival Days are appointed, the Subjects of every such King, ought not by Christ's Example, in celebrating the said Feast, to observe and keep them: or, that all the true Members of the Church are not taught by Christ's Example, in his observing of the Ceremonial Law, being then in force, that they likewise are bound to observe all such Constitutions and Ceremonies, as for Order and Decency, are with all due Cautions established in any particular Church, by the chief Governours of it, until it shall please them the said Governours, to abrogate them: or, that all Christians are not bound by Christ's Example, to refrain all bitterness of Calumniation and Detraction, and to deal temperately and mildly with their Ecclesiastical

T Gover-

Governours, in respect of their Authority, that it be not brought into contempt, though they find some imperfections, either in their Persons, or in their Proceedings; as he our said blessed Saviour, in the same respect, dealt with the Priests of the Jews, though they had many ways transgressed, and were his mortal Enemies: or, that Christ, by whipping Buyers and Sellers out of the Temple, did either impeach the Authority of the Priests, or practise therein any Pontifical or Temporal Power, as if he had been a temporal King, or did the same by any other Authority, than as he was a Prophet: or, that Christians are not now as strongly bound in doubts of Religion, to repair unto the chief Ministers and Ecclesiastical Governours, although they are not always tied to do as they do; as were the Jews in such like Cases bound to repair to them, that sate in Moses's Seat: or, that every true Christian, when for the said Cause he repaireth to the chief Ministers, and Governours of the Church, to be resolv'd by them, is any further now bound to depend upon such their Resolutions, than they are able to shew them unto him out of the Word of God; or than the Jews were bound to believe the Scribes and

Pharisees,

[135]

Pharisees, **though they sat in** Moses's **Chair when they taught them any thing which was not agreeable to that which** Moses **had commanded: or, that Christ's Example in condemning the false Interpretations and Glosses of the** Scribes **and** Pharisees, **and in restoring to the Law the true sense and original meaning of it, hath not ever since warranted learned and godly Men, when they found the Scriptures perverted by those that govern the Church, of purpose to make their own gain thereof, and to maintain their great Usurpations, to free the same by searching the said Scriptures from all such false Interpretations and Glosses, and to make plain (as much as in them did lie) the true sense and meaning of them: or, that our Saviour Christ, when he purged divers parts of the Law from the gross and erroneous Expositions of the** Scribes **and** Pharisees, **did give any other sense and meaning of them; or infer upon it any new Rules of greater perfection, either as he was Man, or as he was a Prophet, than they had, and contained originally, when he first gave them to the** Israelites, **as he was God: or, that it is not an erroneous and fond conceit, like unto that of the Sectaries among the** Jews **(especially of the** Pharisees**)**

T 2   for

for any sort of Persons, (no way able to perform their duties to God, in such manner and sort as they ought) once so much as to imagine, that by the observation of their own rules, they are able to attain to greater perfection, than by the observation of God's rules: or, that it is not as vain and fond an imagination as the former, for any Christian Man to think, that the enjoying of such Possessions and Riches as God hath blessed him with, is repugnant to that perfection which God hath required at his hands; or that the same are otherwise incompatible with the said perfection, than in such cases only, when either they must leave their Worldly Estates, or Christ their Saviour: or, that our Saviour Christ, by laying of some grounds for the future estate of the Church after his Passion, did thereby erect any new Churches apart from that Church which was to continue until his Death: or, that the Example of Christ and his Apostles, in holding Society and Communion with the Jews, in the outward worship and service of God, doth not condemn all such Sectaries as do separate themselves from the Churches of Christ, whereof they were once Members; the same being true Churches by lawful Authority established;

blished, under pretence of they know not what new Christianity: or, that there ought not to be now amongst Christians, Ecclesiastical Courts for Ecclesiastical Causes, as well as there were such Courts amongst the Jews for such kind of Causes: or, that all Christians are not now bound to repair, as well to Ecclesiastical Courts and Governours, for reformation of such Offences, as are of Ecclesiastical Connusance, as the Jews were bound to repair to their Sanhedrims, to have those Evils redressed that were to be reform'd by those Courts: or, that as many as do profess themselves to be true Imitators of Christ in their Lives and Conversation, are not bound to such obedience unto their Princes and Rulers, how evil-disposed soever they be, yea though they seek their Lives) as Christ shewed and performed, both to the Ecclesiastical and Temporal State of the Jews, at what time he knew they were plotting his Death; He doth greatly Erre.

CAP.

CAP. V.

The Sum of the Chapter following.

That our Saviour Chrift, after his Refurrection and Afcenfion, did not alter the form of temporal Government, eftablifht by himfelf long before his Incarnation: and that therefore Emperours, Kings, and Soveraign Princes, though they were then Infidels, were neverthelefs to be obey'd by the Subjects, as formerly from the beginning they had been.

IT hath been before obferv'd by us, that our Saviour Chrift, whilft he lived in the World, was no temporal King, nor had any temporal Dominion, Court, Poffeffions, Regal State, Dukes, Earls, Lords, or any other Subjects, as other temporal Kings had, to obey and ferve him. But perhaps after his Refurrection, it was far otherwife with him. Indeed fo it was; For whereas the Son of God, God himfelf, equal to the Father, by being made Man, did ceafe to put in practice the Glory and Majefty of his Deity in his humane Nature, otherwife than by doing fuch Miracles as he thought neceffary for the Converfion of thofe who were to believe in him : Now after his Refurrection and Afcenfion, the ftate of his humane Nature was become (as it may well be faid) much more glorious ; becaufe his Divine Nature did communicate unto his Humane Nature. So many divine Dignities and operations of his Deity (in refpect of the hypoftatical Union betwixt them) as the fame was capable of, without turning of his Divine Nature into his Humane Nature: It being always to be underftood, that the faid hypoftatical and real Union, notwithftanding there

was

was never any Confusion betwixt the two Natures of Christ; both of them always retaining their distinct and essential Proprieties. Which ground observ'd, we may truly say, that the Attributes are admirable, which in regard of the said Union are and may be ascribed unto our Saviour Christ, as he is Man; especially after his Resurrection and Ascension. For some short proof hereof these following Places may suffice. Before our Saviour Christ commanded his Apostles *to go and teach all Nations, baptizing them in the name of the Father, the Son, and the Holy Ghost*; he told them, (lest they should have doubted whether he had any Authority to make them so large a Commission) *that all power was given him in Heaven, and in Earth.* Matth. 28. 18. He also was before (as the Holy Ghost testifieth of him) *made Heir of all things*, Hebr. 1. 2. and so had a true Interest in them; and after his Resurrection, had the full possession of them. *We see Jesus* (saith the Apostle) *crown'd with glory and honour.* Hebr. 2. 9. And again, *When God raised up Jesus from the dead, he set him at his right hand, in heavenly places, far above all Principality and Power, and Might and Domination, and every Name that is named not in this world only, but in that also which is to come; and hath made all things subject under his feet.* Eph. 1. 20, 21, 22. And again, *The kingdoms of this world are our Lord's and his Christ's.* Apoc. 11. 15. And again, *The lamb is Lord of lords, and King of kings.* ——17. 14. And to conclude, *He hath upon his garment, and upon his thigh, a name written, The King of kings, and Lord of lords.* ——19. 16.

Howbeit, all that we have hitherto said notwithstanding, though all the World doth actually appertain to our Saviour Christ (now in Glory) as he is Man, in respect of the said Unition, or hypostatical Union: yet did he not alter, after his Resurrection and Ascension, the manner of temporal Government, which he had ordained throughout the World before his Incarnation, as he was God (his humane Nature being invested by the power of his Divinity in manner before exprest with

all

all his said Glory, and Authority :) but doth still continue the sole Monarch over all; distributing that his universal Kingdom, as formerly he had done, into divers Principalities and Kingdoms, and appointing temporal Kings and Soveraign Princes, as his Substitutes and Vicegerents to rule them all by the Rules and Laws of Nature, if they be *Ethnicks*, or if *Christians*, then not only by those Rules, but also as well by the Equity of the Judicial Laws, which he gave to the *Jews*, as by the Doctrine of the Gospel, more throughly opened and delivered with all the parts of it, by himself and his Apostles, than in former times it had been. Of Christian Kings, we shall have fitter place to speak hereafter. Now we will prosecute this point, concerning the Regal Authority of Princes that are Infidels, and consider more particularly, Whether they did not, and so consequently do not still, as lawfully enjoy their Kingdoms and legal Soveraignties under our Saviour Christ, after his Resurrection and Ascension, as they did before, either of them; and likewise as they did before his Incarnation; according to that which we have delivered in the former Chapter. And the especial Reason that moveth us so to do, is the audacious temerity of the before-named ignorant *Canonists*, and of their adherents, the new Sectaries of the *Oratory Congregation* : who, with the like Ignorance and Folly that they told us, how all Kings lost their Interest and Authority over their Kingdoms, by the birth of our Saviour Christ, do furthermore endeavour very wickedly and sottishly to pervert such especial places in the Apostles Writings, as are, most aparently, repugnant to their said Fancy, or rather Phrenzy. To make their dealing with one place apparent, is sufficient for our purpose. Whereas St. *Paul*, writing to the *Romans*, willeth them to *be subject to the higher Powers*, or teacheth them (as a late absurd *Canonist* abridgeth the place) *Obediendum esse Principibus, that Princes are to be obey'd : He speaketh not* (saith he) *de Ethnicis, as that place is corruptly*

Rom. 13.

Dr. Mart.
Tract. de Ju-
rid. par. 1. c.
24. n. 38.

ruptly alledged, fed quatenus de illis intellexit, that is, *in such a fenfe as he meant it*. And what the Apoſtle meant, he is not aſhamed to tell us in this fort, faying, (1.) *the Apoſtle fpeaketh of the Roman Empire, which Chriſt had approved, when he bad the Jews pay Tribute to Cæfar*, (2.) *the Text doth expound it felf, for he writeth to Chriſtians; whom he counfelleth to be obedient to Princes, leſt they ſhould fin; for Princes are not to be feared for good works, but for evil: therefore he doth not fimply command Obedience to Ethnick Princes*, &c. (3.) *The like manner of writing, St. Paul ufed in exhorting Servants to honour their Lords, etiam infideles, though they were Infidels, for the Reafons by him there mentioned*. (4.) *By thofe Monitions* (meaning the faid Commandments of the Apoſtle, concerning Obedience of Subjects to their Princes, and of Servants to their Maſters) *juſt Dominion is not founded in the Perfons of Ethnicks, (nam Paulus, qui hoc dicit, non erat fummus Pontifex; for Paul, who faid fo, was not the chief Biſhop*, &c.) (5.) *Furthermore, in that time of the Primitive Church, the Church could not, de facto, puniſh Infidels, and transfer their Kingdoms*, &c. Thus far this audacious and unlearned *Canoniſt*: the very citation of whofe Words, we hold fufficient to refute them; although he alledgeth for himfelf to fupport them very grave Authors; the *Diſtinctions* (forfooth) the *Glofs, Hoſtienfis*, & *Præpofitus*: adding that fome other *Canoniſts* do concur with him. Only we will oppofe againſt him and all his Fellows (to ſhew their Follies by a proof of this Nature) the Teſtimony of the Pope's chief Champion, the only *Jefuit* without Comparifon (now a principal Cardinal) who maintaineth in exprefs Terms, "That Infidel Princes are true and fupream Princes of "their Kingdoms: and writeth thus againſt the faid "Affertion of the *Canoniſt* directly: faying, God doth "approve the Kingdoms of the Gentiles in both the Te- "ſtaments. *Thou art King of kings, and the God of Hea-* *ven hath given thee thy Kingdom and Empire*, &c. *Re-*
ſtore

Matth. 22.

Rom. 13.

store those things unto Cæsar that are Cæsar's. Note, that he saith not *Give*, but *Restore those things that are Cæsar's*; that is, those things which in right are owing unto him. And *Give unto all Men that which is due unto them*; *Tribute to whom you owe Tribute*; *and Custom to whom you owe Custom.* *Et jubet ibidem etiam propter Conscientiam obedire Principibus Ethnicis: At certè non tenemur in Conscientiâ obedire illi, qui non est verus Princeps:* "that "is, and we are commanded in the same place, even "for Conscience, to obey Princes that are Ethnicks: "but assuredly we are not bound in Conscience to obey "him who is no true, lawful, or right Prince. Hitherto the *Cardinal*.

We would not have cited this Man's testimony thus at large, were not All, that he hath said therein, throughly supported by all the Learned Men (as we suppose) of his Society; and sufficient to refel the Vanity of the *Canonists*, and their Fellows in that folly. For if we should insist herein upon the Authority of Men, all the ancient Fathers do fully concur with us: that through the whole course of the Scriptures, Obedience was, and is as well prescribed in the Old Testament to Ethnick Princes, as unto the Kings of *Judah*: and so likewise in the New Testament, as well to Infidel Princes as Christian: the Precepts of the Apostles in that behalf being general, and so to be applied, as well to the one sort as to the other; in that they hold their Kingdoms of Christ equally (as is aforesaid) and therefore ought to be equally obeyed by their Subjects, with that general Caution which was ever understood, *viz.* in those things which they commanded them, and were not repugnant to the Commandments of God. And therefore the Judgments of the ancient Fathers, being in this sort only remember'd by us, we will not much insist upon them; but give that honour which is due (especially in a matter so apparent) unto the sole Authority of the Holy Apostles; who writing by the

direction

direction of the Holy Ghost, those things which Christ himself before had taught them, do give unto all Christians and Subjects, to what manner of Kings soever, these Precepts following.

"Let every Soul be subject to the higher Powers; Rom. 13.
"for there is no Power but of God: for the Powers
"that be, are Ordained of God. Whosoever therefore
"resisteth the Power, resisteth the Ordinance of God;
"and they that resist, shall receive to themselves Judg-
"ment. For Princes are not to be feared for good
"works, but for evil. Wilt thou then be without
"fear? Do well: So shalt thou have praise of the
"same: for he is the Minister of God for thy Wealth.
"But if thou do evil, fear; for he beareth not the
"Sword for nought: for he is the Minister of God to
"take Vengeance of him that doth evil. Wherefore
"ye must be subject, not because of wrath only, but
"also for Conscience sake. For this cause ye pay also
"Tribute: for they are God's Ministers, applying
"themselves for the same thing. In which words of the Apostle, in saying, that Princes have their Power from God, and that he is God's Minister; there is no repugnancy to that which we have abovesaid, concerning the great honour and dignity of the humanity of our Saviour Christ, after his Resurrection and Ascension; to prove that Kings do hold their Kingdoms under Christ, as he is Man, the Lamb of God, and Heir of all the World. For we were very careful to have it still remembred, that all the said Power and Dignity which he hath, as he is Man, doth proceed from his Divinity: and likewise, that by reason of the real Union of the two Natures in our Saviour Christ, that which doth properly belong to the one nature, may very truly be affirmed of the other. So as it may, in that respect, be very well said, and truly; that all Kings and Princes receive their Authority from Christ, as he is Man; and likewise, that they receive their

Authority from Christ, as he is God: and that they are the Ministers of Christ, being Man; and the Ministers of God, without any limitation. But it is plain, that the said words of the Apostle do very throughly refute the vanity mentioned of the Canonists, and their new Companions: in that by the said words it appeareth very manifestly, That Kings do not otherwise hold their Kingdoms of the humanity of Christ, than they did before of his divine nature. They have their Authority (saith the Apostle) from God; and they are God's Ministers. And there is nothing written, either by St. *Paul*, or by any other of the Apostles, which swerveth in any point from this Doctrine, where they write of the obedience due unto all Kings and Soveraign Princes: whose testimonies in that behalf, we are, as we promised, a little further to pursue.

1 Tim. 2. 1. &c.

"I exhort, saith St. *Paul*, that first of all, Supplications, Prayers, Intercessions, and giving of thanks, be made for all Men; for Kings, and for all that are in Authority: that we may lead a quiet and a peaceable Life in all Godliness and Honesty. And

Tit. 3. 1.

again, Put them (that is both old and young, and all sorts of Persons that are purged to be a peculiar People unto Christ) in remembrance, that they be subject to the Principalities and Powers; and that they be obedient and ready to every good work. Also

Pet. 2. 13. &c.

St. *Peter* saith to the same effect, Submit your selves unto all manner of Ordinance of Man for the Lord's sake; whether it be unto the King, as unto the Superiour; or unto Governours, as unto them that are sent of him for the punishment of evil doers, and for the praise of them that do well. For so is the will of God; that by well doing, ye may put to silence the ignorance of foolish Men as free, and not as having the liberty for a Cloak of Maliciousness; but as the Servants of God. Honour all Men; love Brotherly Fellowship;

Fellowship; Fear God; Honour the King. And the same Apostle, describing the nature of false Teachers, which in times to come would thrust themselves into the Church, and by feigned words, make a Merchandise of their Followers; amongst other impieties, he noteth them with these, "That commonly they are "despisers of Government, presumptuous Persons, and "such as stand in their own conceits; Men, that fear "not to speak evil of them that are in dignity: but as "brute Beasts, led with sensuality, and made to be "taken and destroyed, speak evil of those things which "they know not. And with St. *Peter* in this point, the Apostle St. *Jude* doth concur: where speaking of those who in future times should be Makers of Sects, " He "termeth them Mockers, and Men that had not the "Spirit of God. And speaking also of such like wick- "ed Persons as were crept into the Church in the Apo- "stles days; he saith, they did despise Government, "and speak evil of them that were in Authority. In all which places thus by us noted, concerning aswell the dignity and Authority of Sovereign Kings and Princes, as the fear, duty and obedience; which all their Subjects were truly and sincerely, without murmuring or repining, to yield and perform unto them, though they were then Ethnicks: When we consider the manner of their delivery of that Evangelical Doctrine, and their grounds thereof; as also how vehemently they have written against all such Persons, as either did then, or should afterward, oppose themselves unto it, by despising of civil Magistrates, speaking evil of them, or in any other sort whatsoever; We are fully perswaded, that they neither commanded, taught, or writ any thing therein, but what they knew to be the will of God, and did accordingly believe to be true; for we hold it resolutely, That whatsoever the Apostles did either write, teach, or command, they writ, taught, and commanded it, as they were inspired and directed

by

2 Tim. 3. 15.
2 Pet. 1. 21.
Joh. 15. 7. 13.

by the Holy Ghost: becaufe when our Saviour Chrift was to leave the World, he promifed to fend unto them the Holy Ghoft, the *Comforter and fpirit of truth* ; which *fhould lead them*, not into any By-ways, or fhifting conceits, but *into* the direct and plain paths of *all truths* : and did very fhortly after perform that his Promife, when upon the day of *Pentecoft* they were all filled with the Holy Ghoft, as St. *Luke* witneffeth. Befides,

Act. 2. 4.

the Apoftle St. *Paul* himfelf doth profefs , both in his own name , and in the behalf of the reft of the Apoftles, his Fellows , that their Mafter being the truth it felf, after he had fo mercifully and liberally perform'd his faid Promife unto them, they did not deal with the word of God, as Vintners, Regraters or Merchants do with their mixed Wines and adulterated Wares; that is, mingle it with any untruths or fuperftitious conceits, or vent it out otherwife than the truth did therein warrant them ; or did apply it with fraud, either to ferve their own, or any other mens defignments ; or deliver'd it with any fuch inward Refervations, and mental Evafions, as when they did moft feem to their hearers to fpeak one thing directly, they had fuch another meaning, as when time fhould ferve they might make ufe of. But whatfoever

2 Cor. 2. 17.

they faid, they fpake it fincerely, *ficut ex Deo* , as *God did guide them by the Holy Ghoft* ; *coram Deo, as in the fight of God*; unto whom one day they were to give an account of their faid fincerity ; *& in Chrifto,* as their bleffed Saviour himfelf had preached , taught them, and had commanded them.

CAN.

CAN. IV.

Therefore if any Man shall affirm, under colour of any thing that is in the Scriptures, either that the Deity of our Saviour Christ, doth not since his Resurrection and Ascension, otherwise execute the Majesty and Glory thereof in his Humanity, than it did before his Passion: or, that Christ now in Glory, is not actually the Heir of all things, as he is Man so highly exalted, and both King of kings, and Lord of lords: or, that he now sitting at the right hand of God, in Glory and Majesty, as he is Man, hath made an alteration in the manner of temporal Government, ordain'd by himself long before, as he is God: or, that now all the Kingdoms in the World, being but one Kingdom in respect of himself, he doth not allow the distributing of that his one Universal Kingdom, into divers Principalities and Kingdoms, to be ruled by so many Kings, and absolute Princes under him: or, that such Kings and Sovereign Governours, as were Ethnicks, were deprived by Christ's Ascension into Heaven, and most glorious Estate there; from the true Interest and lawful Possession of the

Kingdoms,

Kingdoms, which before they enjoyed: or, that the ancient Fathers were deceived, in holding and maintaining, that all Christians in the Primitive Church were bound to obey such Kings and Princes as were then Pagans: or, that the Subjects of all the Temporal Princes in the World, were not as much bound in St. Paul's time to be subject unto them, as the Romans were to be subject to the Empire, not only for Fear, but even for Conscience Sake: **or, that St.** Paul's **Commandment (by virtue of his Apostleship, and assistance of the Holy Ghost) of Obedience to Princes, then Ethnicks, is not of as great force to bind the Conscience of all true Christians, as if he had been then** Summus Pontifex: **or, that any Pope now hath power to dispense with the said Doctrine of St.** Paul, **as the said** Canonist, **by us quoted, doth seem to affirm; Where after he hath said, That the Apostle St.** Paul, **commanding all Men to be obedient to superiour Powers, was not the highest Bishop, he addeth these Words,** Papa major est administratione Paulo ; & Papa dispensat contra Apostolum in his, quæ non concernunt Articulos fidei: The Pope is greater in Authority than Paul; the Pope doth dispense against the Apostle in those things that do not concern the Articles

cles of Faith: or, that the Primitive Church was not as well restrain'd de jure by the Doctrine of Christ's Apostles, as de facto, from bearing Arms against such Princes as were then Ethnicks, and transferring of their Kingdoms from them unto any others: or, that St. Peter himself (who our Adversaries would make the World believe, was then the highest Bishop) concurring with the Apostle St. Paul, when he commanded the Christians in those days to submit themselves unto the King, as unto the Superiour, (they both of them were assured, commanding therein, as they were inspired by the Holy Ghost) did leave this Doctrine, so jointly taught, to be dispensed with afterward by any Pope, his Vicar; led by what Spirit is easy to be discern'd, being so far different from the Holy Ghost, which spake (as is aforesaid) by the said Apostles: or, that it is not a most wicked and detestable assertion for any Man to affirm, That the Apostles in commanding such obedience to the Ethnick Princes then, did not truly mean as their plain Words do import, but had some mental Reservations, whereby the same might be alter'd, as occasion should serve: or, that the Apostles at that time, if they had found the Christians of sufficient force,

for

for Number, Provision, and Furniture of Warlike Engines, to have deposed those Pagan Princes, that were then both Enemies and Persecutors of all that believed in Christ; would (no doubt) have moved and authorized them to have made War against such their Princes, and absolved them from performing any longer that Obedience, which they (as Men temporizing) had in their Writings prescribed unto them: or, that when afterward Christians were grown able for number and strength, to have opposed themselves by force against their Emperours, being Wicked, and Persecutors; they might lawfully so have done, for any thing that is in the New Testament to the contrary: or, that these, and such like Expositions of the meaning of the holy Apostles, when they writ so plainly and directly, are not very impious and blasphemous; as tending not only to the utter discredit of them and their Writings, but likewise to the indelible stain and dishonour of the whole Scriptures, in that they were written by no other Persons of any greater Authority than were the Apostles, nor by the Inspiration and direction of any other Spirit; He doth greatly Erre.

CAP.

CAP. VI.

The Sum of the Chapter following.

That our Saviour Christ after his Resurrection and Ascension did not in Effect alter the Form of Ecclesiastical Government amongst the Jews; *the essential parts of the Priesthood under the Law (otherwise than as the said Priesthood was typical, and had the Execution of* Levitical *Ceremonies annexed unto it) being instituted and appointed by God to continue, not for a time, but until the End of the World.*

WE have deduced, in our former Book, the joint Descent of the State, as well Ecclesiastical as Temporal, from the Beginning of the World unto the Incarnation of our Saviour Christ. Since whose Birth, seeing we have found no alteration in the Temporal Government of the World, either while Christ lived here upon the Earth, or during the time of his Apostles; assuredly we shall not find that the alteration, which, upon Christ's Death, fell out in the Church, was so great, as some have imagined. For as our Saviour Christ according unto his Divine Nature having created all the World, was the sole Monarch of it, and did govern the same visibly by Kings, and Soveraign Princes, his Vicegerents upon Earth; so he in the same Divine Nature being the Son of God, and foreseeing the Fall of Man, and how thereby all his Posterity should become the Children of Wrath, did of his infinite Mercy, undertake to be their Redeemer; and presently after the Transgression of *Adam* & *Eve*, put that his Office in practice: Whereby, as he was *Agnus occisus ab origine Mundi*, he not only began the Erection of that one Church, selected people, and Society of Believers, which ever since hath been, and so shall continue his blessed Spouse for ever; but also took upon him thenceforward and for ever to be the sole Head and Monarch of it, ruling and governing the same visibly by such Priests and Ministers under him, as in his heavenly Wisdom he thought fit to appoint, and as we have more at large expressed in our said former Book: Especially, when he settled amongst the *Jews* a more exact and eminent Form of Ecclesiastical Government, than before that time he had done. In the which his so exact a Form, he first did separate the civil Government from the Ecclesiastical, as they were both jointly exercised by one Person, restraining the Priesthood, for a time, unto the *Tribe of Levi*, and the civil Government unto temporal Princes, and shortly after, more particularly, unto the *Tribe of Judah*. Concerning the Priesthood thus limited, we need to say little; because the Order and Subordination of it is so plainly set down in the Scriptures. *Aaron* and his Sons after him, by succession, had the first Place, and were appointed to exercise the Office of Highpriests; and under their soveraign Princes and temporal Governours, (as we have shewed in our said first Book, cap. 18.) did bear the chief sway in matters appertaining to God. Next unto *Aaron* there were 24. Priests of an inferiour Degree, that were termed *Principes Sacerdotum*, that governed the third sort of Priests, allotted unto their several Charges: and this third sort also had the rest of the *Levites* at their direction. In like manner these *Levites* neither wanted their chief Rulers to order them, according as the said third sort of Priests did command (which Rulers were termed *Principes Levitarum*, in number 24.) Nor their Assistants the *Gabionites*, otherwise called *Nethinæi*, to help them in the Execution of their baser Offices. Of this notable Form of Ecclesiastical Government, it may be truly said in our Judgments, That the same being of God's own framing,

it

it is to be esteem'd the best and most perfect Form of Church-Government, that ever was, or can be devised: and that Form also is best to be approved and upheld, which doth most resemble it, and cometh nearest unto it.

We said upon a fit Occasion, That by the Death of our Saviour Christ, the Church-Government then amongst the *Jews*, was greatly altered: and therefore do think it very convenient in this place more fully therein to set down our meaning. It is very true, that before the Death of Christ, the outward Service of God did much consist in Figures, Shadows, and Sacrifices; the *Levitical* Priesthood itself (as it was to *Aaron* and his Stock, and in some other Respects) being only a Type of our High Priest, *Jesus Christ*. But afterward, when by his Passion upon the Cross he had fulfilled All, that was signified by the said Figures, Shadows, and Sacrifices; and had likewise not only abolished them, but freed the Tribe of *Levi*, of the charge of the Priesthood, and removed the High Priesthood (as it was typical) from the said Priestly Tribe, unto the Regal Tribe of *Judah*; the same being now setled in himself, our only High Priest, according to the Order, not of *Aaron*, but of *Melchizedech*: He hath by that his Translation of the Priesthood, freed his Church from the Ceremonial Law, which contained in it little but Patterns, Shadows, and Figures of that one Sacrifice offer'd by him upon the Cross, which doth *sanctifie all the faithful, and purge their Consciences from dead works to serve the living God*. Nevertheless in this so great an alteration, although all the said Figures, Shadows, Sacrifices, and whatsoever else was typical in the true Worship of God, and Priesthood of *Aaron*, were truly fulfilled, and had their several Accomplishments according to the Natures of them. Yet we are further to understand, that as from the beginning there was a Church, so there was ever a Ministry; the Essential

l. 2. c. 4.

Hebr. 7. 12.
— 10. 10.
— 9. 14.

parts

parts of whose Office (howsoever otherwise it was burdened with Ceremonies) did consist in these three Duties; *viz.* (1.) Preaching of the Word. (2.) Administration of Sacraments: and (3.) Authority of Ecclesiastical Government: and that none of all the said Figures, Shadows, and Sacrifices, or any other Ceremony of the *Levitical* Law had any such relation to any of the said three Essential Parts of the Ministry, as if either they the said three Essential Parts of the Ministry had only been ordain'd for their continuance until the coming of Christ; or that the accomplishment or fulfilling of the said Ceremonies had in any sort prejudiced or impeached the Continuance of them, or any of them. So as the said three Essential Parts of the Ministry were in no sort abolished by the Death of Christ; but only translated from the Priesthood under the Law to the Ministry of the New Testament: Where, in the judgment of all Learned Men, opposite in divers points one to another, they do or ought for ever to remain to the same End and Purpose for the which they were first ordain'd.

Now concerning the two first Essential Parts of this our Ministry, or Priesthood of the New Testament, there are no Difficulties worthy the insisting upon, how they are to be used. Only the third Essential Part of it, as touching the Power of Ecclesiastical Regiment, is very much controverted, and diversly expounded, extended, and applied. For some Men, relying upon one Extremity, do affirm, That it was in the Apostles time radically inherent only in St. *Peter*; and so, by a certain consequence, afterwards in his supposed Vicar the Bishop of *Rome*, to be derived from St. *Peter* first to the rest of the Apostles and other Ministers, while he lived, and then after his Death, in a fit proportion to all Bishops, Pastors, and Ministers to the end of the World from the Bishops of *Rome*: and that St. *Peter* during his time, and every one of his Vicars, the Bishops of
Rome

Rome succeſsively, then did, and ſtill do occupy and enjoy the like Power and Authority over all the Churches in the World, that *Aaron* had in the Church eſtabliſhed amongſt the *Jews*. There are alſo another ſort of Perſons, that run as far to another extremity, and do challenge the ſaid Power and Authority of Eccleſiaſtical Regiment to appertain to a new Form of Church-Government by *Presbyteries*, to be placed in every particular Pariſh: Which Presbyteries (as divers of them ſay) are ſo many compleat and perfect Churches; no one of them having any dependency upon any other Church: So as the Paſtor in every ſuch Presbytery, repreſenting after a ſort *Aaron* the High Prieſt; there would be by this project (if it were admitted) as many *Aarons* in every Chriſtian Kingdom, as there are particular Pariſhes. And the Authors of both theſe ſo different, and extream conceits, are all of them moſt reſolute and peremptory, that they are able to deduce and prove them out of the Form of Church-Government, which was eſtabliſhed by God himſelf in the Old Teſtament. Howbeit, notwithſtanding all their vaunts and ſhews of Learning, by perverting the Scriptures, Councils, and ancient Fathers; the Mean betwixt both the ſaid extreams is the truth, and to be embraced: *viz.* That the adminiſtration of the ſaid Power of Eccleſiaſtical Regiment under Chriſtian Kings and ſuprèam Magiſtrates, doth eſpecially belong, by the Inſtitution of Chriſt and of his Apoſtles, unto Arch-Biſhops and Biſhops: This Mean bearing the true Pourtraicture, and infallible Lineaments of God's own Ordinance above-mentioned; and containing in it divers Degrees of Prieſts, agreeable to the very order and light of Nature; ſome ſuperiour to rule, and ſome inferiour to be ruled, as in all other Societies and civil States it hath been ever accuſtomed. So as we are bold to ſay, and are able to juſtify it, That as our Saviour Chriſt, as he is God, had formerly ordain'd in his National

tional Church amongſt the *Jews*, *Prieſts* and *Levites* of an inferiour Order, to teach them in every City and Synagogue; and over them Prieſts of a ſuperiour degree, termed *Principes Sacerdotum*; and laſtly, above them all, one *Aaron* with *Moſes*, to rule and direct them: So he, no ways purpoſing by his Paſſion more to abrogate or prejudice this Form of Church-Government ordain'd by himſelf, than he did thereby the temporal Government of Kings and Sovereign Princes; did by the direction of the Holy Ghoſt, and Miniſtry of his Apoſtles, ordain in the New Teſtament, that there ſhould be in every National Church, ſome Miniſters of an inferiour degree, to inſtruct his People in every particular Parochial Church or Congregation; and over them Biſhops of a ſuperiour degree, to have a care and inſpection over many ſuch Parochial Churches or Congregations; for the better ordering, as well of the Miniſters as of the People within the limits of their Juriſdiction: And laſtly, above them all Archbiſhops, and in ſome eſpecial places Patriarchs; who were firſt themſelves, with the advice of ſome other Biſhops, and when Kings and Sovereign Princes became Chriſtians, then with their eſpecial aid and aſſiſtance, to overſee and direct, for the better Peace and Government of every ſuch National Church, all the Biſhops, and the reſt of the particular Churches therein eſtabliſhed. And for ſome proof hereof, We will conclude this Chapter with the teſtimony of one of no mean account and deſert: Who (when Archbiſhops and Biſhops did moſt obſtinately oppoſe themſelves, as being the Pope's Vaſſals, to the Reformation of the Church) was the principal Deviſer of the ſaid Presbyteries (though not in ſuch a manner as ſome have ſince with too much bitterneſs urged) whereof, out of all Queſtion, he would never have dream'd, if the ſaid Biſhops had not been ſo obſtinate, as they were, for the maintenance of ſuch Idolatry and Superſtition, as were no longer to be tolerated.

lerated. "That every Province had amongst their "Bishops one Archbishop; that also in the *Nicene* "Council, Patriarchs were appointed, who were in "Order and Degree above Archbishops; that did ap- "pertain to the preservation of Discipline. And a little after, speaking of the said Form of Government so framed, although he shewed some dislike of the word *Hierarchia*; yet, saith he, *Si, omisso Vocabulo, rem intueamur, reperiemus Veteres Episcopos non aliam regendæ Ecclesiæ formam voluisse fingere, ab eâ, quam Dominus verbo suo præscripsit.*

Calv. in. Instit. l. 4. c. 4. §. 4.

CAN. V.

And therefore if any Man shall affirm, under colour of any thing that is in the Scriptures, either that our Saviour Christ was not the Head of the Church from the beginning of it: or, that all the particular Churches in the World are otherwise to be termed One Church, than as he himself is the Head of it; and as all the particular Kingdoms in the World are called but one Kingdom, as he is the Only King and Monarch of it: or, that our Saviour Christ hath not appointed under him several Ecclesiastical Governours, to rule and direct the said particular Churches; as he hath appointed several Kings and Sovereign Princes, to rule and govern their several Kingdoms: or, that by his Death he did not abolish the Ceremonial Law, and the Levitical Priesthood, so far forth as it was Typical, and had the Execution of the said Ceremonial Law annexed unto it: or, that he did any more abrogate by his Death, Passion, Resurrection and Ascension, the Power and Authority of Church-Government; than either he did the other two Essential parts of the said Priesthood or Ministry, or the Power and Authority of Kings and Sovereign Princes: or, that he did more appoint any one chief Bishop to rule all the particular Churches, which should be planted throughout all Kingdoms, than he did appoint any one King to rule and govern all the particular Kingdoms in the World: or, that it was more reasonable or necessary (as hereafter it shall be further shewed) to have one Bishop to govern all the Churches in the World, than it was to have one King to govern all the Kingdoms in the World: or, that it was more necessary or convenient, to have every Parish, with their Presbyteries, absolute Churches, independent upon any but Christ himself; than that every such Parish should be an absolute Temporal Kingdom, independent of any Earthly King, or Sovereign Magistrate: or, that the Government of every

National

National Church under Christian Kings, and Sovereign Princes, by Archbishops and Bishops, is not more suitable and correspondent to the Government of the National Church of the Jews, under their Soveraign Princes and Kings, than is either the Government of one over all the Churches of the World, or the setling of the Form of that National Church-Government in every particular Church; He doth greatly Erre.

CAP. VII.

The Sum of the Chapter following.

That the Form of Church-Government, which was ordained by Christ in the New Testament, did consist upon divers degrees of Ministers, one above another; Apostles in Preeminence and Authority superiour to the Evangelists; and the Evangelists superiour to Pastors and Doctours: And that the Apostles knowing themselves to be mortal, did, in their own Days (by the Direction of the Holy Ghost) as the numbers of Christians grew, establish the said form of Government in other Persons; appointing several Ministers in sundry Cities, and over them Bishops; as also over such Bishops certain worthy Persons such as Titus *was, who were afterward termed Arch-Bishops; to whom they did commit so much of their Apostolical Authority, as they held then necessary, and was to be continued for the Government of the Church.*

WE had in our former Book the Scriptures at large, containing the Histories and Doctrine both of the Law and the Gospel, after the manner that was then prescribed, from the time of the Creation until the days of the Prophet *Malachy*; that is, for above 3500. years: Whereupon we did ground the particular Points by us therein handled, concerning the Government as well Ecclesiastical as Temporal. And for the Supply of the other years following till the Incarnation of our Saviour Christ, we observed some things to the same purpose out of the *Apocryphal* Books, second to the Scriptures, and to be preferr'd before all other Writers of those times. But now forasmuch as the New Testament is but, in effect, a more ample Declaration

of

the Old; shewing withal, how the same was most throughly fulfilled by our Saviour Christ (without the impeachment of any kind of Government, by himself ordain'd, as before we have exprest) and because the Books of the Evangelists and Apostles do only contain the Acts and Doctrine of our Saviour Christ and his Apostles, with the Form and Use both of the Temporal and Ecclesiastical Government, during the time whilst they lived here upon the Earth; (St. *John*, who lived the longest of them all, dying about sixty six Years after Christ's Passion:) although the Holy Ghost did judge the said Books and Writings sufficient for the Church and all that profess Christianity, to teach and direct them in those things which should appertain either to their Temporal or Ecclesiastical Government, or should be necessary unto their Salvation: Yet for the said Reasons, we were induced, for the upholding of the Temporal and Ecclesiastical Government in the New Testament, to insist so much as we have done upon the Precedents and Platforms of both those kinds of Governments established in the Old Testament; albeit we want no sufficient Testimonies in the New to ratify and confirm as well the one as the other.

First, therefore we do verily think, That if our Saviour Christ or his Apostles had meant to have erected in the Churches amongst the Gentiles any other Form of Ecclesiastical Government than God himself had set up amongst the *Jews*: they would have done it assuredly in very solemn manner, that all the World might have taken publick notice of it: considering with what Majesty and Authority the said Form was erected at God's Commandment by his Servant *Moses*. But in that they well knew how the Form of the Old Ecclesiastical Government, in substance, was still to continue and to be, in time, establish'd in every National Kingdom and Soveraign Principality amongst Christians, as soon as they should become for number sufficient Bodies and ample

Churches

Churches to receive the fame; as before the like opportunity it was not eſtabliſhed amongſt the *Iſraelites*: they did in the mean while, and as the time did ſerve them, attempt the erecting of it in ſuch ſort, and by ſuch fit and convenient Degrees, as by the direction of the Holy Ghoſt, they held it moſt expedient, without intermiſſion, till ſuch time as the work was (in effect) accompliſhed.

It hath been before touched, how our Saviour Chriſt here upon Earth, did not only chuſe to himſelf, for the buſineſs he had in hand, twelve Apoſtles, who were then deſign'd, in time to come, to be the Patriarchs and chief Fathers of all Chriſtians, with ſome Reſemblance (as it hath been ever held) of the twelve Sons of *Jacob*, who had been in their days the Patriarchs and chief Fathers of all the *Iſraelites*: But likewiſe he took unto him (over and beſides his ſaid Apoſtles, 70, or as ſome read 72 Diſciples, to be in the ſame manner his Aſſiſtants, in imitation of *Moſes*, when he choſe 70. Elders to be helpers unto him, for the better Government of the People committed to his charge. None of theſe, either Apoſtles or Diſciples, had then any other Duties committed to them, but only of Preaching and Baptizing: for the Power of Eccleſiaſtical Regiment they might not then intermeddle with, becauſe it did appertain to the Prieſts, and Courts of the *Jews*. But afterward that want, and ſome other defects in them, were throughly ſupplied, when our Saviour Chriſt upon his Reſurrection, and a little before his Aſcenſion, enlarging their Commiſſion, did commit unto his Apoſtles the Adminiſtration of the Keys of the Kingdom of Heaven; and ſhortly after furniſhed, not only them, but the ſaid Diſciples alſo (according to their ſeveral Functions) moſt abundantly with all ſuch Gifts, and Heavenly Graces, as were neceſſary for them in thoſe great Affairs which were impoſed upon them. Whereby we find already two compleat Degrees of Eccleſiaſtical Miniſters,

Ministers, ordained by Christ himself immediately; *viz.* His 12. Apostles, and his 70. Disciples; the one in Dignity and Authority above the other, the Disciples in that respect being termed *Secondary Apostles*; and were the same (as 'tis most probably held) who were afterward called Evangelists. We will not intermeddle with the Prophets in those times, of whom the Scriptures make mention; because divers of them were no Ministers of the Word and Sacraments, of whom only we have here taken upon us to intreat; leaving in like manner the said 70. Disciples, or Evangelists, as before they had been assistants unto Christ, so now to be directed by his Apostles. Touching whose blessed calling it is to be observed, that the end of it was not, that they should only for their own times, by Preaching the Word, Administring the Sacraments, and likewise by their Authority of Ecclesiastical Regiment, draw many to the embracing of the Gospel, and afterward to rule and order them, as that they might not easily be drawn again from it: but were in like sort to provide for a Succession in their Ministry, of fit Persons, sufficiently Authorized by them, to undertake that charge, and as well to yield some further assistance unto them, whilst they themselves lived, as afterward; also, both to continue the same, in their own Persons, unto their lives end; and in like manner to ordain, by the Authority of the Apostles, given unto them, other Ministers to succeed themselves: that so the said Apostolical Authority, being derived in that sort from one to another, there might never be any want of Pastors and Teachers, *for the work of the Ministry, and for the Edification of the Body of Christ*, unto the end of the World.

This being the duty of the said Apostles, and that it may be evident what it was, which they did communicate unto the Ministry; it is to be observed, that some things in the Apostles were essential and perpetual, and was the substance of their Ministry, containing

ing the three Effential Parts before mentioned, of Preaching, adminiftring the Sacraments, and of Ecclefiaftical Government; and that fome were but perfonal and temporary, granted unto them for the better ftrengthning and approving of the faid Miniftry with all the Parts of it; there being then many Difficulties and Impediments, which did many ways hinder the firft Preaching and Plantation of the Gofpel. In the number of the faid perfonal or temporary Gifts or Prerogatives, thefe may be accounted the Chief. (1.) That they were called immediately by Chrift himfelf, to lay the Foundation of Chriftian Faith among the Gentiles. (2.) That their Commiffion to that purpofe was not limited to any Place or Country. (3.) That they had power, through Impofition of their hands, to give the Holy Ghoft by vifible Signs. (4.) That they were directed in the performance of their Office by the efpecial Infpiration of the Holy Ghoft: and laftly, That their Doctrine which they deliver'd in Writing, was to be a Canon and Rule to all Churches for ever. All which perfonal Prerogatives, although they did then appertain, and were then adherent to the Effence of the Apoftolick Function, and were neceffary, at the firft, for the eftablifhing of the Gofpel; yet it is plain, that they did not contain in them any of the faid Effential Parts of the Miniftry, and likewife that they could not be communicated by the Apoftles unto any others. So as either the Apoftles, for the Propagation and Continuance of the Ecclefiaftical Miniftry, did communicate to others the faid three Effential Parts of it, *viz.* Power to Preach, to Adminifter the Sacraments, and Authority of Government: wherein muft be Degrees, fome to direct, and fome to be directed, or elfe they died all with them, which were a very wicked and an idle conceit; the Apoftles having Power to communicate them all alike, as by their Proceedings it will appear. At the firft, they themfelves with the

Evangelifts

Evangelists, and so many of the Prophets as were Ministers of the Word and Sacraments, after they had converted many to the Faith; did execute in their own Persons, agreeably to their several Callings, all those Ecclesiastical Functions, as were afterward of necessity, and in due time to be distinguished, and setled in some others. Whereby it came to pass, that the Church in *Jerusalem*, during that time, had no other Deacons, Priests, nor Bishops, but the Apostles, the Evangelists, and the said Prophets. But afterwards the Harvest growing great, as to disburthen themselves of some charge, they Ordained Deacons; So their own Company, Apostles, Disciples, or Evangelists, and Prophets, coming short of that number of Labourers which the said Harvest required; they did for their future aid, chuse unto themselves, by the Inspiration of the Holy Ghost, certain other new Disciples and Scholars, such as they found meet for that work; and after some good experience had of them, made them by the *Imposition of their* hands, Priests and Ministers of the Gospel; but did not for a time tie them to any particular places, as having design'd them to be their Fellow-Labourers, and Coadjutors. 2 Tim. 1. 5.

These Men the Apostles had commonly in their Company, and did not employ their Pains and diligent Preaching for the speedier Propagation of the Gospel, (which was their first and most Principal Care) but likewise did use to send them hither and thither (their Occasions so requiring) to the Churches already planted, as their Messengers and Legates, sufficiently authorized for the dispatching of such Affairs as were committed unto them. Of this number were *Timothy*, *Titus*, *Marcus*, *Epaphroditus*, *Sylvanus*, *Andronicus*, and divers others; who in respect of such their Apostolical Employments, and because also the Apostles did oftentimes commend them greatly, and join'd their Names with their own in the beginnings of sundry their Epistles to divers Churches, Rom. 16. 21. Phil. 2. 25. Philem. 1. 24.

Z

Rom. 16. 7.
2 Cor. 8. 23.
Phil 2. 25.

Churches, were Men of great Reputation and Authority amongſt all Chriſtians in thoſe days, and had the name it ſelf of Apoſtles given unto them, as formerly it hath been obſerv'd of the 70. Diſciples. And theſe were the Perſons, who were afterward, when they were tied to the overſight of divers particular Churches or Congregations, termed Biſhops, as it will afterward appear. Now becauſe theſe Apoſtolical Perſons were ſtill to attend upon the Apoſtles, and their Deſignments, as is above mentioned; and for that the number of Chriſtians every where did ſtill encreaſe, the Apoſtles held it neceſſary to ordain, by impoſition of their hands, a ſecond degree of Miniſters, who were thereupon ſtill to remain in the particular Churches or Congregations, that were already planted in divers Cities (for in thoſe populous places Churches were firſt ſetled) whilſt the Apoſtles, Evangeliſts, and Prophets, that were Miniſters, with their Coadjutors, were travelling from place to place, as the Holy Ghoſt did direct them, to plant and order other Churches in other Cities elſewhere, as God ſhould bleſs their labours.

The office of this ſecond degree of Miniſters was by Preaching and Adminiſtring the Sacraments, to confirm and encreaſe, to their utmoſt ability, the number of Chriſtians in thoſe Cities, where they kept their reſidence; and likewiſe in the abſence of the Apoſtles, by their common and joint counſel, to adviſe and direct every particular Congregation, and Member of it, as well as they could, when any difficulties did occur. Beſides, it appertained unto them by Preaching of the Goſpel, and of the Law, and upon Conference with ſuch as were Penitent, to bind and looſe Mens Sins, and to keep back from receiving the holy Communion, ſuch as were notorious and obſtinate Offenders, until either willingly by their perſwaſion, or afterwards by the Apoſtles further Chaſtiſements, they were brought to Repentance. Only they wanted Power and Authority

rity of Ordination to make Ministers, and of the Apostolical Keys to Excommunicate. For the Apostles had reserv'd in their own hands those two Prerogatives, and were themselves (during those first times, now spoken of by us) not so far from the said Cities, Churches, and Ministers, but that they well might, and did throughly supply all their wants whatsoever, and also set an order in all matters of difficulty, when they fell out amongst them, concerning either Doctrine or Discipline, sometimes themselves in their own Persons, and sometimes by their Letters, or Messengers, as the importance of those Causes did require. In these times it may well be granted, that there was no need of any other Bishops but the Apostles, and likewise, that then their Churches, or particular Congregations in every City, were advised and directed touching points of Religion, in manner and form aforesaid, by the common and joint advice of their Priests or Ministers. In which respect, the same Persons who then were named Priests or Ministers, were also in a general sense called Bishops. Howbeit this course dured not long, either concerning their said common direction, or their names of Bishops so attributed unto them; but was shortly after order'd far otherwise, by a common Decree of the Apostles, to be observ'd in all such Cities where particular Churches were planted, or (as one speaketh) *in toto Orbe, throughout the World*. For the number of Christians growing daily in every City throughout those Provinces and Countries, where the Apostles, Evangelists, Prophets, with their Coadjutors, first travelled to plant the Christian Faith; it was still more and more necessary, that they should be distinguished into more Congregations than they were before, and that also the number of their said Ministers that were to be resident amongst them, should be accordingly encreased. By reason of which encrease, as well of Christians and particular Congregations, as of their said Ministers; as also for that

Act. 14. 23.
2 Tim. 1. 6.
2 Thess. 3. 14.
1 Cor. 4. 21.
2 Cor. 13. 2.
1 Cor. 5. 3, 4

Jerom. in Ep. ad Tit. c. 1.

Rom. 16. 17.
2 Cor. 1. 11.
& 3. 4.
Gal. 1. 6. & 3. 1.
Phil. 3. 2, 3.
Col 2. 4, 8. 18.

1 Theff. 4. 13.
2 Theff. 2.2, 3.
Act. 20. 29, 30.
2 Pet. 2.1. &c.
1 Joh. 2. 18.
& 4. 1.

that now it began to come to pass, that neither the Apostles, nor the Evangelists, nor their Coadjutors and Messengers could be always so ready, and at hand, or present with them, as before they had been; many Questions, Dissentions, and Quarrels, fell out amongst them (both Ministers and particular Congregations mentioned) as by the places quoted in the Margent it is evident; the People being as apt, through affection and private respects, to adhere to one Man more than to another, as sundry of their Ministers then were

2 Cor. 1. 24.
4. 17. 10. 12.
18. 11. 5, 23.
12. 11.

prompt for their own glory to entertain all Comers, and to embrace every occasion that might procure them many Followers; not sparing to oppose themselves in their Pride against the very Apostles, and to charge them with ambitious seeking of preheminence above their Brethren Ministers; as if they had meant to tyrannize

3 Joh. 9.

and domineer over all Churches. Insomuch as St. *John* complain'd in his time of such Insolencies: and St. *Paul* was driven to purge himself; but yet in such sort, as he stood upon the Justification of his Apostolical Authority; I grant, saith he, *That they are Ministers of Christ*; but withal he addeth these words, *I am more*; protesting, that although he was more than they were, yet he sought *to have no Dominion over the Faith of any*. The places quoted in the Margent deserve due consideration, and many other to the same purpose might be added unto them.

Now forasmuch as the Apostles did well understand the said Oppositions, Dissentions, and Emulations; and that the People had as well Experience, what Equality wrought amongst their Ministers in every place, whilst each Man would be a Director as he list himself, and accordingly broach his own Fancies without Controulment, or sparing of any that stood in his way; as also how themselves (the people) were distracted and led to the embracing of Divers Sects and Schisms: they (the said Apostles) having now no such leisure and opportunity,

portunity, as that they could themselves every where appease these Quarrels, did find it necessary to settle another Course for the redress of them by others. For whereas before, the Apostles held it convenient, when they first planted Ministers in every City, to detain still in their own hand the Power of Ordination, and the authority of the Keys of Ecclesiastical Government (because they themselves, for that time, with the Evangelists and others their Coadjutors, were sufficient to oversee and rule them:) Now for the Reasons abovementioned they did commit those their said two Prerogatives, containing in them all Episcopal Power and Authority, unto such of their said Coadjutors, as upon sufficient tryal of their Abilities and Diligence, they knew to be meet Men; both, whilst they themselves lived, to be their Substitutes, and after their deaths to be their Successors, both for the Continuance of the work of Christ, for the further building of his Church, and likewise for the perpetual Government of it. And in this manner, the Ministers of the Word and Sacraments, who had the charge but of one particular Church or Congregation, and were of an inferiour Degree, were distinguished from the first and superiour sort of Ministers, termed (most of them) before, *The Apostles Coadjutors*; and now and from thenceforth called *Bishops*. Unto which sort of worthy and selected Coadjutors, and unto some others also of especial Desert so advanced to the Titles and Offices of Bishops, the Apostles did commit the charge and oversight of all the particular Congregations, Ministers and Christian people that dwelt in one City, and in the Towns and Villages thereunto appertaining. And such were the Angels of the seven Churches in *Asia*, who were then the *Bishops* Apoc. 1. 11. of those Cities, with their several Territories; and so in all times and ages that since have succeeded, have ever been reputed. And unto some others the most principal and chief men of the said Number, the Apostles did

likewise

likewise give Authority, not only over the particular Congregations, Ministers and People in one City, and in the Towns that did belong unto it; but likewise over all the Churches in certain whole Provinces and Countries, as unto *Timothy* all that were in *Asia the less*, and unto *Titus* all that were planted throughout the Island of *Crete*. And this sort of Bishops who had so large Jurisdictions over the Bishops themselves in particular Cities, were afterward called Archbishops: Over whom, in like manner, as likewise over all the rest, Bishops and Ministers, and particular Churches, the Apostles themselves as the chief Fathers and Patriarchs of all Churches, had whilst they lived, the chief preheminence and oversight to direct and over-rule all, as they knew it to be most convenient and behoofull for the Church: communicating notwithstanding unto the said Bishops and Archbishops (now their Substitutes, but in time to be their Successors) as full Authority in their absence (with the limitations mention'd) for the ordering of Ministers, for the use of the Keys, and for the further Government of all the Churches committed to their charges, by the good advice and counsel of the inferiour sort of Priests, or Ministers under them, when Causes so required; as if they (the Apostles themselves) had been present, or could have always lived to have performed those duties in their own Persons; their Patriarchal Authority for Government not ceasing, or dying with them. Of this Authority of Ordination and Government, given to Bishops by the holy Apostle St. *Paul*, he himself hath left to all Posterity most clear and evident Testimonies; where writing to two of his said Bishops, *Timothy* and *Titus*, he describeth very particularly the Essential parts of their duties, and Episcopal Office, in manner and sort following.

" For this cause I left thee at *Crete*, that thou shouldst
" continue to redress the things that remain; and
" shouldst

marginal notes:
1 Tim. 1. 3.
Tit. 1. 5.

Tit. 1. 5.

"shouldst Ordain Priests or Elders in every City, as I 1 Tim. 5. 22.
"appointed thee. Lay hands hastily on no Man; nei- —— 3. 10.
"ther be Partaker of other Mens Sins. Let them first —— 5. 19.
"be proved, then let them minister, if they be found
"blameless. Against a Presbyter or Priest, receive no
"accusation but under two or three Witnesses. Them
"that sin rebuke openly, that the rest may fear. I —— 1. 3, 4, 7.
"pray thee to abide at *Ephesus*, to command some, that
"they teach no strange Doctrine, neither that they
"give heed to Fables and Genealogies which are end-
"less, and do breed Questions rather than godly Edifi-
"cation, which is by Faith. They would be Doctors
"of the Law; and yet understand not what they
"speak, neither whereof they affirm. There are ma- Tit. 1. 10, 11.
"ny disobedient and vain Talkers and Deceivers of
"Minds; whose Mouths must be stopped; which sub-
"vert whole Houses, teaching things which they ought
"not, for filthy lucre's sake. Stay foolish questions and —— 3. 9.
"contentions; reject him that is an Heretick after one —— 10.
"or two warnings. These things speak and exhort, —— 2. 15.
"and rebuke with all Authority: See that no Man de-
"spise thee. What things thou hast heard of me, the
"same deliver to faithful Men, which shall be able to
"teach others also. Put them in remembrance, and
"protest before the Lord, that they strive not about 2 Tim. 2. 2.
"words, which is to no profit, but to the perverting —— 2. 14.
"of the Hearers. Stay profane and vain bablings; for —— 15.
"they shall encrease unto more ungodliness. Put away —— 23.
"all foolish and unlearned Questions; knowing that
"they engender strife. I charge thee before God, and
"the Lord Jesus Christ, and the Elect Angels, that 1 Tim. 5. 21.
"thou observe these things, without preferring one to
"another; and do nothing partially. Divers other
particulars might be hereunto added, were it not that
these are sufficient for our purpose, to show as well
what Power was given to the said *Timothy* and *Titus*
(two Apostolical Bishops newly designed unto their
Episcopal

Episcopal Functions) as also what Authority the Apostle himself had, whilst he lived, both of prescribing rules unto them, and also of exacting the due observation of them: He retaining still in his own hands, as full power and ample Jurisdiction over them, as they the said Bishops had received from him over the rest of the Ministry, within their several charges.

And thus we see, how by degrees the Apostles did settle the Government of the Church amongst the Gentiles converted to Christ, most suitable and agreeing with the Platform ordain'd by God himself amongst the *Jews*. Ministers are placed in particular Congregations, as *Priests* or *Levites* were in their Synagogues. Four and twenty Priests termed *Principes Sacerdotum*, had in that Kingdom the charge over the rest of the Priests: and amongst Christians, one sort of Priests named Bishops or Arch-Bishops (as their Jurisdictions were extended) had the oversight of the rest of the Ministry or Priesthood. Lastly, as over all the Priests, of what sort soever, and over the rest of all the *Jews*, *Aaron* had the chief preeminence; so had the Apostles over all the Bishops and Priests, and over the rest of all Christians. There was only this want to the full accomplishment of such a Church-Government, as was settled amongst the *Jews*, that during the Apostles times, and for a long season afterward, it wanted Christian Magistrates to supply the rooms of *Moses*, King *David*, King *Solomon*, and of the rest of their worthy Successors. There is no mention in the Scriptures of the particular success that the rest of the Apostles had in planting of Churches throughout all *Africa* and *Asia the great*, and a great part of *Europe*: but we doubt not, but that they followed that same course in those parts nearer, or better known to us; they proceeding within their limits, as St. *Paul* did within his. And moreover, we have sufficient warrant by the said Practice of our Apostles to judge, that if all the Kings, and Soveraign Princes

of

of the World would have received the Gospel whilst the Apostles lived, they would have setled this Platform of Church-Government under them in every such Kingdom, and Sovereign Principality: that as the three Essential parts of the Priesthood under the Law, were translated to the Ministry or Priesthood in the New Testament; so the external shew or practice of them, might have been in effect the same under Christian Princes that it was under the godly Kings and Princes of *Judah* : Christians of particular Congregations to be directed by their immediate Pastors; Pastors to be ruled by their Bishops; Bishops to be advised by their Archbishops; and the Archbishops, with all the rest, both of the Clergy and Laity, to be ruled and governed by their godly Kings and Sovereign Princes.

CAN. VI.

AND therefore if any Man shall affirm, under colour of any thing that is in the Scriptures, either that the Platform of Church-Government in the New Testament, may not lawfully be deduced from that Form of Church-Government, which was in the Old: or, that because the Apostles did not once for all, and at one time, but by degrees, erect such a like form of Ecclesiastical Government, as was amongst the Jews, therefore it is not to be supposed, that they meant at all to erect it: or, that their expectation of fit opportunity to establish that kind of Government in the

A a   Churches

Churches of the Gentiles, being converted to Christ, hath any more force to discredit it, than had the want of it for many years amongst the Jews to blemish the dignity of it, when it was there established: or, that the Apostles had no further Authority of Church-Government committed unto them, after the Resurrection and Ascension of Christ, than they had before his Passion: or, that there was not as great necessity of sundry degrees in the Ministry, whilst the Apostles lived, one to rule, another to be ruled, for the establishing and government of the Church, as there was whilst the Priesthood of Aaron endured: or, that Christ himself did not, after a sort, approve of divers degrees of Ministers, some to have præheminence over others, in that having chosen to himself twelve Apostles, he did also elect 70. Disciples, who were neither superiour nor equal to the Apostles, and were therefore their inferiours: or, that he did not very expresly, after his Ascension appoint divers Orders and degrees of Ministers, who had power and præheminence one over another; Apostles over the Prophets and Evangelists, and the Evangelists over Pastors and Doctors: or, that the Authority of Preaching, of Administration of the Sacraments,

craments, and of Ecclesiastical Government, given to the Apostles, was not to be communicated by the Apostles unto others, as there should be good opportunity in that behalf: or, that because there were some personal Prerogatives belonging to the Apostles, which they could not communicate unto others, therefore they had not power to communicate to some Ministers, as well their Authority of Government over other Ministers, as their Authority to preach and administer the Sacraments: or, that in the Authority of Government so to be communicated unto others by the Apostles, there are not included certain degrees to be in the Ministry, some to rule, and some to be ruled: or, that it was not lawful for the Apostles to choose unto themselves Coadjutors, and to make them Ministers of the Word and Sacraments, though they tied them for a space to no certain place, more than they themselves, and the Evangelists, were limited or tied; but kept them in their own Company, as if they had been (in a manner) their Fellows, and employ'd them in Apostolical Embassages, as there were occasions: or, that the Apostles might not lawfully ordain a second Order of Ministers, by Imposition of their hands, to Preach and administer the Sacraments, and to tie them to particular Churches and Congregations, there to execute those their duties: or, that the Ministers of that second degree and Order, so tied unto their particular Charges, had any power committed unto them, either at all to make Ministers, or to pronounce the Sentence of Excommunication against any of their Congregation, but by the direction of the Apostles, when they had given the Sentence, during all the time that the Apostles kept in their own hands the said two points of Ecclesiastical Authority: or, that it was not expedient for the Apostles to retain in their own hands, the Power and Authority of Ecclesiastical Government for a time, and whilst they were able to execute the same in their own Persons, or by their Coadjutors, as they should direct them; and not to communicate the same, either to any their said Coadjutors, or other Persons of the Ministry, until they themselves had good experience and tryal of them; and that the particular Churches also in every City, found the want of such Men, so authorized, to reside amongst them: or, that when the said Ministers, placed in divers particular Churches in sundry Cities, fell at variance amongst themselves,

themselves, which of them should be most prevalent amongst the People, and drew their Followers into divers Sects and Schisms; it was not high time for the Apostles (seeing by reason of their great affairs and business otherwise, they could not attend those particular brawls and inconveniencies) to appoint some worthy Persons in every City, to have the rule, government, and direction of them: or, that when such Men were to be placed in such Cities, the Apostles did not make especial choice of them, out of the number of their said Coadjutors, and likewise out of the rest of the Ministry, to execute those Episcopal duties, which did appertain to their Callings: or, that when they had so design'd and chosen them to be Bishops, they did not communicate unto them, as well their Apostolical Authority of Ordaining of Ministers, and power of the Keys, as of Preaching and Administring the Sacraments: or, that it was not the meaning of the Apostle St. Paul, that such Persons, as Timothy and Titus were, ought to be made Bishops in such Cities and Countries as were that Province of Ephesus, and Kingdom of Crete, to have the like Authority and Power given them in their several Cities, with their Suburbs,

Diocess,

Diocefs, or Province, that was committed to Timothy and Titus, for the ruling of those Ministers and Churches under them: or, that the Authority given by the Apostle St. Paul, or by any other of the Apostles to Timothy and Titus, and such like other Bishops or Archbishops, did any more diminish the Power and Authority which the Apostles had in their own hands, before they appointed any such Bishops and Archbishops, to rule and govern them all; than their giving Power and Authority of Preaching and Administring the Sacraments, did impeach their own Authority so to do; He doth greatly Erre.

CAP.

CAP. VIII.

The Sum of the Chapter following.

That the Churches and godly Fathers, that were immediately after the Apostles times, and all the Ancient Fathers since, did account the Form of Church-Government, established by the Apostles (of Priests and Ministers for more particular Charges; of Bishops superiour to the said Priests; and of Arch-Bishops to have the care and oversight of the said Bishops and Churches committed unto them) not to have been ordain'd for their times only, but to be continued to the End of the World; the same reasons exacting the continuance of it, which moved the Apostles (by the Direction of the Holy Ghost) first to erect it.

WE have pursued the Form of Ecclesiastical Government, so far forth as it is expressed in the Scriptures, and as it was put in practice during the Apostles times. For the further proof whereof, we have thought it expedient briefly to observe, what the primitive Church, Ancient Fathers, and the Ecclesiastical Histories, have in their Writings testified, and said of this matter: as whether they held, that *Timothy* and *Titus* were Bishops in the Apostles times, and had Authority over the Churches and Ministry committed to their Charge: and whether that Form of Church-Government in the Apostles times, wherein were divers Degrees of Ministers, one sort to direct and rule, *viz.* Bishops, and the other to be directed and ruled, was only necessary for the first plantation of the Churches, but not so afterward, when the Churches were planted; as if it had been a lawful Form of Government, whilst the Apostles lived, but upon their Deaths,

it

it became prefently to be unlawful. It is very apparent and cannot be denied, That in many *Greek* Copies of the New Teſtament, *Timothy* and *Titus* are termed Biſhops in the Directions or Subſcriptions of two Epiſtles, which St. *Paul* did write unto them. Theſe are the words of the ſaid Directions: *The ſecond Epiſtle written from Rome unto Timotheus, the firſt Biſhop elected of the Church of Epheſus*, And again, *To Titus elect the firſt Biſhop of the Cretians, written from Nicopolis in Macedonia*. Moreover, agreeable to the ſaid Subſcriptions, the ancient Fathers generally, having (no doubt) upon their due ſearching the Scriptures fully conſidered of the Form of Eccleſiaſtical Government, whilſt the Apoſtles lived, do with one conſent, whenſoever they expound the Epiſtles of St. *Paul* to *Timothy* and *Titus*, or have Occaſion to ſpeak of the Authority of thoſe two Perſons, very reſolutely affirm, That they were by the Apoſtles made Biſhops. And the ſame alſo, they do teſtifie of St. *James* the Apoſtle himſelf, called the *Lord's Brother*; that he was made by the reſt of the Apoſtles, his Colleagues, Biſhop of *Hieruſalem*: and ſo alſo of the *Seven Angels* of the Churches in *Aſia*, that they

Tertull. contra Marcion. l. 5. Chryſoſt. Hom. 10. in 1 Tim. Ambr. in 1 Tim. c. 6. Oecum. in 1 Tim. c 6.

were ſo many Biſhops of the Apoſtles Ordination. Beſides, the ſaid ancient Fathers did very well know that when St. *Paul* ſaid to *Timothy*, *I charge thee in the ſight of God, and before Jeſus Chriſt, that thou keep this Commandment without ſpot, and unrebukable, until the appearing of our Lord Jeſus Chriſt*; that it was impoſſible for *Timothy* to obſerve thoſe things till the coming of Chriſt, he being to die long before: and that therefore the Precepts and Rules which St. *Paul* had given unto him, to obſerve in his Epiſcopal Government, did equally appertain as well to Biſhops, his Succeſſors, as to himſelf, and were to be executed by them ſucceſſively after his Death unto the Worlds End, as carefully and diligently as he himſelf, whilſt he lived, had put them in Pra-

Ambr. ibid.

ctice. One of the ſaid Fathers doth write followeth:
" With

"With great Vigilancy and Providence, doth the Apo-
"ſtle give Precepts to the Ruler of the Church: for
"in his Perſon doth the ſafety of the People conſiſt.
"He is not ſo circumſpect, as fearing *Timothy*'s care,
"but for his Succeſſors; that after *Timothy*'s Example
"they ſhould obſerve the Ordination of the Church,
"and begin themſelves to keep that Form which they
"were to deliver to thoſe that came after them. A-
gain, it is evident by the Eccleſiaſtical Hiſtories, that
not only St. *James*, *Timothy*, and *Titus*, were made
Biſhops by the Apoſtles; but that likewiſe *Peter* him- Euſeb. l. 3. c.
ſelf was Biſhop of *Antioch*; ſo termed, becauſe of his 35.
long ſtay there: and that the Apoſtles likewiſe made Iren. l. 3. c. 3.
Evodius Biſhop of *Antioch* after St. *Peter*, and St. *Mark* 23.
Biſhop of *Alexandria*, and *Polycarpus* Biſhop of *Smyrna*;
and that St. *John*, returning from *Patmos* to *Epheſus*,
went to the Churches round about, and made Biſhops
in thoſe places where they were wanting: and alſo,
that divers others of the Apoſtles Coadjutors, beſides
Timothy and *Titus*, were made by them Biſhops, and
did govern the Cities and Provinces where they were
placed, according to the ſame rules, that were preſcri-
bed to *Timothy* and *Titus*: as *Dionyſius the Areopagite* Origen.inRom.
was the firſt Biſhop of *Athens*; *Caius* the firſt Biſhop of c. 16. Ambr.
Theſſalonica, *Archippus* the firſt Biſhop of the *Coloſſians*; in Coloſſ. c. 4.
and we doubt not, but many more by diligent reading
may be found, that were in the Apoſtles times made
Biſhops.

 Furthermore it is apparent by the teſtimonies of all
Antiquity, Fathers, and Eccleſiaſtical Hiſtories, that
all the Churches in Chriſtendom, that were planted
and govern'd by the Apoſtles, and by ſuch their Coadjutors, Apoſtolical Perſons, as unto whom the Apoſtles had to that end fully communicated their Apoſtolical Authority; did think, that after the Death, either
of any of the Apoſtles, which ruled amongſt them, or
of any other the ſaid Biſhops ordained by them, it was

the meaning of the Holy Ghost, testified sufficiently by the practice of the Apostles, that the same Order and Form of Ecclesiastical Government should continue in the Church for ever. And therefore upon the death of any of them, either Apostles or Bishops, they (the said Churches) did always supply their places with others the most worthy and eminent Persons amongst them: who with the like Power and Authority, that their Predecessors had, did ever succeed them. Insomuch as in every City and Episcopal See, where there were divers Priests and Ministers of the Word and Sacraments, and but one Bishop only; the Catalogues of the Names, not of their Priests but of their Bishops, were very carefully kept from time to time, together with the Names of the Apostles, or Apostolical Persons, the Bishops their Predecessors, from whom they derived their Succession. Of which Succession of Bishops, whilst the Succession of Truth continued with it, the ancient Fathers made great account and use, when any false Teachers did broach new Doctrine, as if they had received the same from the Apostles; choaking them with this, that they were not able to shew any Apostolical Church that ever taught as they did. Upon such an occasion, *Irenæus* Bishop of *Lyons*, within 75 years (or thereabout) after St. *John*'s Death, doth write in this sort: *Habemus annumerare eos, qui ab Apostolis instituti sunt Episcopi in Ecclesiis, & Successores eorum usq; ad nos, qui nihil tale docuerunt, neq; cognoverunt, quale ab his deliratur.* And so likewise, not long after him, *Tertullian*, to oppress some, who (as it seemeth) drew Companies after them, saith thus: *Edant Origines Ecclesiarum suarum; Evolvant ordinem Episcoporum suorum ita per Successiones ab initio decurrentem; ut primus ille Episcopus aliquem ex Apostolis, aut Apostolicis viris, qui tamen cum Apostolis perseveraverit, habuerit autorem, & Antecessorem: Hoc enim modo Ecclesiæ Catholicæ sensus suos deferunt.* And St. *Augustin, Radix*

Iren. adv. hæres. l. 3. c. 3.

Tertull. de præscrip. adv. hæres.

Aug. Epist. 24.

dix Christianæ Societatis per sedes Apostolorum, & Successores Episcoporum certâ per Orbem propagatione diffunditur.

Again, forasmuch as it was thought by our Saviour Christ, the best means for the building and continuing of his Church in the Apostles times, to ordain sundry degrees of Ministers in Dignity and Authority one over another, when such a kind of preheminence might have been thought not so necessary, because the Apostles by working of Miracles, might otherwise (as it is probable) have procured to themselves sufficient Authority: How can it with any reason be imagined, but that Christ much more did mean to have the same still to be continued after the Apostles days, when the gifts of doing Miracles were to cease, and when Mens Zeal was like to grow more cold, than it was at the first. It favoureth assuredly, We know of what Faction, Indiscretion, or Affection for any Man, either to think that Form of Church-Government to be unfit for our times, that was held necessary for the Apostles times; or that Order, so much commended amongst all Men, and is most properly termed *Parium, dispariumq; rerum sua cuiq; loca tribuens Dispositio,* should be necessary to build the Church, but unfit to preserve it; or, that the same Artisans, that are most meet to build this or that House, are not the fittest both to keep the same in good Reparations, and likewise to build other Houses when there is cause. No Man can doubt (who is of any reading) but that, when the Apostles died, there were many defects in many Churches: and that likewise there were a number of places in the World, where the Apostles had never been, and where there were no Churches planted, or established. Whereupon it followeth of necessity, that if the said Form of Government in the Apostles days was then necessary for the planting and ordering of Churches; that the same did continue to be as necessary

neceſſary afterward, for the ſupplying of ſuch defects, as were left in ſome Churches, and for the planting and ordering of other Churches in thoſe places, that had not received the Goſpel, whilſt the Apoſtles lived. And to this purpoſe it doth much avail, that for ought we can find, there can no one Nation or Country be named ſince the Apoſtles days, neither in times of Perſecution nor ſince; but when it firſt received the Faith of Chriſt, it had thereupon both Biſhops and Archbiſhops placed in it for the Government of the Churches, that were there planted; imitating therein for their more certain direction the Government of the Churches, that were erected by the Apoſtles, and had been deduced from them, agreeable (in ſubſtance) with the Form of Eccleſiaſtical Government, that was once amongſt God's own People the *Jews*. Which was no new conceit amongſt the ancient Fathers; as it may appear by the words of one of them; "Who ſaith (in effect) "that Biſhops, Prieſts and Deacons, may challenge "now that Authority in the Church, which *Aaron* and "his Sons, and the *Levites*, had in times paſt; and "that the Apoſtles in eſtabliſhing of their Government "in the New Teſtament, had reſpect to that which "was in the Old; for as much as concern'd the Eſſen- "tial parts of that Prieſthood.

<small>Jeron. Ep. ad Evagr.</small>

Moreover the Primitive Churches, preſently after the Apoſtles times, finding in the New Teſtament no one perſon to have been ordain'd a Prieſt, or Miniſter of the Goſpel, mediately by Men, but either by Impoſition of the Apoſtles hands, or of their hands to whom they gave Authority in that behalf, as unto *Timothy* and *Titus*, and ſuch other Biſhops as they were; and knowing that the Church of Chriſt ſhould never be left deſtitute of Prieſts and Biſhops for the work of the Miniſtry: they durſt not preſume upon their own heads to deviſe a new form of making of Miniſters, nor to commit that Authority unto any other, after their own

Fancies;

Fancies; but held it their bounden duty to leave the same where they found it, *viz.* in the hands of *Timothy* and *Titus*, and confequently of other Bifhops their Succeffors. Whereupon it followeth very neceffarily, that none of the Primitive Churches, or ancient Fathers, did ever fo much as once dream, that the Authority given by St. *Paul* to *Timothy*, and to *Titus*, and to the reft, who were then made Bifhops, as well for the ordering of Priefts, as for the further order and government of the Church, did determine by the death of the Apoftles: Confidering, that prefently after, as long as they were in being, and lived, and ever fince till very lately, it was held by them altogether unlawful, for any to ordain a Prieft or Minifter of the Word, except he were himfelf a Bifhop: and no one approved Example for the fpace of above 1500. years, can be fhewed (for ought we find) to the contrary. It is true, that one *Coluthus*, being himfelf but a Prieft, would needs take upon him to make Priefts, in fpleen againft his own Bifhop (the Bifhop of *Alexandria*) with whom he was then fallen at variance: and that the like attempt was made by one *Maximus*, fuppofing himfelf to have been a Bifhop, where he was indeed but a Prieft, as it was decided by the firft *Council of Conftantinople.* Howbeit fuch their Ordinations were accounted void, and utterly condemn'd as unlawful; they themfelves not efcaping fuch juft reproof, as fo great a Novelty and prefumption did deferve. We acknowledge, that for the great dignity of the Action of Ordination, it was decreed by another Council, That Priefts fhould lay their hands, with the Bifhop, upon him that was to be made Prieft: but they had not thereby any Power of Ordination; but only did it to teftifie their confent thereunto, and likewife to concur in the blef-fing of him: neither might they ever in that fort impofe their hands upon any without their Bifhops.

Again,

Again, the said Primitive Churches and ancient Fathers, finding how the Apostles, by the Inspiration of the Holy Ghost, had ordained Bishops, *Timothy*, *Titus*, and such like, for the ordering and appeasing of such Quarrels and Contentions as arise amongst the Ministers and People, for want of some amongst them of Authority to govern them; they might thereby have been confirmed more and more in their Judgments (if at any time they had doubted of it) concerning the necessity of that Apostolical Form of Government, that it was for ever to continue, to the end the Schisms and contentious Persons might be still, by the same means, suppressed, that they were whilst the Apostles lived. For they ever observed what the want of Bishops would work in the Church; and how the contempt of them, and disobedience to their directions, was always a chief cause of Sects and Schisms. Which made them easily to discern, that if the Apostles had not provided for the continuance of their Apostolical Authority in Bishops, who were to succeed them in the Government of the Church; but had left an equality in the Clergy, that every one might have proceeded in his own particular Church after his own Fashion; there would have been nothing in the Church but Disorder, Scandals, Sects, Schisms, and all manner of Confusion. One of the ancient Fathers perceiving in his time, what Pride and Contempt certain unstaid and contentious Persons shewed toward their Archbishops, did lay it upon them as a property of Hereticks, and feared not to compare them to the Devils. These are his words, *Quilibet hæreticus*, &c. *loquens cum Pontifice, nec eum vocat Pontificem, nec Archiepiscopum, nec Religiosissimum, nec Sanctum; sed quid? Reverentia tua; & nomina illi adducit communia, ejus negans autoritatem. Diabolus hoc tum fecit in Deo: Ero similis Altissimo. Non Deo, sed Altissimo.* And another Father, long before the days of the former, did accordingly observe, that Hereticks and Schismaticks did usually

ally spring from no other Fountain, but this, *Quod Sacer-* Cypr. l. 1. Ep.
doti Dei non obtemperatur ; nec unus in Ecclesia ad tempus 3.
Sacerdos ; & ad tempus Judex vice Christi cogitatur: that
the Priest of God (meaning every such Bishop as he himself was in his own Diocess) *was not obey'd*; nor one Priest
in the Church acknowledg'd for the time to be Judge in Christ's
stead. And again, *Unde Schismata & Hæreses abortæ sunt,* Id. l. 4. Ep. 8.
& oriuntur ; nisi dum Episcopus qui unus est, & Ecclesiæ
præest, superbâ quorundam præsumptione contemnitur ?
Whence have Schisms and Heresies sprung up, and do spring:
but whilst the Bishop, which is one and ruleth the Church, is
by the proud Presumption of certain men despis'd? A third
Father also, though at some times he had a sharp tooth
against Bishops, as they carried themselves in his time,
doth confess nevertheless, That *when Schisms first began,*
Bishops were ordain'd, Ut Schismatum semina tollerentur;
and in another Place, *in Remedium Schismatis, ne unus-*
quisq; ad se trahens Christi Ecclesiam rumperet. Also
where the same Father doth write against the *Luciferi-* Hieron. adv.
ans, and undertaketh the defence of Bishops in a right Luciferianos.
point, untruly by them impugn'd, he speaketh of their
Authority within their several Diocesses after this sort,
Ecclesiæ salus in summi Sacerdotis dignitate pendet: Cui si
non exors quædam, & ab hominibus eminens detur potestas,
tot in Ecclesiis efficientur Schismata, quot Sacerdotes: that
is, *The safety of the Church doth consist in the dignity of*
the chief Priest: unto whom, if an extraordinary and emi-
nent Power from other men be not yielded, there will be as
many Schisms in Churches, as there are Priests.

Lastly it is to be observed, that in the Apostles times
the *Roman* Empire had wrought a great confusion in all
the Kingdoms and Countries about it ; whilst in the
greediness of Honour in that state they had subdued
their Neighbour Kings and Princes, and turn'd their
Kingdoms and Principalities into Provinces and Consul-
ships and divers other such like Forms of Regiment ;
leaving the same to the Government of their own Substitutes

stitutes, to whom they gave sundry and different titles. Which course, held by that state, caused the Apostles, in their planting of Churches, when they could not perform that which otherwise they would have done, to frame their proceeding as near unto it, as they could. In the chief Cities, which had been Heads of so many Kingdoms, and were still the Seat then of the principal *Roman* Officers, principal Persons were placed, who were Bishops, and more than Bishops: as St. *James* at *Jerusalem*, (although *Jerusalem*, notwithstanding it was honoured with the name and title of the See of St. *James*, was not the Metropolitan Seat, or Archbishoprick of that Province, but *Cæsarea*; whose Right is saved in the giving that honour to *Jerusalem* in the first *Nicene Council*;) St. *Peter* first in *Antioch*, and then in *Rome*; and St. *Mark* in *Alexandria*: who remain'd in those places, as was then most behooveful for those Churches, as so many principal Archbishops, Patriarchs, to rule and direct all the Bishops, Priests, and Christians, in *Palestine, Syria, Italy*, and *Egypt*. And in other Cities also and Countries, not so famous then as the said four, there were appointed, according to the largeness of their Extents, in some, Bishops, to govern the Ministers which were in such Cities; and in some others, such as *Timothy* and *Titus* were, who (as we have shewed in the former Chapter) had the oversight committed unto them, as well of Bishops, as of the rest of the Churches within their limits. All which particulars, so put in practice by the Apostles, were very well known to the Primitive Churches, and ancient godly Fathers, that lived the first 300. years after Christ; and gave them full assurance, that they might lawfully pursue in those days that Form of Church-Government which the Apostles themselves had erected: the state and condition of the times remaining still one and the same, that it was, when the Apostles lived. Whereupon, by their Example,

ample, they did not only continue the Succession of Bishops and Archbishops, in those places where the Apostles had setled them: supplying other Churches, either not throughly setled, or not at all planted, when the Apostles died (as before hath been mention'd) with the like Church-Governours: but did likewise preserve, and uphold in those parts of the World, where Christianity did then chiefly flourish, the Succession of Patriarchal Archbishops in the above-mention'd four most principal Cities, *Jerusalem*, *Antioch*, *Rome*, and *Alexandria*. Insomuch as it is commonly held, that this Apostolical Order was thus distributed, and setled by the Fathers of the Primitive Church long before the *Council of Nice*; and that then in that holy Assembly, it was only but so acknowledged and continued, *idq; ad Disciplinæ conservationem*, as a very worthy Man hath observed. *Calvin.*

   The consideration of all which particular points, concerning the placing of Archbishops and Bishops in the Territories of the *Romans*, according to the Dignities and chief honours of the Cities and Countries where they were placed; doth very throughly perswade us, that (as we observed in the former Chapter) if all the said Kingdoms, and Sovereign Principalities, then in subjection to the *Roman* Empire, had been freed of that servitude, and governed by their own Kings and Princes, as they had been before: the Apostles (though the said Kings and Princes had refused to receive the Gospel) would notwithstanding as much as in them lay, have setled in every one of them, for the Government of the Church there, the like Form that God himself did erect amongst the *Jews*, and that they themselves did establish in their time in the like Heathenish places, as is aforesaid; that is, in every such Kingdom Ministers in particular Churches, or Congregations; Bishops over Ministers, and Archbishops to oversee and direct them all. And assuredly, if when Christian Kings

Kings and Sovereign Princes did free themselves from the Yoke of the Empire, they had either known or regarded the Ordinance of the Holy Ghost, for the Government of the Churches within their Kingdoms and Principalities; they would have been as careful to have deliver'd their Churches from the bondage of the Bishop of *Rome*, as they were their Kingdoms from subjection to the Empire. For all, that is commonly alledged to the contrary, is but the fume of presumptuous Brains. The chief Archbishops, either in *France* or *Spain*, have as full Power and Authority under their Sovereigns, as the Bishops of *Rome* had in times past over *Italy*, under their Emperour: and by the Institution of Christ, they ought to depend no more upon the See of *Rome*, than they do now one upon the other: or than the Archbishops of *England*, under their most worthy Sovereign, do depend upon any of them: as it will hereafter more plainly (we hope) appear by that which we have to say of that infinite Authority which the Pope doth vainly challenge to himself.

CAN. VII.

AND therefore if any Man shall affirm, under colour of any thing that is in the Scriptures, either that the Subscriptions, or Directions of the second Epistle of St. Paul to Timothy, or of his Epistle to Titus, though they are found in the ancient Copies of the Greek Testament, are of no Credit or Authority: or, that such an Impeachment and Discredit laid upon them, is not very prejudicial to the Books and Writings of the Holy Ghost: or, that

it

it is not great presumption for Men in these days, to take upon them to know better, Whether Timothy and Titus were Bishops, than the Churches and godly Fathers did, which were planted and lived either in the Apostle's times, or presently after them; except they have some especial Revelations from God: or, that whilst Men do labour to bring into discredit the ancient Fathers and Primitive Churches, they do not derogate from themselves such credit as they hunt after, and as much as in them lieth, bring many parts of Religion into a wonderful uncertainty: or, that it is probable, or was possible for Timothy to have observ'd those Rules that St. Paul gave him unto the coming of Christ; except (as the Fathers expound some of them) he meant to have them first observed by himself and other Bishops in that Age, and that afterward they should so likewise be observed by all Bishops for ever: or, that the ancient Fathers, and Ecclesiastical Histories, when they Record it to all Posterity, that these Men, and those Men, were made by the Apostles, Bishops of such and such places, are not to be held to be of more credit than any other Historiographers, or Writers: or, that when the ancient Fathers did collect out of the Scriptures and practice of the Apostles, the continuance for ever of that Form of Church-Government which was then in use, they were not so throughly illuminated with the Holy Ghost, as divers Men of late have been: or, that it was an idle course held by the Primitive Churches, and ancient Fathers, to keep the Catalogues of their Bishops, or to ground Arguments in some Cases upon their Succession, in that they were able to deduce their beginnings, either from the Apostles, or from some Apostolical Persons: or, that the Form of Government, used in the Apostle's times, for the planting and ordering of Churches, was not, in many respects, as necessary to be continued in the Church afterward; especially considering, that many Churches were not left fully ordered, nor in some places were at all planted, when the Apostles died: or, that true and perfect Order, grounded upon the very Laws of Nature and Reason, and established by the Holy Ghost in the Apostles times, was not fit for the Churches of God afterward to embrace and observe: or, that any Church, since the Apostles time, till of late years, when it received the Gospel, had not likewise Archbishops and Bishops for the Government of it: or, that divers of

the

the ancient Fathers did not hold, and that very truly (for ought that appeareth to the contrary) that our Saviour Christ and his Apostles, in establishing the Form of Church-Government amongst the Gentiles, had an especial respect to that Form which God had setled amongst the Jews, and did no way purpose to abrogate or abolish it: or, that any since the Apostles times, till of late days, was ever held to be a lawful Minister of the Word and Sacraments, who was not Ordain'd Priest or Minister, by the Imposition of the hands of some Bishop: or, that it is with any probability to be imagin'd, that all the Churches of Christ, and ancient Fathers from the beginning, would ever have held it for an Apostolical Rule, That none but Bishops had any Authority to make Priests, had they not thought and judged, that the same Authority had been derived unto them the said Bishops from the same Apostolical Ordination, that was committed unto Timothy and Titus, their Predecessors: or, that the Apostles, and all the ancient Fathers, were deceived, when they judged the Authority of Bishops necessary at all times for the suppressing of Schisms; and that without Bishops, there would be in the Churches

as

as many Sects as Ministers: or, that when Men find themselves, in regard of their disobedience to their Bishops, so fully and notably described and censured by all the ancient Fathers for Schismaticks and contentious Persons, they have not just cause to fear their own Estates, if they continue in such their willfulness and obstinacy: or, that the Church-Government, by us above treated of, is truly to be said to savour of Judaism, more than the observation by godly Kings and Princes, of the Equity of the Judicial Law, given to the Jews, may truly be said to favour thereof: or, that it doth proceed from any other than the Wicked Spirit, for any sort of Men, what godly shew soever they can pretend to seek to discredit (as much as in them lieth) that Form of Church-Government, which was established by the Apostles, and left by them to continue in the Church to the end of the World, under Archbishops and Bishops, such as were Timothy and Titus, and some others, then called to those Offices by the said Apostles, and ever since held by the Primitive Churches, and all the ancient Fathers to be Apostolical Functions; or to term the same, or any part of it to be Anti-Christian; He doth greatly Erre.

CAP.

CAP. IX.

The Sum of the Chapter following.

That our Saviour Christ, upon his Ascension into Heaven, did not commit the Temporal Government of the whole World unto St. Peter. That the Apostles and whole Ministry did succeed Christ, not as he was a Person immortal and glorious after his Resurrection; but as he was a Mortal Man here upon the Earth before his Passion. That Christ left neither to St. Peter, nor to the Bishops of Rome, nor to any other Archbishops or Bishops any temporal Possessions; all, that since any of them have gotten, being bestowed upon them by Emperours, Kings and Princes, and other their good Benefactors. And that the Imagination of St. Peter's Temporal Sovereignty, is very idle; the same being never known unto himself, (for ought that appeareth) and argueth great Ignorance of the true nature of the Spiritual Kingdom of Christ: for the erecting whereof the spiritual working of the Holy Ghost with the Apostles, and the rest of the Ministry of the Gospel, was, and is only necessary.

IT hath been shewed by us before that our Saviour Christ, after his Resurrection and Ascension, became actually in the State of the Heir of all things, Governour of all the World, and King of kings, even as he was Man: his divine Nature working more gloriously in his Humanity, than formerly it had done. Howbeit although we also made it plain, that notwithstanding the said Glory, Power, Rule, Dominion and Majesty, wherewith Christ is really possest, sitting in Heaven at the right hand of his Father; he made no alteration in the Form, and manner of Temporal

poral Government; but left the whole World to be ruled by Kings and Soveraign Princes under him, as it had been before; himself retaining still in his own hands, the Scepter and chiefest Enfigns of Royal and highest Majesty, to direct and dispose them all according to his divine pleasure: Yet the Parafitical, and fottish Crew of *Romish Canonists*, with the new Sectaries, their Companions, will assuredly moil and repine thereat: telling us by the Pen of one of their Fellows (the veriest Idiot we think amongst them,) "That "all Power, Dominion, and Worldly Principality, was "left by Christ, after his Ascension, unto St. *Peter*: "That two times are to be considered in Christ; the "one before his Passion, when *propter humilitatem*, he "refused to judge, that is, to shew himself a Tempo- "ral Magistrate, the other after his Resurrection, and "then he said, All Power is given unto me, in Heaven "and in Earth: That Christ, after his Resurrection, gave his Power to St. *Peter*, and made him his Vicar, and that *ex potestate Domini*, the Power of his Vicar is to be measured. And to advance that Power, as highly as he can, supposing, that what he can say thereof doth belong to St. *Peter*, he quoteth a number of places out of the Scriptures, concerning the Dignity, Honour, Royalty and Majesty, attributed to our Saviour Christ after his Resurrection and Ascension, by reason of the Union so oft before by us mentioned: and doth conclude, "That *cessantibus rationibus humilitatis, necessita-* "*tis, atq; paupertatis*, that the reasons of his former "humility, necessity, and poverty ceasing, Christ did "shew himself to be the Lord of all; *ut ascensurus ad* "*Patrem eandem potestatem Petro relinqueret*. And more- "over he is peremptory, that *Peter* did exercise this "temporal Power *in suâ propriâ naturâ temporaliter*, in "the proper nature of it temporally: for it is said in "the *Acts*, c. 5. that he condemn'd *Ananias* and *Sap-* "*phira, pro crimine facti ad panam civiliter*, for the crime
"of

"of a fact to a punishment civilly. Now if *Peter* were
"so great a Temporal Monarch, whilst he lived, what
"must we think of his Vicar, the Pope; and how
"royal is the Estate of all Archbishops and Bishops,
"that have any dependency upon him? For as the
"especial *Jesuit* and *Cardinal* (an Enemy to the *Cano-*
"*nists* in this point) doth infer, *Si Papa est Dominus*
"*totius orbis Christiani supremus, ergo singuli Episcopi sunt*
"*principes temporales in oppidis suo Episcopatui subjectis:*
"*If the Pope be Lord of all the Christian World, then it fol-*
"*loweth, that all particular Bishops are temporal Princes in*
"*the Cities and Towns subject to their Bishopricks.*

<small>Bellarmin. de Rom. Pont. l. 5. c. 3.</small>

To the manifestation of all which the said *Canonist*
his so absurd and gross assertions, before we proceed
any further; We hold it not unfit, for the reasons
elsewhere specified by us (when we shewed, that Christ
was no temporal Lord, nor had any temporal Dominion after the manner of other Kings) First to hear the
Cardinal, how he shaketh the very ground-work and
foundation of all these Vanities. For whereas his Op-
posites would make St. *Peter*, and consequently the
Pope, his Successor, to derive such their infinite Power,
and temporal Authority from Christ, after his Resurrection, as he was then a Man, immortal and glorious,
having cast off his former infirmities and mortality.
The *Cardinal* is resolute to the contrary, and doth reason in this sort. "*Christus, ut homo, dum in terris vixit,*
"*non accepit, nec voluit ullum temporale Dominium. Sum-*
"*mus autem Pontifex Christi Vicarius est, & Christum no-*
"*bis repræsentat, qualis erat, dum hic inter homines vive-*
"*ret: Igitur summus Pontifex, ut Christi Vicarius, atq;*
"*adeo ut summus Pontifex est, nullum habet temporale Do-*
"*minium.* Christ, as he was Man, and lived upon the
Earth, neither did, nor would receive any temporal Dominion: But the Pope is Christ's Vicar, and doth represent
Christ unto us, in that Estate and Condition that he lived
in here amongst Men: therefore the Pope, as Christ's
Vicar,

<small>Bellarm. de Rom. Pont. l. c. c. 4.</small>

Vicar, *and so as he is the highest Bishop*, *hath no temporal Dominion*. And again, "*Dicimus, Papam habere illud* "*Officium, quod habuit Christus, dum in terris inter homi-* "*nes humano more viveret. Neq; enim Pontifici possumus* "*tribuere officia, quæ habuit Christus, ut Deus, vel ut homo* "*immortalis, & gloriosus; sed solum ea, quæ habuit, ut* "*homo mortalis. We say, that the Pope hath that Office that Christ had, when he lived in the Earth amongst Men, after the manner of Men : for we cannot ascribe unto him those Offices which Christ hath, as he is God, or as he is Man, immortal and glorious ; but only those which he had as a mortal Man.* Neither doth he stay here, but goeth on forward, saying ; Add, *that the Pope hath not all that Power which Christ had as a mortal Man. For He, because he was God and Man, had a certain Power, which is called a Power of Excellency; by the which he govern'd both faithful Men and Infidels : but the Pope hath only committed unto him his Sheep ; that is, such Persons as are faithful.* Again, *Christ had Power to institute Sacraments, and to work Miracles by his own Authority ; which things the Pope cannot do. Also Christ might absolve Men from their Sins, without the Sacraments, which the Pope cannot.*

Nay the *Cardinal* was so far from believing, that all Power and Worldly Principality was left by Christ unto St. *Peter*, and so unto his Successors; as he confesseth in effect, that neither St. *Peter*, as he was Bishop of *Rome*, nor any of his Successors can challenge so much as a rural Farm, or any other kind of temporal Possessions, which have not been given unto them by the Emperours, and other Temporal Princes. And lest such gifts might be held by any to be unlawful ; he, to prove the contrary, alledgeth, that they were godly Princes who so endowed the Church of *Rome*. These are his words: "*Qui donaverunt Episcopo Ro-* "*mano, aliisq; Episcopis Principatus temporales, pii homi-* "*nes fuerunt, & eâ de causâ præcipuè à totâ Ecclesiâ com-* "*mendati*

Idem ibid.

Bell. de Rom. Pont. l. 5. c. 9. § quartóq;

" *mendati sunt : ut patet de Constantino, Carolo magno,*
" *& Ludovico ejus filio, qui inde Pius appellatus est.* They
who gave to the Bishop of Rome, *and other Bishops, temporal Principalities, were godly Men, and for that cause especially were commended by the whole Church* ; *as appeareth of*
Constantine, Charles *the Great, and* Lewis *his Son, who
in that respect was called* Lewis *the Godly*. Again, *That* Id. ibid. § Jam
the Pope holdeth in right that Principality which he hath, vero.
may easily be perceived, quia dono Principum habuit, be-
cause he had it by the gift of Princes. Of which gifts, he
saith, the Authentical Instruments remain still in *Rome:*
adding neverthelefs,that if they had been loft, " *abunde*
" *sufficeret præscriptio octingentorum annorum* ; *that a* Id. ibid. § Ie
prescription of 800. *years, were abundantly sufficient to
prove the Pope's right.* And unto these words of *Bernard,* Id. ibid. c. 10.
" *Forma Apostolica hæc est* ; *interdicitur Dominatio* ; *indi-* § tertio obji-
" *citur Ministratio* ; he answereth, that *Bernard* doth cit.
" speak of the Bishop of *Rome, secundum id, quod habet*
" *ex Christi institutione.* Also *Gregory the First,* de-
" nouncing a Curse against that Bishop, *qui jubet ali-*
" *cui Agro more fiscali Titulum imprimi* , *who doth
challenge to hold any Possessions , as an absolute Temporal
Prince, in right of his Church,* the Cardinal doth answer,
That it is not to be marvelled , that Gregory *would not
have Bishops, nor the prefects of the Patrimony of the Church
of* Rome *to use,* More *fiscali, in recovering the Possessions
of the Church* ; For, saith he, " *Nondum habuerat Eccle-*
" *sia politicum principatum* ; *sed possidebat Bona temporalia*
" *ad eum modum, quo privati homines possident. Itaq;*
" *æquum erat, ut Agros, quos suos esse censebat Ecclesia* ; *si*
" *forte ab aliis occuparentur, in Judicio legitimo eos repete-*
" *ret* ; *non autem More fiscali propriâ sibi Autoritate ven-*
" *dicaret :* that is, *for as yet* (meaning when *Gregory*
lived, which was 600. years after Christ) *the Church
had no political Principality, but did possess her temporal
goods in the same manner, whereby other private Citizens
possessed theirs. And therefore it was agreeable to Equity,*

Dd 2 *that*

that if perhaps the *Possessions* which the Church supposed to be hers, were occupied by other men ; she was to require them, *Judicio legitimo* , in a temporal Court of the Prince, of whom the same were held; and might not challenge them to her self, by her own proper Authority, More *fiscali*, as Sovereign Princes do, when their right is detained from them.

<small>Calvin. Instit. l. 4. c. 11.</small> Lastly, the *Cardinal* is so far driven by a worthy Man, and some others of our side, who held it unlawful for the Bishops of *Rome*, or any other Bishops, to be absolute Worldly Princes (whosoever do bestow that Soveraignty upon them) the same being directly against Christ's words, *Vos autem non sic* , and for many other reasons; as he flieth to the times of the *Maccabees*, when the Ordinances of God, as touching the High-Priesthood, were utterly neglected, and nothing (in effect) left in the Church, but Pride, Presumption, Blood and Confusion (as we have declar'd in our first Book, *cap.* <small>Bell de Rom. Pont. l. 5. c. 9. § deniq; probatur.</small> 32.) and would gladly thereby uphold the Pope's Regalities. These are his words, *Although perhaps it were absolutely better, that Bishops should deal with Spiritual matters, and Kings with temporal : Yet in respect of the malice of times, experience doth cry, that some temporal Principalities were not only profitable, but also of necessity ; and by the singular Providence of God, given to the Bishop of* Rome, *and to other Bishops. For if in* Germany *the Bishops had not been Princes , none had continued to this day in their Seats. As therefore in the Old Testament, the High-Priests were for a long time without temporal Authority, or Empire ; yet in the latter times Religion could not have continued , and been defended , except the High-Priest had been King, (that is, in the time of the Maccabees :) So we see it hath faln out to the Church ; that she, which in her first times had no need of temporal Principality to defend her Majesty, doth now seem necessarily to have need of it.* As though he should have said; Now, that the Church of *Rome* hath in her Pride and Presumption, determined still to Tyrannize over all Kings, Priests, Kingdoms

doms and Churches, contrary to the rules and prescription of our Saviour Christ, and of his blessed Apostles; the Popes must needs be temporal Kings.

Thus far we have followed the *Cardinal*; who is bold to affirm, That neither St. *Peter*, nor the Popes, his pretended Successors, nor any other of the Apostles, nor of their Successors, Archbishops, or Bishops, nor any other Minister, nor all the Ministers in the World, (if they were together) do succeed Christ, as he was after his Resurrection or Ascension, a Man immortal and glorious; but only as he was a mortal Man, and lived here in that Estate upon the Earth, without the enjoying of any temporal Kingdom, or Regal Possessions; contenting himself to be only a Spiritual King, and to have in this World a Spiritual Kingdom, that is, his Church; so termed, because he ruleth only in those Mens hearts which are true Members of it; the Gospel also being named *Evangelium Regni*, because it containeth the Doctrine of our *Messiah*, and Spiritual King, and how he doth establish his Spiritual Kingdom, in and amongst Men. Of which Spiritual Kingdom some little further consideration, and how our Saviour Christ obtained it, and then did, and still doth govern it, will make the folly of those Men more apparent, which cannot apprehend the Excellency of it, except it have joined with it all Worldly Principalities, and Authority. None is ignorant, that hath any sense of Christianity, how all Men by nature were the Children of wrath; and how before they embraced Christ by Faith, *they walked according to the course of this World,* Ephes 2. 2. *and after the Prince that ruleth in the air, even the Spirit that still worketh in the Children of Disobedience.* Which wicked Spirit being termed *the Spirit of darkness*, all his Rom. 13. 12. Subjects and Servants, and whatsoever they take in Ephes. 5. 11. hand, are called the *Children and works of darkness*. From whose Service, had not our Saviour Christ delivered us, and by subduing, and vanquishing this wicked Prince,

taken

taken actually the possession of our hearts, where the Devil before raigned; we had been still in the state of wrath and damnation. Whereas now *through Grace, and by Faith Christ dwelling in our hearts, we are no more darkness, but light in the Lord: nor are to hold any longer fellowship with the unfruitful works of darkness, or of the flesh; but are bound, being replenished with God's holy Spirit, to bring forth the fruits and operations of the same.* To this vanquishment of Satan, by our Saviour Christ, these Scriptures following have relation. *If I, by the Finger of God, do cast out Devils, doubtless the Kingdom of God is come unto you: When a strong Man armed keepeth his Palace, the things which he possesseth are in Peace: but when a stronger than he cometh upon him, and overcometh him, he taketh from him all his Armour, wherein he trusted, and divideth the spoils.* Again, *Now is the Judgment of this World; now shall the Prince of this World be cast out.* And again; *We cease not to pray for you,* &c. *That you might walk worthy of the Lord,* &c. *Giving thanks to God the Father,* &c. *Who hath deliver'd us from the power of darkness, and hath translated us into the Kingdom of his dear Son, in whom we have Redemption through his Blood.* Again, *Christ putting out the hand-writing of Ordinances, that was against us,* &c. *He took it out of the way, and fastned it upon the Cross, and hath spoiled the Principalities and Powers, and hath made a shew of them openly, and hath triumphed over them in himself.* And lastly, *He that committeth Sin is of the Devil; for the Devil sinneth from the beginning. For this purpose appeared the Son of God, that he might loose the works of the Devil.*

Ephef. 5. 8.
Gal. 5. 16, 22.
Luc. 11. 22. &c.
Joh. 12. 31.
Col. 1. 9. &c.
Col. 2. 14, 15.
1 Joh. 3. 8.

Now our Saviour Christ did, by fullfilling the Law for us, and the Sacrifice of himself once offered upon the Cross, vanquish both the Devil, Death, and Hell; to the end, that *as many as believed in him, might not perish, but have life everlasting.* And therefore knowing Faith to be the Means of so unspeakable a Benefit, he vouchsafed not only to be our Priest, but our heavenly Prophet;

Prophet; labouring, by Preaching and Miracles, to beget Faith in the Hearts of his Hearers, that, Satan being expel'd thence, he himself with his Father might abide and make their Mansion in them. To the performance of which most admirable work, how our Saviour Christ, being equal with his Father, became a Servant for our sakes (as it was the will of God, whereunto, of his own accord, he conform'd himself) and what a poor Estate he held, whilst he was upon the Earth; how he was born in Poverty, lived in Poverty, and died in Poverty; how maliciously and scornfully he was oftentimes entreated; how as, when he spake the truth, his Enemies said he *blasphemed*; So, when he cast out Devils, they told him, that *he cast them out by Beel-* Matth. 12. 24. *zebub the Prince of the Devils*; how in the whole course of his Life, he was so far from being a temporal King, or having possession of any Regal State, as he had not so much as an House of his own to rest his head in, but was glad to lodge now with one man, and then with another, as the Occasions and Times served; and how in the end, he was content to satisfie the Malice of his Enemies, by submitting himself for our sakes, unto the Death of the Cross, it were a needless labour for us to pursue; the *Evangelists* have so plainly set down all these particulars and many more besides to that purpose. Likewise it shall be sufficient for us sparingly to recount how our Saviour Christ was not only content to preach and work Miracles himself for the conversion of those that heard him: but did to the same end, as well before his Passion as after, authorize likewise his twelve Apostles and seventy Disciples to preach and work strange Miracles; and furthermore ordain a Succession of the Ministry, for the encreasing of this his Kingdom unto the end of the World; himself never forsaking his Church and Ministers, but still assisting them in that their spiritual Charge, which he had committed unto them. For although that he himself by his Death and Passion hath

vanquished

[204]

vanquished Satan, and ruleth in the Hearts of the Faithful; yet by reason of our Infirmities and Weakness of Faith, and through the Malice of the Devil, who never ceaseth, *like a roaring Lyon, to seek whom he may devour*; this spiritual Kingdom of Christ is but now begun in us, and upheld in us by the most merciful hand of our Saviour Christ, through the operation of the Holy Ghost, and by the labour of the Ministry. But in the end, through the Virtue of Christ's Passion, shall be brought to pass,

1 Cor. 15. 54. &c. that which is written, *Death is swallowed up in victory. O Death, where is thy sting? O Hell, where is thy victory? The sting of Death is sin; the strength of sin is the Law: But thanks be unto God, who hath given us victory thrô*

Apoc. 20. 10. 14. *our Lord Jesus Christ*. And again, *Death, Hell, and the Devil shall be cast into the lake of fire and brimstone*. In the mean while, and during the time of this our Pilgrimage,

Ephes. 4. 27. we are for the continuance of Christ's *dwelling in our Hearts*, to follow the Counsel and Direction of the Holy Ghost, That in no sort *we give any place to the*

Jam. 4. 7. *Devil: but that we resist him with all the force we are able, for in so doing he will fly from us*. And for our better Resistance, that we might be able to stand against the Assaults of Satan, we have a notable and compleat armour appointed us by the said Holy Spirit which is agreeable to the Nature of the Enemies we have to fight with. For (saith the holy Apostle) *we wrestle not against flesh and blood; but against principalities, against powers, and against worldly*

Ephes. 6. 11, 12. *governors, the princes of darkness of this world; against spiritual wickednesses which are in the high places.*

And thus we have a brief and short Idea of the Spiritual Kingdom of Christ: Whereof when the Apostles, after they were replenished with the Holy Ghost, upon the day of *Pentecost*, had full understanding and notice: they never dreamed (for ought that appeareth to the contrary in the Scriptures) of any Worldly preheminence or Principalities; who should sit here, and who should sit there: but contented themselves with the

the same estate and condition of life that their Master had led before them; remembring how he had described the same unto them, when he first sent them to preach amongst the Jews. *Behold* (saith he unto them) *I send you as sheep in the midst of Wolves. Beware of men; for they will deliver you up to the Councils, and will scourge you in the Synagogues. And ye shall be brought to the Governours and Kings, for my sake, in witness to them and the Gentiles. And ye shall be hated of all Men for my sake. When they persecute you in this City, flee into another: the Disciple is not above his Master, nor the Servant above his Lord: If they have called the Master of the House* Beelzebub; *how much more them of his Houshold? Whosoever will be a perfect Disciple, shall be as his Master. Verily, Verily, I say unto you, that ye shall weep and lament, and the World shall rejoice. The time shall come, that whosoever killeth you, will think that he doth God service.* And as Christ did thus foretel them, so it came to pass. For no sooner did they begin to Preach the Gospel, after the Ascension of Christ; but they were whipped, scourged, cast into Prison, bound with Chains, and most cruelly entreated. St. *Paul* doth testify somewhat hereof; when writing in the name, both of himself and of the rest of the Apostles and Ministers, he saith thus; *In all things we approve our selves as the Ministers of God; in much patience, in afflictions, in necessities, in distresses, in stripes, in prisons, in tumults, in labours, by watchings, by fastings, by long sufferings, by dishonour, by evil report; as Deceivers, and yet true; as unknown, and yet known; as dying, and behold we live.* Besides, that which he speaketh of his own particular condition, doth argue the estate and condition of his Fellows; though one would have thought, that little more could have been added to the barbarous Cruelty last mentioned to have been Executed upon them. For comparing himself, and his pains, with certain false Brethren, that were crept into the Church amongst the Apostles, and sought

Matth. 10. 16, &c.

Joh. 16. 20.

— 2.

2 Cor. 6. 4.

for their own commendation to impair the credit of this our Apostle; he writeth in this manner. *They are Ministers of Christ; I am more: in labours more abundant, in stripes above measure, in Prison more plenteously. Of the Jews five times received I forty stripes, save one. I was thrice beaten with Rods. I was once stoned. I suffered thrice Shipwrack. Night and day have I been in the deep Sea. In Journying I was often, in perils of Water, in perils of Robbers, in perils of mine own Nation, in perils amongst the Gentiles, in perils in the Wilderness, in perils in the Sea, in perils amongst falseBrethren; In weariness and painfulness, in watching often, in hunger and thirst, in fastings often, in cold and nakedness. Besides these things which are outward, I am cumber'd daily, and have the care of all the Churches.* Much is not written of St. Peter, by the Evangelist St. *Luke:* but it is not to be doubted, that his Case was as bad as any of his Fellows. When he began to Preach, he was call'd in question with great eagerness; and vehemently threatned. Also with some other of the Apostles, he was cast into Prison, and beaten. Likewise when *James* was killed by *Herod*'s Commandment, *Peter* was again Imprisoned, and loaden with Irons; and had assuredly, in all likelyhood, escaped hardly with his Life; but that the Angel of the Lord delivered him. In a word, after many Afflictions, Injuries, Calamities and Miseries, endured by the Apostles, whilst they lived in this World; they were in the end (as well St. *Peter* as almost all the rest) most spitefully and cruelly, by the Enemies of Christ, and of their own Salvation, put to Death. During the course of whose lives, in so great dangers and manifold distresses; out of question, they would greatly have marvelled, their hard Estates consider'd, but especially St. *Peter*, if he had known himself to be the sole Monarch, under Christ, over all the World; and that the Emperour, and all other Kings, had been at that time his Vassals; and that likewise they (the rest

of

of the Apostles) had been under St. *Peter*, so many Soveraign and Temporal Princes, to have commanded and ruled amongst them throughout the whole World. Neither do we see any true cause, that might have moved St. *Peter* to have concealed that his so eminent temporal Power and Authority; if he had thought it to have been the Ordinance of God : or, at least, if he for modesty would have been silent, why the rest of the Apostles should not have published it ; that the civil and temporal States in those times, who knew no such Ordination made by Christ, might have been left inexcusable. Besides, the concealing of a truth of so great importance, was an injury offered to all the faithful in those days; who had they been truly taught in these Mens conceits, ought to have left their Obedience to the Emperour in all temporal Causes; and for the dignity of the Gospel, to have adher'd unto St. *Peter*, to have been directed in them, by him their temporal Monarch. The consideration of all which inconveniences and consequents, doth perswade us to think, that none of the Apostles ever dreamed of any such temporal Soveraignty ; notwithstanding, that they knew well the Scriptures; how Christ told them, That All Power in Heaven and Earth, was given unto him ; how St. *Peter* had two Swords ; and how *Ananias* and *Sapphira*, for lying to the Holy Ghost, were stricken suddenly from Heaven with Death.

Touching the two first of which places, the same being notoriously abused, and wrested by the *Canonists* and their Adherents, to prove the Popes temporal Monarchy ; the said *Cardinal* doth very resolutely reject the Arguments which are thence by them deduced. And to the first he answereth ; " *Potestatem, de quâ hic* " *loquitur Dominus, non esse potestatem temporalem, ut* " *Regnum terrenorum; sed vel tantùm spiritualem, ut B.* " *Hieronymus, & B. Anselmus exponunt ; qui hunc esse* " *volunt sensum eorum verborum; Data est mihi omnis* " *potestas*

Bell. de Rom. Pont. l. 5. c. 5. §. sed occurrunt.

"*potestas in cœlo, & in terrâ,* i. e. *ut sicut in cœlo Rex*
"*sum Angelorum, ità per fidem regnem in cordibus homi-*
"*num: vel, ut addit Theophylactus, esse potestatem quan-*
"*dam summam in omnes creaturas, non temporalem, sed*
"*divinam, vel divinæ simillimam, quæ non potest commu-*
"*nicari homini mortali:* That the Power, whereof the Lord
here speaketh, is not a temporal Power, like the Power of
terrene *Kings*; but it is either a spiritual Power, as *St.*
Hierom, and *St.* Anselm *do expound the said place*; who
will have this to be the sense of those words; All Power is
given me in Heaven and Earth; which is to say, that as in
Heaven I am *King* of Angels, so by Faith I do reign in
the hearts of Men: or, as Theophylact *addeth*, it is a certain supream Power, not temporal, but divine, or most like
to the Divine Power, which cannot be communicated to any
mortal Man.

And for the second Argument, drawn from St. *Peter*'s two Swords, the same is set down by our said *Cardinal* in these words. "*Secundò objiciunt Scripturam,*
" Luc. 22. *Ubi Dominus duos gladios* Petro *concedit. Cùm*
" *enim Discipuli dicerent, Ecce, duo gladii hic: Dominus*
" *non ait, nimis est; sed satis est. Quare* B. Bernardus
" l. 4. *de Consid. &* Bonifacius *octavus in Extravag.*
" *Unam sanctam, de Majoritate, & Obedientiâ, ex hoc loco*
" *deducunt, Pontificem duos gladios ex Christi institutione*
" *habere*: that is, Secondly, they object the Scriptures, Luc.
22. Where the Lord doth grant two Swords to Peter. For
when the Disciples said, Behold, here are two Swords; the
Lord answered not they are too many, but they are sufficient.
Therefore St. Bernard, and Boniface the eighth, do hence
deduce, that the Bishop of Rome, by Christ's Institution,
hath two Swords. Unto which objection our *Cardinal*
saith thus. " *Respondeo, ad Literam, nullam fieri mentionem in eo loco Evangelii de gladio spirituali, vel temporali Pontificis; sed solum Dominum illis verbis monere*
" *voluisse Discipulos tempore Passionis suæ in iis angustiis,*
" *& metu ipsos futuros fuisse, in quibus esse solent, qui tunicam*
" *vendunt,*

Ibidem §. secundò objiciunt.

"*vendunt, ut emant gladium; ut ex Theophylacto, aliisq;*
"*Patribus colligitur.* I answer, that according to the Letter, there is no mention made in that place of the Gospel, either of the spiritual, or temporal Sword of the Bishop of Rome : but that Christ meant only in those words, to admonish his Disciples, how they should be in the time of his Passion in those straights and fear wherein Men are accustomed to be, who sell their Coat to buy them a Sword; as it is to be collected out of Theophylact, and other Fathers. And for *Bernard* and *Boniface* he saith, They did expound the said place mystically, and meant not to have their words so far extended, as the Objector would have them. Which answer, it is likely *Bernard*, if he were now alive, would take in good part : but assuredly, if any *Cardinal* in *Bonifacius*'s days had made it, he would have smarted for it; and might perhaps have tried the depth of *Tiber*. Neither do we suppose, that the now Pope will give him any great thanks for it : nor that in all likelyhood he hath received any greater commendation for his plain dealing, in answer to another Objection, which is grounded upon the Authority of Pope *Nicholas*. Who in an Epistle of his to *Michael*, the Emperour of *Constantinople*, doth write thus : " *Christus* B. " *Petro, vitæ æternæ clavigero, terreni simul & cælestis* " *Imperii Jura commisit.* Christ did commit to St. Peter, the Key-bearer of Everlasting Life, the right and interest, both of the Earthly, and of the Heavenly Empire. To which saying of Pope *Nicholas*, the Cardinal maketh two answers. " *Ad testimonium* Nicolai *dico*; *Impri-* Bell. ibidem " *mis, illud citari à* Gratiano d. 22. Can. *Omnes*; *sed non* §. Ad testimonium. " *inveniri inter Epistolas* Nicolai Papæ. To the testimony of Pope Nicholas, I answer; First, that the said is cited by Gratian, but it is not to be found amongst the Epistles of Pope Nicholas : As if he should have said, That testimony is forged. And the effect of his second Answer is, That if any Man shall urge, that Testimony of Pope Nicholas, in the sense objected, they make him directly

repugnant

repugnant to himself, *in the rest of the said Epistle*.

And concerning the other Argument, by our said *Canonist* alledged, of the Death of *Ananias* and *Sapphira*; the ancient Fathers, in the Primitive Church, would certainly have scorn'd it, if ever they had heard of it. *Peter*, knowing by the instinct of the Holy Ghost, that Satan had possessed both their hearts, and how they lied not to Men, but to God; did only pronounce that Sentence of Death upon them, which the holy Spirit did suggest unto him. Wherein although there may appear, what force the Sword of the Spirit, which is the Word of God, had, when it was brandished by St. *Peter*, through the Operation of the Holy Ghost; there was assuredly no use of any material and civil Sword: for if there had, another manner of Form of outward Justice would first have been held, before they had been Executed. And to conclude this point, We do freely profess, That the nature of Christ, his Spiritual Kingdom being throughly weighed, we cannot find to what purpose, either St. *Peter*, or any of his Successors, should have been made temporal Monarchs over all the Civil Magistrates in the World: because all their temporal Forces, and Swords joined together, had not been able to have vanquished one wicked Spirit of the Air, or have open'd the door of any one Man's heart for Christ, or the Holy Ghost to have entered and have made their habitation in it.

CAN.

CAN. VIII.

IF therefore any Man shall affirm, under colour of any thing that is in the Scriptures, either that our Saviour Christ hath otherwise committed the World to be governed under him by Kings, and Soveraign Princes, but so, as he himself, with his Regal Scepter, doth rule and govern them all, according to his Divine Pleasure: or, that it is not a sound Argument, that the Bishops of Rome, in taking upon them to be temporal Kings, have wholly perverted the Institution of Christ in that behalf; in that they are driven to justify their facts therein, by the Examples of the Maccabees, and those times of so great confusion: or, that our Saviour Christ, whilst he was here upon the Earth, did not fully content himself to be only a Spiritual King, to rule in Mens hearts: or, that to the end he might erect such a Spiritual Kingdom, he did not conquer the Devil, Sin, Death, and Hell, and thereby took possession in the hearts of all true Believers: or, that before our Saviour Christ doth begin to reign in Man's heart, he doth not first, by the Ministry of his Word, beget a lively Faith in
it;

it: or, that whilst he lived here in the World, he did not satisfy himself, for our sakes, with a very mean and poor Estate, being in himself most rich, because he was God, and in his humanity, the Heir of all things: or, that he did not Institute and Ordain a Priesthood, or Ministry, to continue to the end of the World, for the continuance and augmenting of his Spiritual Kingdom: or, that the Children of God, notwithstanding that they are redeemed, through Faith by Christ, and delivered out of the Jaws of Hell, and Satan, are not still to take heed, and beware of him, and to arm themselves accordingly against his Forces: or, that our Saviour Christ, when he told his Apostles and Disciples, That the Servant is not above his Lord, but that whosoever would be a perfect Disciple, should be as his Master, did not mean, that his Apostles, and after them their Successors, Archbishops, Bishops, and the rest of the Ministry, should hold their Services and Offices under him, to do as he did, when he was a Mortal Man of poor Estate, and subject to many bad Usages, and Injuries: or, that because our Saviour Christ, after his Resurrection and Ascension, when he was become a Man Immortal and Glorious,

rious, did then enlarge the Commission of his Apostles, and ordain'd by them a succession of the Ministry for the government of the Church he did thereby make them any more partakers of his Regal Authority, whereof his humane nature was then actually possessed, for the state and exercise thereof, by reason of the free and unrestrained Operation of his Deity, than he made their natural and corruptible Bodies, incorrupt and spiritual Bodies, or endowed them in this life, with any of that Glory, Power, and Heavenly Estate, which they were to enjoy after their Deaths, and blessed Resurrection: or, that the Apostles after Christ's Death (not exempting St. Peter) did not find their Estates in this World very suitable to their Master's, whilst he lived with them, all things happening unto them, as he had foretold them: or, that either St. Peter, or any of the Apostles, or of their Successors, either then, or since that time, could challenge so much as this, or that one temporal farm, by virtue of their Ecclesiastical Functions, more than their Master had, or that either they were themselves possessed with), as their own, before they were called to that Ministration, or than was afterward given unto them by godly Emperors, Kings and
F f Princes,

Princes, and other devout and religious Persons: or, that if St. Peter had known himself to have been under Christ the sole temporal Monarch of the World, it had not been his duty to have made the same known; at least, to the Apostles, and such as were converted to Christ, to the end they might have honour'd him accordingly, as his dutiful and loyal Subjects: or, that it had not in all probability, if St. Peter meant to shew himself to be a temporal King, by the Deaths of Ananias and Sapphira, been much more expedient for the success of the Gospel in those days, if he had used such his Regal Authority against those civil Magistrates, which were Enemies to Christ, and to all that Preached in his name: or, that it may be rightly imagin'd, with our dutiful regard of St. Peter's Sincerity, that ever he would have been so earnest with the dispersed Jews, to have submitted themselves for the Lord's sake unto Kings, and other Governours, to have obey'd them and honour'd them, if he had known them to have had temporal Authority, because they did not acknowledge themselves to be his Vassals: or, that it did not proceed from the great Wisdom of God, to abridge in the Apostles of Christ (even in St. Peter himself) that great Power and
Authority

Authority which Christ had; as appeareth by his Words, when he said, that if he had thought it fit, he could have twelve Legions of Angels at his Commandment, to have Defended him from all his Enemies (the Scribes and Pharisees, with all their partakers;) in that perhaps the Apostles, even St. Peter himself, might have abused it: or, that it is not more than probable, that howsoever St. Peter would have used the said Power and Authority, if he had had it, if the Bishops of Rome had received it from him, they would certainly have made great havock and confusion in the World with it: or, that if all the Kings and Sovereign Princes in the World had been subject to St. Peter, and were thereupon in the like subjection to the Bishops of Rome, they (both St. Peter, and his Successors) might not have had ready at their Commandment (if Kings and Princes had done their duties) more than twelve Legions, to have confounded all Men, that should have disobey'd them: or, that therefore it is not as absurd an imagination and conceit for any Man to think, that Christ did give so great temporal Authority, either to St. Peter, or any of his Successors, over temporal Kings and Princes, that they might have so great Ar-

Ff 2   mies,

unes, when they list, at their directions; as if any Man should hold, that because they are Christ's Vicars, they may have twelve Legions from Heaven to do them service, if perhaps temporal Kings and Princes should be negligent, or refuse to be at such charges at their Commandment: or, that it is not a kind of madness (the true nature of Christ's spiritual Kingdom and Church, here upon Earth consider'd) for any Man to conceive, and thereupon maintain, that any such Omnipotency of temporal Power in St. Peter, ever was, or ever shall be, available to vanquish the Devil, or remove him out of his Palace, or to spoil him of all his Principalities, or to beget Faith in the Children of God, or to erect in their hearts a Tabernacle for Christ, and the Holy Ghost; which are only the peculiar and proper actions of our Saviour Christ, as he is our Spiritual King, and of St. Peter, and the rest of the Apostles, with all their Successors in their degrees, and as they are his Spiritual Ministers; He doth greatly Erre.

CAP.

CAP. X.

The Sum of the Chapter following.

That the Bishops of Rome *have no temporal Authority indirectly, over Kings and Princes, throughout the Christian World, to depose them from their Kingdoms, for any cause whatsoever.*

Because we have been bold to use the Authority of the *Cardinaliz'd Jesuit* against the ridiculous *Canonists*, and their Companions, the new Sectaries of the *Oratory-Congregation*, concerning the Pope's temporal Authority over all Kings and Princes in the World directly : We may not do him so much injury, as once to pretend, that he favoureth either us, or any point of truth (for our sakes) that we defend. It may rather be ascribed unto him for a singular virtue (his bringing up, and course of life consider'd) if he study not to impugn it with all the strength that he hath, either of his Wit or Learning. Nevertheless, albeit he hath travelled exceedingly in his Books *de Romano Pontifice*, to advance the Papacy to his uttermost Ability; and had no purpose therein (we are well assured) to give us any advantage (who do oppose our selves against the whole drift of those his Books:) Yet he hath so muster'd and marshall'd his matters and Forces together, as whilst he endeavours to fortifie the Pope's Authority, and to encounter the Assaults that have been made against it, he hath done more for us, against his Will, to the prejudice of his Master, whom he laboureth to uphold, than we could ever have expected at his hands. Insomuch, as we are verily perswaded, the time will come before it be long, that his Works will

be

be thruft into the Catalogue *Librorum prohibitorum*; becaufe dealing with our Arguments, as he did in the faid Books *de Romano Pontifice*, and thinking that he would no further yield to the truth, by way of Objection, than as he fhould be able fufficiently to refel it; it hath often fall'n out with him, as it will ever do with all Impoftors, that the very meaning of the truth, according to the nature of it, hath (notwithftanding all his cunning) very much prevail'd againft him, to the everlafting glory of her own name, and forcible ftrength to difcover Errors, like to the Sun's to expel Darknefs. We will not here otherwife make proof hereof, than, as by the matter we have in hand, and are purpofed to profecute, we are after a fort urged and compelled. For albeit hitherto he hath feemed to have joined with us (as he hath indeed, more than now, we are perfwaded, he doth well vouchfafe) yet forefeeing what tempefts he was otherwife, like to have endured, in affirming fo peremptorily (as he did) that the Pope had no temporal Authority at all, as he was either Chrift's, or St *Peter*'s Vicar: he minced his matter in the titles of his Chapters to that purpofe with the word *Directè* (whereof in his reafons he never made mention;) and then falleth upon this Iffue, That *Indirectè*, the Pope hath Authority over all Emperours, Kings, and Soveraign Princes, to hurry them hither and thither; to depofe and remove them from their Regal Eftates and Dignities; to difpofe of their Kingdoms according to his own Pleafure; to releafe their Subjects of their Oaths and Obedience, and to thruft them into all Rebellions, Treafons, Furies, and what not againft them. In the which his courfe this is our comfort, that by direct dealing, the *Cardinal* did find no ways or means how to withftand the truth; but is driven by in fretir fhifts and by-paths, to oppofe his labours (we f— , *reclamante Confcientiâ*) how to fave his own Wo— — credit, he might caft a mift

upon

upon the truth; if not to deprefs it (which was not in his power) yet at the leaft to obfcure it, to darken it, and perplex it.

Some of the principal Reafons, which he hath ufed to this purpofe mentioned, are of this kind and confequence. "*Bona corporis,* the good things that do ap- "pertain to the Body, as health efpecially, are to be "preferr'd before *Bona fortunæ,* as the Philofophers call "them; that is, Riches and all other Worldly Digni- "ties and Preferments whatfoever: Therefore the cal- "ling of Phyficians, the end whereof is the health of "Mens Bodies, is to be preferr'd before all other tem- "poral Callings that are in the World Or thus; Na- "tural Parents, be they Emperours, Kings, or Sove- "reign Princes, do give unto their Children their na- "tural Being only: but Schoolmafters do adorn by In- "ftruction, and beautify their Minds: therefore School- "Mafters are more to be honour'd by young Lords and "Princes, than are their Lords and Kings, their natu- "ral Parents. Or thus; One end why Men were firft "Created, and afterward born, be they Kings or Prin- "ces, Priefts or private Perfons, was to live in the "World: but for the fupporting of Mens Lives, Huf- "bandry, and many other Occupations, are of greater "Importance and Neceffity, than are either Kings, "Princes, Lords, or civil Magiftracy: therefore thofe "Mens bafe Callings are to be preferr'd before the Cal- "lings of the other. Or, as if a Man fhould reafon thus; "They, that have the chiefeft charge of Souls com- "mitted unto them, are to be efteem'd, as Men in this "World, of the higheft Calling: but all Chriftians "generally, have every one of them a greater charge "committed unto them of their own Souls, than any "fort of Priefts or Minifters have: therefore every "Chriftian is in that refpect, in Calling and Dignity, "to be preferred before the Calling of any one Paftor, "Prieft, Prelate, or Pope. Now after he hath dallied

Bell. de Rom. Pont. l. 5. c.5.

with

with such sophistications and comparisons betwixt the Body and the Soul, the Flesh and the Spirit, he falleth upon some particulars; the more fully (as he saith) to express what he had formerly delivered. The sum of which particulars is, That although the Pope, as he is Pope, cannot *ordinariè*, ordinarily depose temporal Princes, or make civil Laws, or judge *de rebus temporalibus*; yet *in ordine ad Spiritualia*, he may do them all. And this he taketh upon him to prove by five main reasons, grounded (God knoweth) upon very weak Foundations. Of which his odd number, for the glory of them, this which followeth is the first.

_{Bell. de Rom. Pont. l. 5. c 6.}

_{Ibidem, c. 7.}

" Civil Power is subject to Spiritual Power, when " they are both part of a Christian Commonwealth: " therefore the Spiritual Princes may command tempo- " ral Princes, and dispose of their temporal affairs *in* " *ordine ad Bonum spirituale,* in order to a spiritual good. The Antecedent of which Argument may briefly be refuted, for ought that he hath said to justify it, in manner as followeth. For in saying, that this subjection of the temporal Power to the Spiritual, is, but where both these Powers are part of one and the same Christian Commonwealth, he maketh the Estate of Christian Kings and Princes, inferiour and worse than the Estate of those that be Infidels: Whose political Power being no part of any Christian Commonwealth, is not subject to the Ecclesiastical. Again, to prefer the Ecclesiastical Authority of the Church, for honour and dignity in this World, before the temporal Authority of Kings and Princes, is in effect, to prefer the poor and base Estate of our Saviour Christ, as he was a mortal Man here upon Earth, subject to many wants, oppressions, and injuries, before the glory and majesty of his Divine Nature: in that Kings have their Authority and Calling from Christ, as he is God: Whereas all Ministers, even St. *Peter* himself, and consequently the Pope, are but Christ's Vicars and Substitutes, as he

was

was Man, subject to the said wants, miseries, and Oppressions. Moreover, in that *every Soul*, by the testimony of St. *Paul*, is subject to the Power and Authority of temporal Princes; and that they must be so, not *because of wrath only, but also for Conscience sake*: forasmuch, as the points of subjection there specified, are commanded to all Men to be observed, *& Sacerdotibus, & Monachis, non solùm sæcularibus*, to Bishops and Monks, and not to secular Priests only (as *Chrysostom*, saith by our Interpretation, adding to these words of the Apostle. *Let every Soul be subject to the higher Powers, Etiamsi Apostolus sis, si Evangelista, si Propheta, sive quisq; tandem fueris, although thou art an Apostle, or an Evangelist, or a Prophet, or whosoever thou art*:) and because, for ought we have read, none of the ancient Fathers do herein dissent from *Chrysostom*; We hold it to be very plain, and evident to our understandings, that the Ecclesiastical Authority, to be exercis'd in this World, by any manner of Ecclesiastical Persons whosoever, is inferiour, and of a lower degree, than is the Authority and Power of temporal Kings and Princes. For if the Authority of such Ecclesiastical Persons, whether Apostles, Evangelists, Prophets, Bishops or Priests, either Regular or Secular, cannot exempt them from the Authority of Kings, it must follow of necessity, that it is subject and inferiour to their temporal Power and Authority.

Hom. in Rom. 13.

Another of the *Cardinal*'s Reasons, whereby he would gladly prove the Pope's indirect temporal Power (to omit the rest of his absurd trifling about the first) is built upon a very traiterous Position, never heard of in the Church in the times of the principal ancient Fathers. For how earnest soever he seem'd before in refuting their Opinions, who hold, That no Princes are to be obey'd, if they be Infidels; he thinketh he is able to shift off that in effect with his jugling and indirect Fetches. These are his traiterous words. It is

"not

Bell. de Rom. Pont. l. 5. c. 7.

" not lawful for Christians to tolerate a King, being an
" Infidel, or an Heretick, if he endeavour to draw his
" Subjects unto his Heresy or Infidelity: but to judge,
" whether a King doth draw his Subjects to Heresy or
" no, doth belong to the Pope, unto whom is commit-
" ted the charge of Religion, and therefore it belongeth
" to the Pope to judge, whether a King is to be depo-
" sed or not. Concerning the Assumption of this Argument, touching the presupposed charge of the Pope,
in matters of Religion, over all the Churches in the
World, we shall have a fitter occasion to touch it, after
a sort, in the next Chapter: Now we will only briefly
handle the falshood of his Proposition, *Of the Power of
Subjects over their Soveraigns.* Where, after he hath
abused a place in *Deuteronomy*, and spent some idle conceits of his own, he writeth in this sort. " Although
" Christians in times past did not depose *Nero* and *Dio-*
" *clesian*, and *Julian the Apostate*, and *Valens* the *Ar-*
" *rian*, and such like; *id fuit, quia deerant vires tempo-*
" *rales Christianis*; it came to pass, because Christians
" did then want temporal Forces. For that otherwise
" they might lawfully so have done, appeareth by the
" Apostle, 1 *Cor.* 6. Where he commandeth new
" Judges of temporal Causes to be appointed by Chri-
" stians, that Christians might not be compelled to
" plead their Cause before a Judge, that was a Perse-
" cutor of Christ. Upon which Text the *Cardinal* ma-
" keth this Gloss. *Sicut novi Judices constitui potuerunt;*
" *ita & novi Principes, & Reges propter eandem causam,*
" *si vires adfuissent :* as new Judges might have been
" appointed; so might new Princes and Kings for the
" same cause, if the Christians then had been able, by
" reason of their Forces, to have created, to themselves,
" such new Kings and Princes. Thus the *Cardinal :*
Who undoubtedly was brought into some hard streight,
or else he would never have written in this sort. St.
Peter and St. *Paul* lived and dyed under *Nero*, who
was

was a Persecutor: and shall we think, that St. *Peter* and St. *Paul* had taught the Christians in those days, to have thrust *Nero* from his Imperial Seat, by force of Arms, if they had been able? Certainly it is a blasphemous assertion, and worthy of as great a Censure, as if he had termed those holy Men, in plain terms, Dissembling Traytors, or denied the Scriptures to have been written by the Inspiration of the Holy Ghost. Again, he himself is not ignorant, how grosly he lieth, even against his own Conscience, in saying, that it was for want of strength, that the Christians in the days of the other persecuting Emperours, did not rebel against them; *Tertullian* in express terms affirming the contrary: "First, that they, the Christians in his "times, wanted no Forces to have born Arms, and en- "danger'd the whole Empire; And secondly, That "it was far from their hearts so to do, because they "had been taught otherwise by the Doctrine of Christ "in his holy Gospel. Besides, it is apparent, that in and about *Tertullian*'s time, these four were Bishops of *Rome*, *Victor*, *Zephyrinus*, *Calixtus*, and *Urbanus*: so as the *Cardinal* doth in effect cast a great Imputation upon them of negligence, or insincerity; that the Christians in their days, wanting neither number nor strength to have bridled their bad Emperours, they by their Papal Authority did not depose them. *Dioclesian* began his Empire about the year 288. during the time of whose Government, *Gaius*, *Marcellinus*, and *Marcellus*, were Popes, when the number of Christians was greatly encreased throughout all the World: and yet, for ought that appeareth to the contrary, no Man living, either Pope, Priest, or Prelate, did so much as then dream of this damnable Doctrine. *Julian the Apostate* began his Reign about the year of Christ 360. and *Valens* 8. years after him; in whose times *Liberius* and *Damasus*, were Bishops of *Rome*; which *Damasus* was a Man that wanted no Courage: nevertheless we do not read, that either he, or *Liberius*, ever attempted to Excommunicate, or depose, either of those Emperours, or that they held it lawful for them so to have done. In the space of time betwixt *Nero*, and *Damasus*, the most principal Men of all the ancient Fathers lived, as *Justinus Martyr*, *Irenæus*, *Clemens Alexandrinus*, *Tertullian*, *Origen*, *Cyprian*, *Athanasius*, *Jerom*, and *Augustin*: who never had learned, nor did in their times teach it for sound Doctrine, either that the Christians had Authority to bear Arms against their Soveraigns; or that the Bishops of *Rome* might lawfully depose Kings and Princes, either for Heresy, or for Cruelty, and thrust their Subjects (to serve their turns) into such furious and rebellious courses. So as it was great boldness, for the *Cardinal* of his own Head, to broach so palpable an untruth; especially seeing it carrieth with it so many Arguments to convince his want herein of all Honesty, Sincerity, and Conscience.

But why should we be so earnest with the Man? considering, that although it be certain, that neither St. *Peter* not St. *Paul*, nor any of the said ancient Fathers or Popes ever thought it lawful to depose such Emperours and Kings as before we have spoken of, when they should be able through the Numbers and Forces of Christians so to do; Yet the same did proceed in the most of them from their Ignorance and want of Learning. " For (saith he) that Christians, if they had been able, " might so have done, is apparent by the Apostle's " words: where it is plain, that they had authority to " make Judges; and consequently, that if they had " been able, they might have thrust the said wicked " Emperours from their Thrones, and have made to " themselves new Kings of their own. Assuredly the Devil himself did never abuse any place of Scripture (for ought that we remember) so palpably and grosly, as the *Cardinal* doth this: and therefore we will

bestow

bestow no great Pains to refute him. It shall be sufficient briefly to observe, that in the Judgments of *Jerom*, *Austin*, *Ambrose*, and *Chrysostome*, the Judges which here the Apostle speaketh of, were only such, as might by way of Arbitrement, end such Suits, as arose amongst Christians in those days; and not such Judges, as by Law and Authority might have compelled them to have stood to their Sentences: for that had been indeed to have encroached upon the Authority of the civil Magistrate; which was far from the Apostle's intent and meaning. "And therefore, saith *Theodoret, Sciendum est*, &c. It is to be observed, that "these words (of chusing Arbiters) do not repugn to "those things which are written to the *Romans* For "here the Apostle doth not command Christians to re- "sist the Magistrates, but willeth them that are injured, "not to use the Magistrates: meaning, that it was fitter "for Christians to compound their causes and quarrels a- "mongst themselves, rather than to the dishonour of their "Profession, contend before such Magistrates as were In- "fidels, and were like enough to despise and contemn "them, because they could not better agree amongst them- "selves. And the *Cardinal*'s own Doctor, commenting "likewise upon this place doth write in this sort, "*Sed* "*videtur*, &c. But that which is here said by the Apostle "doth seem to be contrary to that which St. *Peter* saith, "*Be subject to every humane Creature for God, whether to* "*King as excelling, or to Rulers as sent by him.* For it doth "appertain to the Authority of a Prince to judge of his "Subjects, and therefore it is against the Law of God, "to prohibit, that a Subject should submit himself to "the Judgment-Seat of his Prince, if he be an Infidel. "*Sed dicendum*, &c. But it is to be answered, that "the Apostle doth not here forbid, but that faithful "Men, living under Princes that are Infidels, may ap- "pear in their Judicial Seats if they be called; for this "were against the Subjection which is due unto

Theodoret. in 1 Cor. 5.

Aqu. in 1 Cor. 6.

1 Pet. 2.

"Princes:

"Princes : but he forbiddeth, that faithful Men do not "of their own accord, voluntarily choose the Judgment- "Seat of Infidels. But if these Authorities will not serve, we will be bold to present against him the Judgment of a whole College, first published in *Rhemes*, and then set out again the second time, by the same College at *Doway*, approved in both Places; at *Rhemes* by *Petrus Remigius*, *Hubertus Morus*, *Johannes Lebesque*, *Guil. Balbus*; and at *Doway* by *Will. Estius*, *Barth. Petrus*, *Judocus Heylens*, all of them great Doctors of Divinity in those Places, and one a Doctor of the Canon Law, Vicar general of the Archbishoprick of *Rhemes*. The said College writing upon these words [*But brother with brother contendeth in Judgment, and that before Infidels*] saith thus; "To be given much to Brabling and Litigious-"ness for every trifle, to spend a pound rather than lose "a penny, the Apostle much reprehendeth in Christian "Men. For a Christian Man to draw another to the "Judgment-Seats and Courts of Heathen Princes "(which then only raigned) and not to suffer their "Controversies and Quarrels to be taken up among "themselves, Brotherly and peaceably, was a great "fault. What the *Cardinal*'s Friends will say, of his perverting the Apostle's meaning with so desperate an Exposition, we are uncertain: but of this, we are sure, that the Estate of that Church must needs be very miserable, that cannot be upheld without so apparent injury done to the Holy Ghost. Which observation we thought fit to make in this place; because he once having past the bounds of all Modesty, or rather Piety, is grown to that presumption and hardness of heart, against the truth, as that he dareth to ground another of his Reasons, to prove, that the Pope hath Authority indirectly, to depose Kings and Princes, upon these words spoken to St. *Peter*, *Pasce oves meas*, *Feed my Sheep*. Touching which words, because we have a fitter place to entreat, we will here be silent, and address

Rhem. Test. in 1 Cor. 6. 6.

dress our selves to his fourth Reason, as idle, and as false, as any of the rest.

These are his words. "When Kings and Princes "come to the Church, that they may be made Chri- "stians, they are received *cum pacto expresso, vel tacito*, "with a condition expressed or implied, without any "mention made of it, that they do submit their Scep- "ters unto Christ; and do promise, that they will "keep and defend the Faith of Christ, *Etiam sub pœnâ* "*Regni perdendi*, even under pain of losing their King- "doms: Therefore, when they become Hereticks, or "do hinder Religion, they may be judged by the "Church, and also deposed from their Principality, and "there shall be no injury done unto them, if they be "deposed. For answer whereof; first, we say, That in all the Forms of Baptisms which hitherto have been published, we cannot learn, that there was ever any such express Covenant, as the *Cardinal* here mentioneth, required of any King, when he came to be Christned. Baptism is the Entrance, ordain'd by Christ, into the Church, which is his spiritual Kingdom; and agreeably to the nature of that Kingdom, all who are thereby to enter into it, of what Calling or Condition soever they are, as well poor as rich; private Persons as Princes, are (according to the Rules of Baptism practised in all the particular Churches in the World, for ought that is known to the contrary) either themselves in their own Persons, or if they be Infants, by their Sureties to profess their belief in Christ, and to Promise, that *they will forsake the Devil, and all his Works, the vain Pomp and Glory of the World, with all covetous desires of the same, and carnal desires of the Flesh; and that they do constantly believe God's holy word, and that they will keep his Commandments*. The willful breach of any of which points, and perseverance in it without Repentance, doth indeed deprive every Christian Man, of what Calling soever he be, from the interest he had

(by

(by his said profession and promise, when he was Baptized) to the Spiritual Kingdom of Christ in this Life, (that is, from being a true and lively Member of the Church and mystical Body of Christ) and from the Kingdom of Glory in the Life to come. But that any Man, by the breach of any Promise made when he was Baptized, should lose that which he gain'd not by his Baptism; or that the Church did never receive any King or Prince to Baptism, but either upon condition in express terms, or by implication made either by himself, or by his Godfathers, that he would submit his Scepter unto Christ, that is, unto the Bishop of *Rome* (as the *Cardinal*'s drift sheweth his meaning to be) and promise to keep and defend the Faith of Christ under pain of the loss of his Kingdom, is certainly *a Doctrine of Devils*, and was never heard of in the Church of Christ for many hundred years; but is utterly repugnant to the Analogy of Scripture, and to the true nature of Christian Baptism. These secret intentions (for, as we have said, there was never any Form of Baptism, that contain'd any such express contract, as the *Cardinal* speaketh of) Mental Reservations, and hidden Compacts, such as Men were never taught in the Primitive Church, nor ever dream'd of, or suspected to be thrust into one of the holy Sacraments, may well become the Impostors of *Rome*, but are altogether contrary to the meaning of Christ, and of his holy Apostles: In whose days, he *that believed was baptized in the name of the Father, the Son, and the Holy Ghost*, without any such jugling, or snares laid to hazard and entangle Mens temporal Estates. There is nothing in the Gospel, whereof Men ought to be ashamed, or which will not abide the touchstone of truth, if it be compared with the rest of the Scriptures; or, that doth not promote the Spiritual Kingdom of Christ, it being called in that respect, Evangelium Regni, *the Gospel of the Kingdom*. Now whether this underhand

bargaining

bargaining be suitable or no, with the sincerity of the Holy Ghost; or whether if it had been known in the Primitive Church, that all Men, who would submit themselves to the Doctrine of the Gospel, and be baptized, did thereby bind themselves to be subject, and at the Commandment of the Bishop of *Rome* for the time being, under pain to lose all their Worldly Estates; the knowledge thereof would not rather have hinder'd, than either promoted or further'd the good success of the Gospel; no Man is so simple, but he may easily discern it. Assuredly the *Grecians*, who did so long oppose themselves against the Authority which the Bishops of *Rome* did challenge over all Churches, were ignorant of this mystical point of Baptism: and so were all the Churches in the World for many Ages, or else there would not have been so great stirs in the World about the continual Usurpations and Encroachments of the Bishops of *Rome*, as are many ways testified by sundry Ecclesiastical Histories. But we insist too long upon this so ridiculous and impudent a fiction, and therefore will come to the *Cardinal*'s principal reason of the Pope's said indirect temporal Authority, to toss Kings and Kingdoms up and down as he list.

"The Ecclesiastical Commonwealth *(saith he)* must
" be perfect and sufficient of her self, in order to her
" own end; (for such are all Commonwealths that
" are well instituted) and therefore she ought to have
" all necessary Power to the obtaining of her own end.
" But the Power of using and disposing of temporal
" things, is necessary to the Spiritual End; because o-
" therwise Evil Princes might, without punishment,
" nourish Hereticks, and overthrow Religion: and
" therefore the Ecclesiastical Commonwealth hath this
" Power. Hitherto the *Cardinal*. The substance of whose Argument is, that the Church of Christ cannot attain to her Spiritual End, except the Bishop of *Rome* have Authority to dispose of temporal Kingdoms, and

to

to punish Kings by depoſing them from their Crowns, if he hold it expedient: For the refutation of which vain and falſe Aſſertion, there are very many moſt direct and apparent Arguments: We will only touch ſome few of them. Our Saviour Chriſt in his days, and the Apoſtles in their times, and the Primitive Churches for the ſpace of 300. years, brought the Eccleſiaſtical Commonwealth (as here it is termed) unto her Spiritual End, as directly and fully, as either the Biſhops of *Rome*, or any other Biſhops have at any time done ſince: and yet they took no Power and Authority upon them, nor did challenge the ſame, of diſpoſing of temporal Kingdoms, or Depoſing of Princes. Beſides, if ſuch an indirect temporal Power be ſo neceſſary in theſe days, for the upholding the Eccleſiaſtical Commonwealth, as that without the ſame ſhe cannot attain the Spiritual End, or be a perfect Eccleſiaſtical Commonwealth, when there are ſo many Chriſtian Kings and Princes; then was the ſame much more neceſſary for the attainment of the ſame end, in the ſaid times of Chriſt, of his Apoſtles, and of the Churches in the Ages following for 300. years, when the civil Magiſtrates were Pagans and Infidels, and for the moſt part, Perſecutors of the truth. But we hope, we may be bold without offence to ſay, that there appeared then no ſuch neceſſity of this pretended temporal Power and Authority, in any Eccleſiaſtical Perſons, over Kings and Kingdoms, for the diſpoſing of them; and that neverthelefs, the Eccleſiaſtical Commonwealth, in thoſe times, did attain her Spiritual End, and was as perfect an Eccleſiaſtical Commonwealth, as it is now under the Pope's Government, notwithſtanding all his temporal Sovereignty, wherein he ſo ruffleth. Again, we are perſwaded, that it cannot be ſhewed out of any of the ancient Fathers, or by any general Council, for the ſpace of above 500. years after Chriſt, that the Biſhops of *Rome* were ever

imagin'd

imagin'd to have such temporal Authority to depose Kings, as now is maintained; much less was it ever dream'd of, during that time, that such Authority was necessary for the attaining the Spiritual End, whereunto the true Church of Christ ought to aim; or, that the Ecclesiastical Commonwealth, ordain'd by Christ and his Apostles, could not be perfect without it. It were a miserable shift, if any should either say, that during all the times above-mention'd, first the Apostles, and then the holy Bishops, Martyrs, and Fathers after them, were ignorant of this new temporal Power, or at least did not so throughly consider of the necessity of it, as they might have done; or that whilst they lived, there could indeed no such matter be collected out of the Scriptures, for that in those days the Scriptures had not received such a sense and meaning as might support the same: but that afterward, when the Bishops of *Rome* did think it necessary to challenge to themselves such temporal Authority, over both Kings and Kingdoms, the sense and meaning of the Scripture was alter'd. But be this shift never so wretched or miserable, yet (for ought we perceive) they are in effect, and still will be, both in this cause and many others, driven unto it: the Scriptures being in their hands a very *Rule of Lead*, and *Nose of Wax*, as in another more fit place we shall have occasion to shew: moreover, if the Bishops of *Rome* have this great temporal Authority over Kings and Soveraign Princes, to preserve the State of the Church here upon Earth, that she may attain her Spiritual End; assuredly he hath made little use of it to that purpose. For it is well known, and cannot be denied, that for the first 300. years of Christ, the Doctrine of the Gospel did flourish far and near, in *Greece, Thracia, Sclavonia, Hungary, Asia minor, Syria, Assyria, Egypt,* and throughout the most part of *Africk,* where there were many very worthy Apostolical, and notable Churches; in the most of which places, there are scarce in these days any footsteps or visible Monuments of them. And although afterward during the space of above 700. years, much mischief was wrought in these parts of the World, better known unto us than the rest, by sundry sorts of *Scythians*, and *Northern People:* yet after the days of *Gregory the Seventh*, when the Bishops of *Rome* did most vaunt of this their Soveraign Power over Kings and Princes, the *Turks* gained and encroached more upon Christendom, still retaining that which they then had so gotten, than at any time before. Whereby it is to us very evident, that neither Christ, nor his Apostles, ever ordained, that the means of building of the Church of Christ, and the conservation of it, should consist in the temporal Power or Authority of any of their Successors, to deprive Emperours or Kings from their Imperial or Regal Estates: and that the Bishops of *Rome* may be ashamed, that having had so great Authority in their own hands, extorted from the Emperours, and other Kings, *per fas & nefas*, since *Gregory* the Seventh's time, they have made no better use of it; but suffer'd so many famous Countries and Kingdoms to be utterly over-run and wasted by Pagans and Infidels; considering that they pretend themselves to have so great an Authority for no other purpose, but only the preservation of the Church, that she might not be prevented of her Spiritual End. But what should we speak of the shame of *Rome*, whose forehead hath been so long since hardned? or ever imagine, that Almighty God either did, or will bless her Usurpations and Insolencies against Emperours, Kings and Princes, for any good to his Church, other than must accrue unto her through her Persecutions and Afflictions? For it were no great labour to make it most apparent by very many Histories, if we would insist upon it, that the Bishops of *Rome*, in striving first to get, and then to uphold (after their scrambling manner) this their wicked and usurped

usurped Authority of troubling and vexing Christian Kingdoms and States with their manifold Oppressions and quarrels, have been some special means, whereupon the *Saracens*, *Turks* and *Pagans* have wrought, and by degrees brought so great a part of Christendom under their Slavery, as now they are possessed of. For it is but an idle and a vain pretence, that the preservation of as much of Christendom, as is yet free from the *Turk* and Paganism, is to be ascribed to the Bishop of *Rome*, and his Authority, that so the *Catholick Church* might attain her Spiritual End, which ought to be the planting of Churches and Conservation of 'em: it being most manifest, to as many as have any wit, experience, and sound Judgment, that as the very situation of the said Countries, which now Pagans enjoy, made them very subject unto the Incursion and Invasions of *Saracens* and *Turks*, God himself, for his own Glory, having his Finger and just operation therein; so through his most merciful goodness, and care of his Church, he blessed the situation of the rest of Christendom, being now free in that respect from those kind of violences, and endowed the hearts of Christian Kings and Princes with such Courage and Constancy, in defence of Christianity, and of their Kingdoms, as notwithstanding that the Popes did greatly vex them in the mean while, they did mightily repel the Forces of their Enemies, and most religiously uphold and maintain the profession of Christ: So, as the preservation of the Gospel in these parts of the World, may more truly be attributed to the working of the Spirit of God in them, than to the Bishops of *Rome*; who have been the chief Authors and occasions of many incredible mischiefs.

Now lastly, and for conclusion of this point; had not Satan with all Power and Signs, and lying Wonders, so inveigled and seduced the hearts and minds of the adherents to the See of *Rome*, as that by degrees,

they

they leaving the love of the truth, are therefore *given over by God unto such strong delusions, that they should believe lyes* (as the Apostle speaketh;) amongst many other of the gross errours maintained by them, we might marvel at this, that ever they durst take upon them, in these times of so great light, to write and defend it with such resolution and confidence, that the Ecclesiastical Commonwealth (as they term it) cannot be perfect, nor attain her Spiritual End, except the Pope may have the said temporal Power and Authority to depose Kings: considering how far the true nature of the Church, which is the Spiritual Kingdom of Christ; and the true Means and Armour, that Christ, our Spiritual King, hath indeed ordained and appointed, for the Edification and Defence of this his Spiritual Kingdom, and for the attainment of the supernatural, and right end and beauty of it, are repugnant to these their Carnal, and Worldly conceits. Touching the true nature of the Church, and Spiritual Kingdom of Christ, we have before spoken: and the true Spiritual End of the Church, being by teaching the ways of truth, to bring as many as possibly they can, to the knowledge of their Salvation, through Christ, so as by Faith they may become true Members of his Spiritual Kingdom in the Life to come; the means ordain'd for that purpose, do contain the full duty and office of all Bishops and Ecclesiastical Ministers; who are furnished by Christ, neither with temporal Swords, nor Imperial Authority to depose Kings and Soveraign Princes, but ought to carry themselves toward all Men, especially towards Kings and Princes, if they be either Pagans, or Enemies to Religion, as Christ himself, and his Apostles did; by Preaching and Praying for them, by Humility and Patience, to endure whatsoever punishment shall be thought fit to be imposed upon them for doing of their duties; and never to intermit such their pains and diligence, to the end, that

2 Thess. 2. 10, 11.

if

if it please God to bless those their Ministerial so great labours, their Auditors of all sorts, private Persons, Kings and Princes, may be brought to the knowledge of the truth; that so Satan being expelled out of their hearts, Christ by Faith may raign in them. To the effecting of which so great and so divine an alteration, and change in Mens Souls, there is no Worldly Force, nor temporal Sword, which will serve the turn. And therefore the Apostle, speaking of this matter, doth write in this sort; *The Weapons of our Warfare are not carnal:* as if he should have said; We do not come with Troops of Men to promote the Spiritual Kingdom of Christ; but with Weapons of another nature, with the glad tidings of the Gospel, with the Doctrine of Salvation to all Believers, and with the Furniture of the Holy Ghost: which Weapons are not weak, but mighty through God, and able to cast down holds, that is, all the carnal Forces of Men, all Principalities and Powers, that shall presume to rise up against Christ. And through the assurance and experience, which both St. *Paul*, and the rest of the Apostles, had in the force of these Weapons, he saith further, *that with them they overthrew Councils, and every high thing, that did exalt it self against the knowledge of God; and that they brought into Captivity, all imagination or understanding to the obedience of Christ:* away then with the Pope's Carnal Weapons, and with all their Illusions, and Juglings, that seek to uphold them: for such Weapons were never ordain'd by Christ for his Apostolical Warfare.

2 Cor. 10. 4, &c.

C A N,

CAN. IX.

AND therefore if any Man shall affirm, under colour of any thing that is in the Scriptures, either, that the external Callings in this World of those Men (as Ministers and Schoolmasters) that have to deal with the information of Mens Minds and Souls, are superiour, and to be preferr'd in Honour and Worldly Dignities, before the Callings of Kings and Soveraign Princes: or, that because health is better, and more to be desired in this Life, than any Worldly Preferments, therefore the Calling of Physicians, who are ordain'd for the health of Mens Bodies, ought to be superiour to all other Worldly Callings: or, that the Regal, and Political Power of the King, when it is part of a Christian Commonwealth, is thereby brought into greater servitude and thraldom, than is the Regal and Political State of Ethnick Princes, when the same are no parts of a Christian Kingdom: or, that to prefer the Ecclesiastical State for Worldly Authority, before the State of Kings and Soveraign Princes, is not (in effect) to prefer the humbled Estate of Christ, as he was Man, living here

here upon the Earth, before his glorious Estate, after his Ascension, and before the glory and majesty of his Divine Nature: or, that any Ecclesiastical Authority, which the Apostles ordained, did either free them, or any of their Successors, from subjection to Kings and Princes, and to their temporal Authority: or, that St. Peter, being an Apostle, and so subject to the civil Sword of Temporal Authority, could lawfully, by any indirect device, challenge any temporal power and Dominion over Kings and Princes; for that had been to have extorted the temporal Sword out of their hands to whom it appertain'd, and to have incurr'd again the commination of his Master, when he told him, how all that take the Sword shall perish with the Sword: or, that it is not a most profane impiety, tending altogether to the discredit of the Scriptures, for any Man to hold, that St. Peter and St. Paul had so instructed the Christians in their times, as that they knew, if they had been able, they might without offence to God, have deposed Nero from his Empire: or, that the Christians in Tertullian's time, when they professed, that notwithstanding their numbers and forces were so great, as they had been able to have distressed very greatly the Estate

I i of

of the Emperours (being then Persecutors) they might not so do, because Christ their Master had taught them otherwise; ought not to be a sufficient Warrant for all true Christians to detest those Men in these Days, and for ever hereafter, who contrary to the Example of the said Christians in the Primitive Church, and the Doctrine of Christ, which was then taught them, do endeavour to perswade them, when they shall have sufficient Forces, to Rebel against such Kings and Emperours at the Pope's Commandment, and to thrust them from their Kingdoms and Empires: or, that this Devilish Doctrine of animating Subjects to Rebellion (when they are able) against their Soveraigns, either for their Cruelty, Heresy, or Apostasie, was ever taught in the Church of Christ by any of the ancient Fathers abovementioned, during the Reigns of Dioclesian, or Julian the Apostate, or Valens the Arrian, or of any other the Wicked Emperours before them: or, that it is not a Wicked perverting of the Apostles Words to the Corinthians (touching their choice of Arbitrators, to end dissentions amongst themselves, rather than draw their Brethren before Judges that were Infidels) to infer thereof, either that St. Paul intended thereby by to impeach, in any sort, the Authority of the civil Magistrates as if he had meant they should have chosen such Judges, as by civil Authority might otherwise have bound them, than by their own consents to have stood to their Award; or to authorize Christian Subjects, when they are able, to thrust their lawful Soveraigns from their Regal Seats, and to choose unto themselves new Kings into their places: or, that any of the said ancient Fathers, or godly learned Men, for many hundred years after Christ, did ever so grosly and irreligiously expound the said place of the Apostle, as our Cardinaliz'd Jesuit hath done: or, that it can be collected out of the Scriptures, that either Christ, or any of his Apostles, did at any time teach or preach, that they, who meant to be Baptized, must receive that Sacrament upon Condition, that if at any time afterward, they should not be obedient to St. Peter, for his time, and to his Successors, they were to lose and be deprived of all their temporal Estates and Possessions: or, that it can be proved, either out of the Scriptures, or by any of the said ancient Fathers, or shewed in any ancient Form of Administration of Baptism, that ever there was any such Covenant made, by any such

faithful

faithful Persons, when they were Baptized, or required of them to be made by any that Baptized them: or, that if such a Covenant were by Christ's Ordinance to be made in Baptism, it ought not as well to be made by Farmers, by Gentlemen possessed of Mannours, and by Lords of greater Revenues and Possessions, as by Kings and Soveraign Princes: or, that it were not an absurd Imagination to think, that Christ and his Apostles did only mean, that Emperours, Kings and Soveraign Princes, should be received to Baptism upon the said Condition: or, that all Christian Men ought not to judge, that the eleven Apostles, if they had known of any such bargain, or condition in Baptism, would have dealt as faithfully with the Church, and in the behalf of St. Peter, in preaching and teaching the same, as now our Cardinal, and other such like Persons of the Roman strain, do by their Writing, Publishing, and maintaining of it in the behalf of the Bishops of Rome: or, that either Christ, or his Apostles, knowing that Baptism ought to be received with such a Condition, did think it convenient, that the same should be concealed, not only whilst they lived, but for many hundred years afterward,

until

until the Bishops of Rome should be grown to such a head and strength, as that they might without fear of any inconveniencies, make the whole Christian World acquainted with it: or, that it is not an idle conceit for any Man to maintain, that the Renunciation of the effects of Baptism, doth deprive Men of their temporal Lands and Possessions which they did not hold by any force of Baptism; or make them subject in that behalf to the deprivation of the Bishops of Rome: or, that Apostasy from Christ, put on in Baptism, doth any further extend it self, than to the Souls of such Apostates in this Life, in that the Devil hath got again the possession of them, and so depriveth them in this World of all the comfort and hope they had in Christ, leading them on to the bane, both of their Bodies and Souls in the Life to come: or, that any Ecclesiastical Person, hath any other lawful means, to reclaim Wicked, Heretical, or Apostated Kings, from their Impiety, Heresy and Apostasy, than Christ and his Apostles did ordain to be used, for winning Men at the first to embrace the Gospel: or, that Christ himself, while he lived, did attempt, either directly or indirectly, to Depose the Emperour, by whose Authority he was

himself

himself put to death, as holding, that the Church could not attain to her Spiritual End, except he had so done: or, that by the death of Christ, the Church did not attain to her Spiritual End, without the Deposition of any Emperours or Kings from their Regal Estates: or, that ever the Apostles in their days, either preached or Writ, that the Ecclesiastical CommonWealth could not be perfect, except St. Peter for his time, and after him the Bishops of Rome, should have temporal Power and Authority to Depose Emperours and Kings, that the Church might attain her Spiritual End: or, that the Church in their days did not attain to her Spiritual End, although no such Authority was then, either challenged, or put in practice: or, that the Church could have attain'd to that her Spiritual End in the Apostle's times, if the said temporal Power and Authority had been then necessary for the attaining of it: or, that our Saviour Christ and his Apostles, did propound a Spiritual End unto his Church, and left no other necessary means for the obtaining of it, than such as could not be put in practice, either in their days, or for many hundred years after: or, that the Churches of Christ, after the Apostle's times, for the
space

space of 300. years, being wonderfully oppressed with sundry Persecutions, did not attain to their Spiritual End, without this dream'd off Temporal Authority of Deposing Kings and Emperours, then their mortal Enemies, not in respect of themselves, but of the Doctrine of Salvation, which they taught to their Subjects: or, that this new Doctrine of the Necessity, that the Bishops of Rome should have temporal Authority, either directly or indirectly, to Depose Emperours and Kings, for any cause whatsoever, (or that else the Church of Christ should not be able to attain to her Spiritual End) was ever heard of, for ought that appeareth for many hundreds of years after the Apostles times, either in any Ecclesiastical History, or in any of the ancient Fathers, by us abovementioned: or, that the Bishops of Rome, With all their Adherents, Whilst they would make the World believe, that the Church of Christ cannot attain her Spiritual End, except they have temporal Authority, indirectly to Depose for some Causes, Emperours, Kings, and Soveraign Princes, are more learned now, than either the ancient Fathers, or the Apostles themselves were; and that they know the sense of the Scriptures

ptures better, than either they the said ancient Fathers did, or the Apostles that writ them; who (for ought that was known for many hundred years) never preached, taught, or intended to have any such Doctrine collected out of their Writings and Works: or, that it may, without great Impiety, be once imagined, that if such a necessary point of Doctrine, concerning the said great temporal Power in the Pope over Princes, as without the which, the Church of Christ could not attain her Spiritual End, had been known to the Apostles and Ancient Fathers, they would not have been as careful and zealous to have preached and divulged the same unto all Posterity, as now the Bishops of Rome, and their Adherents are: or, that we ought not rather to believe, that the Bishops of Rome, and their Adherents, through their forsaking the love of the Truth, are given over by God unto those strong Illusions, that they should believe lies, and maintain them as stifly as though they were true, than once to conceive, that the holy Apostles and ancient Fathers, were either ignorant of this supposed temporal Authority to Depose Kings and Princes, for the end so often mentioned, or thought it fit to dissemble it, or to Write

of

of it so darkly, as for many hundred years it could not be understood: or, that God hath not wonderfully blinded the hearts and understandings, both of the Popes, and all their Adherents in this particular matter (amongst many others) in that the nature of the Church, and Spiritual Kingdom of Christ considered, they dare presume to maintain it so confidently, that the said Spiritual Kingdom of Christ, cannot attain to her Spiritual End, without the Bishop of Rome, his Temporal Authority, indirectly in some Cases, to Depose Kings and Soveraign Princes: or, that the true Spiritual End of the Church consisting in this, that the Devil being banished out of the hearts of all her true Members, Christ may retain his Possession of them, through their Faith and Diligence, to repel Satan, who daily laboureth to regain to himself his own Possession; it is not more than a kind of phrensy, to hold and maintain, that any temporal Authority, managed by the Pope, or by his Commandment, against Kings and Princes, hath any force or power, to work or procure this Spiritual End, either by expelling or repelling of Satan, or to nourish Faith, or to continue the reigning of Christ in any Mens hearts: or, that it

K k is

is not an impious and a profane assertion for any Man to defend, that the Weapons and Armour of this Spiritual Warfare, undertaken by Christ, and his Apostles, and by all godly Bishops, and true Priests and Ministers of the Gospel, are not sufficient of themselves to procure to the Church her Spiritual End, without the Pope's carnal Weapons, or temporal Authority to Depose Kings, when to him, with the assistance of his Cardinals, it shall seem expedient; He doth greatly Erre.

CAP.

CAP. XI.

The Sum of the Chapter following.

That there is no more necessity of one visible Head of the Catholick Church, than of one visible Monarch over all the World.

IN the 35th and 36th Chapters of our first Book, We have shewed at large, that our Saviour Christ, the Son of God, having created the World, and taken upon him to be the Redeemer of Mankind, after their transgression through *Adam*'s Fall, did not only, as he was the Son of God, govern all the World (the same being in that respect but one Universal Kingdom) and appoint several Kings and Sovereign Princes, as his Substitutes, to rule the same under him in their several Countries and Kingdoms, leaving no one Emperour, or temporal Monarch to govern them all; but likewise, as he was the blessed Lamb, slain from the beginning of the World, he did (for his own Glory, and our endless Comfort) erect for himself, in this World, a Spiritual Kingdom, called his Church, consisting of such Men, disperfed throughout the World, as did profess his name; and being himself the only Head and Governour of it (in which respect it is rightly to be termed, but One *Catholick Church*) did appoint no one Priest over the whole *Catholick Church*, but several Priests, and Ecclesiastical Ministers, to rule and govern the particular Churches in every Province, Country, and Nation. And in such manner and form, as our Saviour Christ did rule and govern his Universal Kingdom, and *Catholick Church*, before his Incarnation; So doth he still rule and govern the same: notwithstanding any of those vain pretences,

pretences, and ridiculous Usurpations, which the Bishops of *Rome*, or any of their Adherents, are able to alledge and maintain to the contrary.

Extravag. l. 1. c. 1. de Major. & Obed. unam sanctam.

In the Gloss of one of the Books of the Canon-Law, not long since Printed, and approved by *Gregory* the Thirteenth, a Glossographer, and now an Authentical Canonist, doth write in this sort. " *Dicò, quod potestas* " *Spiritualis debet dominari omni creaturæ humanæ*. *I say, that the Spiritual Power ought to domineer over every humane Creature*. And why saith he so? Forsooth, " *Per* " *rationes, quas Hostiensis inducit in summa: for certain causes and reasons, which* Hostiensis (another Canonist) *doth alledge in his sum*. But he stayeth not there: he hath another motive, which he setteth down thus: " *Item, quia Christus, &c*. *Also, because Jesus Christ, the Son of God, when he was in the World, and also from everlasting was the natural Lord; and by the natural Law he might have given Sentences against the Emperour, and any other whatsoever, of Deposition and damnation, and any other Sentences;* " *Utpote in personas, quas creaverat;* " *& donis naturalibus, & gratuitis dotaverat, & etiam* " *conservabat: As against Persons, whom he had created and endowed with natural and free gifts; and also whom he did preserve:* " *& eadem ratione Vicarius ejus potest: and by one and the same reason* (saith he) *his Vicar may so do*. What? would Pope *Gregory*, by his Canonists, make Men to believe, that all Emperours, Kings, and Soveraign Princes, are Persons of the Pope's Creation? or, that he doth bestow on them freely, any gifts or benefits of Nature? or, that their preservation doth depend upon his good favour and Providence? But the idle Canonist, his Wit doth serve him no better, than to make (in effect) this fond Collection: Christ, the Creator of all things, doth govern, rule, dispose, and preserve all his own Creatures: therefore the Pope must likewise govern, rule, dispose and preserve them all, though he created none of them. And why must he

so

so do? he wanteth not a very substantial reason that moved him so to collect; which followeth in his own words: "*Nam non videretur Dominus discretus fuisse* "*(ut cum Reverentiâ ejus loquar) nisi unicum post se talem* "*Vicarium reliquisset, qui hæc omnia posset. Fuit autem* "*iste Vicarius ejus Petrus. Et idem dicendum est de Suc-* "*cessoribus Petri; cùm eadem absurditas sequeretur, si post* "*mortem Petri humanam naturam à se creatam sine regi-* "*mine unius personæ reliquisset.* For Christ *should not have been thought a Person of sufficient discretion (that with his Reverence, I may so speak) except he had left behind him one such Vicar, who might do all these things. And this his Vicar was* Peter. *And the same is to be said of the Successors of* Peter: *seeing the same absurdity must follow, if after* Peter's *Death he had left Mankind created by himself, without the regiment of one Person.* And Mr. Harding, one of our own Countrymen, doth wholly concur with this profound Canonist; saving that he dealeth more civilly with Christ, in using the word *Providence* instead of the Canonist's *Discretion.* Thus he writeth. *Except we should wickedly grant, that God's Providence doth lack to his Church; reason may soon induce us to believe, that to one Man, the chief and highest of all Bishops, the Successor of* Peter, *the Rule and Government of the Church, by God, hath been deferred.* And he further doth express his opinion to this effect; *That if God had not ordain'd such a Monarchical Church-Government, he should have brought in amongst his faithful People, that unruly confusion and destruction of all Commonwealths, so much abhorred of Princes, which the Grecians call an Anarchy; which is a State, for lack of order in Governours, without any Government at all.*

That our Saviour Christ is the sole Governour, Head, and Archbishop of his *Catholick Church*, as he is the only Governour, Ruler, and Monarch, over all the World: and that his Discretion, and Divine Providence, is no more to be blemished, or impeached, by the

Harding's Confut. of Juel's Apol. § 19.

[250]

the Cavils of any Impostors, in that he hath appointed no one Priest, Archbishop, or Pope, to be his Vicar-General, over the whole Catholick Church, than for that he hath not assigned any one King, Emperour, or Monarch, to rule the whole World under him; this is the point, that here we purpose to make good: taking it in this place for granted, that there was never any one Man in the World, to whom our Saviour Christ did commit the Government of it, after the time that it was Peopled, and throughly inhabited; that is, from *Noah*'s Flood at the least hitherto. They, that labour to prove, that the Bishop of *Rome* is Head of the Universal Church, and that Christ should have shewed little Discretion, or Providence, if he had not so ordain'd it, do insist very much upon the grounds of natural reason and philosophy; telling us out of *Plato, Aristotle, Plutarch, Isocrates, Stobæus, Hesiodus, Euripides, Homer, Herodotus,* and divers others, That of all the kinds of Government that are, the Monarchical Government is the best; " That in a great Host, consisting of Souldiers of divers Nations and Countries, and perhaps " of many Soveraign Princes, and Kings, there must " be one General to govern them all; That all things " naturally have a propension and aptness to Monarchi- " cal Government; That Bees of every Hive have " their King; That in every Flock of Sheep there is a " principal Ram; That every Herd of Cattel hath a " Leader; That Cranes do not fly promiscuously, and " in heaps, but have one whom they do all very orderly " follow; That amongst Cœlestial Spheres, there is but " one *Primum Mobile*; That in the number of the lights " of the World, one is greater than the rest; That " there is a certain Principality in the Elements; That " the Fountain is but one, from whence divers times " there flow sundry Streams; That into one Sea all " Rivers do run and return; That the thing which is " most one, is less easily divided; That it is rather
" one,

Bell. de Rom. Pont. l. 1. c. 2.

Sand. de visib. Monarch. l. 3.

¥ one, which is simply one, than a multitude conspi-   Bell. de Rom.
"ring in one ; And that for these, and many other   Pont. l. 1. c.9.
like reasons, seeing the Monarchical Government is
best, and that we may be sure, that Christ would
have his Church governed by the best manner of Government, (except we should think him to have dealt
absurdly, as a Person void, both of good Discretion
and Providence) ; It followeth therefore, that Christ
committed the Government of it unto one ; first to St.
Peter; and then to his Successor, the Bishop of *Rome*
for the time being. If this one *Jesuit* and his Fellows,
would upon the said Philosophical premises, have concluded thus, That it therefore had followed, that
Christ himself doth not only retain in his own hands,
the sole Government of his Catholick Church, as he is the
only Redeemer of it, but likewise the sole Government
of the whole World, as he is the Creator of it; the
Conclusion had been true, although the premises had
not enforced it. But how stifly soever they meant to
insist upon the said Conclusion, without any regard of
truth, so they may blear the Eyes of the simpler sort
with such their vain Illusions ; We may be bold (as
we hope) resolutely to defend and maintain it, that
the said natural reasons are of as great strength to prove,
That there ought of necessity to be one temporal Monarch over all the World , as one Ecclesiastical Monarch over the whole *Catholick Church :* although in
very deed they are far too feeble and weak, to prove
either the one or the other. For who knoweth not,
that when the Philosophers did write in commendation
of the Monarchical Government, they only had Relation to particular Nations and Countries ; endeavour-
ing to prove, that it was better for them severally to be
ruled by that Form of Government, which is called
Monarchical, than by any of the rest, Aristocratical,
Democratical, or any other ? And it was so far from
their meaning, to have their said reasons wrested to
prove,

prove, that one mortal Man ought to have the Government of the *Catholick Church*, the Spiritual Kingdom of Chrift; as they never dreamed (for ought that appeareth) that one Man, in their Judgment, was fit or able to take upon him the Temporal Government of the whole World: To which purpofe, a principal Lawyer amongft our Adverfaries, doth write in this fort. *Naturâ ipfâ inftitutum non eft, quòd univerfus Orbis uni Principi fubditus fit.* It is not ordain'd by nature, that the whole World fhould be fubject to one Prince. If then it be an idle vanity for any Man to go about by natural reafon to prove, that one Man ought to be the temporal Monarch of all the World, which nature her felf did never intend: it is then certainly a kind of madnefs or phrenzy, to rely upon fuch proofs for the Popes fpiritual Authority over the whole *Catholick Church*; neither of them both being comprehenfible, or fubject to the apprehenfions of nature.

Covarruv. 2. parc. Relect. § 9. tom. 1. num. 5.

Again, thefe Patrons for the Pope, and his Primacy, over the whole *Catholick Church*, have not only fuch Arguments, as we have heard, drawn from natural reafon, but fome likewife deduced from fundry fimilitudes, and thofe out of the Scriptures; upon which they rely with fome more confidence, as reafon is they fhould: faying, that God made all Mankind, *ex uno Adamo, of one Adam*; to fignify thereby, that he would have all Men to depend, *ab uno, of one*: but the Old Teftament was a figure of the new; and that therefore, as there was but one High-Prieft amongft the *Jews* to govern that one Church; fo now there muft be but one Pope to govern all the Churches in the World: that *Aaron* was not only a figure of Chrift, but likewife of St. *Peter*: that the Church is compared to *an Hoft well order'd; to a humane Body; to a Kingdom; to a Fold; to an Houfe; to a Ship*; and that therefore fhe muft have but one Captain; one humane Head; one King; one Paftor; one Houfholder; and one Pilot: that although there

Bell. de Rom. Pont l. 1 c. 2.

there be but one, and proper Head of the Church, which is Chrift, that governeth the fame fpiritually; yet fhe hath need of one vifible Head, or otherwife the Bifhop of *Rome*, and all other Bifhops, Paftors, Doctors, and Minifters, were needlefs: that although Chrift be the Head of the Church, yet he ought to have one underneath him, by whom fhe may be governed; as a King, when he is prefent, may govern his Kingdom himfelf; but being abfent, doth ufually appoint another under him, who is called his Vice-Roy: that every Diocefs and Province hath her Bifhops and Archbifhops, to govern the particular Churches under them, within their feveral Charges; and that therefore there muft be one Bifhop of the whole Catholick Church, to rule and govern them all: Laftly, That as there is but one God, one Faith, and one Baptifm; fo there muft be in the *Catholick Church*, but one chief Bifhop and Judge, upon whom all Men ought to depend. Many more are the reafons, grounded upon divers other fimilitudes, which our Adverfaries have heaped up together, to uphold the Pope's Authority: all of them being as vain and frivolous as the former. For it is certain and manifeft, that as the *Catholick Church* is refembled in the Scriptures, to an Hoft well ordered, to a humane Body, to a Kingdom, to a Flock of Sheep, to an Houfe, and to a Ship: fo Chrift only is intended thereby to be her only General, her only Head, her only King, her only Shepherd, her only Houfholder, and her only Pilot. Neither can any other thing be inforced from the words mentioned of one Faith, and one Baptifm, but that as we are only juftified through a lively Faith in Chrift, fo there is but one Baptifm ordain'd, whereby we have our firft entrance into his Spiritual Kingdom, and are made particular Members of his *Catholick Church*. Befides, in the like fenfe, that the *Catholick Church* is refembled to an Hoft well order'd, to a humane Body, to a Kingdom, to a Flock, to an

L l Houfe,

House, to a Ship; so may the Universal Kingdom of Christ over the whole World, as he is the Creator of it, be resembled to them all, and the aforesaid Titles respectively attributed unto him. The whole World is an Host, under him, well order'd, and he is the General of it. The whole World is but as one Body, whereof he is the Head; being the Life of all Men, from whom, as from their Head, they have their Sense, Understanding, and Motion. The whole Universal World is but his Kingdom, and he is the King of it, ruling and disposing it, as seemeth best to his divine Wisdom. The whole World is with him but one Flock, and he is the Shepherd of it, all Men in it being the Sheep of his Pasture, to whom he giveth food and sustentation in due season. Also he ordereth all the affairs in the World, as a good Housholder doth order and direct all the businesses and troubles appertaining to his Family. Likewise the whole World may aptly be compared to a Ship, in that the State of all Mankind, living in it, is subject, as a Ship on the Sea, unto all manner of contrary Winds, Tempests, and Storms; of which Ship were not Christ, as he is the Creator of the World, the only Pilot, the World could not subsist. And as the *Catholick Church* is resembled to a Fold, which containeth in it all that believe in Christ; so may the universal Kingdom of Christ, over all the World, be compared unto a Fold, in that it containeth in it all Mankind generally, his Heavenly Care and Providence evermore protecting them.

Moreover, as there is but one *Catholick Church*, one Head, or Spiritual Ruler of it, (Christ our Redeemer) one Christian Faith, one Baptism, one Gospel, one Truth, one and the self-same Form or Nature of all the several Theological Virtues, and one Inheritance; which are all of them to be taught, embraced, and expected by all that are true Members of the *Catholick Church:* So there is but one Universal Kingdom in all

the

the World (the Creator of it being the sole Emperour and Governour of it) one moral Faith, one Nature of Truth to be observed amongst all, one rule and nature of Justice, one moral Law, one nature of Equity, one Kind, Form, or Nature of all the several Virtues, both Moral and Intellectual, which are to be put in practice, as occasion requireth, in this one Empire, by as many, as expect from Christ, their Emperour, any happy success in their Worldly affairs. But as all these Unities in the temporal Monarchy of Christ, are no sufficient grounds to warrant this assertion, that there ought to be one temporal King or Emperour under Christ to govern the whole World; so the aforesaid Spiritual and Ecclesiastical Unities, are not able to establish, or uphold this Inference; That one Pope must of necessity have the Government under Christ of the whole *Catholick Church*. Also from the authority of Scripture, that God made all Mankind of one *Adam*, to signify, that he would have all Men to depend upon one; why may it not as well be collected, that he meant, that all the Men in the World should depend upon one Emperour for causes Temporal, as upon one Pope in Causes Ecclesiastical? Likewise it is a very absurd conceit, that our *Jesuit* maintaineth, when he saith, That although Christ be the Head of the Church, yet he ought to have one underneath him, by whom she may be governed; as a King, when he is present, may govern his Kingdom himself, and when he is absent, appoint his Vice-Roy. Of likelyhood this Fellow would perswade us, that Christ is sometimes absent from his Church; to the end, that the Pope may be his grand Deputy: For otherwise, by his own Example, Christ may govern the *Catholick Church* without the Pope; as the King, ruling himself in his own Kingdom, needeth no Vice-Roy. That Christ is never absent from his Church; but doth by his Power, Grace and Virtue of the Holy Ghost, still defend and protect

protect it. It is plain by his own words, where he saith, *Lo, I am with you always unto the end of the World.* It is true, that he told his Apostles, that *he was to depart from them*; meaning, that they must be deprived of his Corporal presence: but did he signify unto them, that for their comfort he would leave St. *Peter* in his place, and after him the Bishops of *Rome*, St. *Peter's* Successors, to govern his Church to the end of the World? No such matter. These are our Saviour Christ's words. *It is expedient for you, that I go away: for if I go not away, the Comforter will not come unto you; but if I depart, I will send him unto you.* Again, *When he is come, which is the Spirit of truth, he will lead you into all truth.* Again, *I will pray to my Father, and he shall give you another Comforter, that he may abide with you for ever; even the Spirit of Truth.* Again, *The Comforter, which is the Holy Ghost, whom the Father will send in my Name, he shall teach you all things.* And again, *I will not leave you comfortless; but I will come unto you.* Which he doth continually, when he upholdeth his Church daily against Satan, and all that do malign it. So, as we may far more rightly and safely, term the Holy Ghost to be Christ's Vicar-General over all the *Catholick Church*, than we may ascribe that title to the Pope: the Holy Ghost being ever present and ready, not only to defend the Church generally, but to aid and comfort every particular Member of it, wheresoever they are dispersed upon the face of the Earth; which we suppose the Pope is not able to perform.

We have before laboured to make it manifest, that our Saviour Christ is the Creator of the World, and the Governour of it; that he hath redeemed and sanctified unto himself his Church, whereof he is the sole Monarch; that he hath neither appointed any one Emperour under him to govern the whole World, nor any one Priest or Archbishop, to rule the whole *Catholick Church*; that, as in respect of Christ, the Creator, all

all the World is but one Kingdom, whereof he is the only King; ſo, in reſpect of Chriſt our Redeemer, all that believe in his name, whereſoever they are diſperſed, are but one *Catholick Church*; and that the ſaid one *Catholick Church* is not otherwiſe viſible in this World, than is the ſaid one Univerſal Kingdom of Chriſt, the Creator of it; *viz.* by the ſeveral and diſtinct parts of them, as by this, or that National Church, by this, or that temporal Kingdom. For our Saviour Chriſt having made the external Government of his *Catholisk Church* ſuitable to the Government of his Univerſal Monarchy over all the World, hath by the Inſtitution of the Holy Ghoſt order'd to be placed in every Kingdom (as before in another place we have obſerved) Archbiſhops, Biſhops, and inferiour Miniſters, to govern the particular Churches therein planted; Prieſts, Miniſters in every particular Pariſh, and over them Biſhops within their ſeveral Dioceſſes; as likewiſe Archbiſhops to have the Inſpection and charge over all the reſt, according to the Platform ordain'd (in ſubſtance) by himſelf in the Old Teſtament; as he hath in like manner appointed Kings and Sovereign Princes, with their inferiour Magiſtrates of divers ſorts, to rule and govern his People under him, in every Kingdom, Country, and Sovereign Principality; ſome of their ſaid inferiour Magiſtrates having Authority from their Soveraigns in particular Pariſhes, ſome in Hundreds, ſome in Shires or Countries, and ſome in Governments of larger extents; there being amongſt them all divers degrees of Perſons, one over another; and their Kings and Sovereign Princes, excelling them all in Power and Authority, as the Perſons appointed by God, to rule and direct all their Subjects; of what calling ſoever, in the right uſe of the Authority and Magiſtracy, which they have committed unto them.

And we cannot but wonder, as well at our ſaid *Jeſuit*, where he ſaith, That although there be but one,

and

and proper Head of the Church, which is Chrift, that governeth the fame fpiritually; yet fhe hath need of one vifible Head, or otherwife the Bifhop of *Rome*, and all other Bifhops, Paftors, Doctors, and Minifters, were needlefs; as likewife at our Countryman *Harding*, who faith (as is above-noted) that if God had not deferred to one Man, that is, to *Peter* and his Succeffors, the Rule and Government of the Church, he fhould have brought, amongft his faithful People, that unruly Confufion which is called an Anarchy. For, were thefe their vain conceits and imaginations true, then would it by the fame reafon follow, that albeit there be but one, and proper Monarch over all the World (which is Chrift that created it) yet the fame hath need of one vifible Monarch; or otherwife Emperours, and all other Kings, Princes, and civil Magiftrates, were needlefs; or otherwife, Chrift fhould have left amongft his People throughout the World, that unruly confufion and deftruction of all Commonwealths, fo much abhorred of Princes, which the *Grecians* call an Anarchy; which is a ftate, for lack of order in Governours, without any Government at all. The fondnefs of which two confequents, do fo plainly argue the folly and falfhood of the two former, as we need no other refutation of them. For if all Chriftian Kingdoms, and Soveraign Princes, would banifh the Pope, with his Ufurped Authority, as the Monarchy of *Britany* hath done, and retain under them the Apoftolical Form of Church-Government, by Archbifhops and Bifhops, with other degrees of Minifters (as before we have divers times fpecified) they fhould find the Churches, in their feveral Dominions, as well governed by them (the faid Archbifhops and Bifhops) without one Pope to rule the whole *Catholick Church*; as they have experience of the fufficiency of their own Regal and Soveraign Form of Government in their feveral Kingdoms and Countries, notwithftand-

ing

ing there be no one Monarch over all the World to command or direct them. And for an Example not to be controlled, to make this good that here we affirm; we leave unto them God's own Form both of Temporal and Ecclefiaſtical Government, eſtabliſhed by himſelf amongſt his own people the *Jews*. Nay, why ſhould we doubt, but that Kings and Soveraign Princes, notwithſtanding the Miſts and Darkneſs wherewith the Biſhops of *Rome* have daily ſought to dim their Eyes, have had long ſince a Glimpſe of this Light, and Truth? About 400. and ſome odd Years ſince, in the latter end of the Reign of *Henry the ſecond*, and in the days of *Richard the firſt*, both of them Kings of *England*, firſt *Baldwin* and then *Hubertus* being Archbiſhops of *Canterbury*, there was a mighty Controverſy betwixt them and the Biſhops of *Rome*, about the erecting of a new Cathedral Church in *Lambeth* ; the ſaid Kings and Archbiſhops having a reſolution utterly to baniſh out of this Kingdom the Popes Authority, if the Monks of *Canterbury* in their Allegation to Pope *Celeſtine*, againſt the ſaid Cathedral Church, did inform him truly. Theſe are their Words, as they are recorded by *Reginaldus*, one of the ſaid Monks (as it ſeemeth) then living, who hath written a whole Book of that matter. *In tantum enim jam opus proceſſit, quod ibi ordinatur Decanus, Præpoſitus, & pluſquam quadraginta Canonici de Bonis Cantuarienſis Eccleſiæ fundati, genere nobiles, divitiis affluentes, cognati Regum & Pontificum. Quidam ipſi Regi adhærent; quidam Fiſci negotia adminiſtrantes, familiares Epiſcopi, & iiſdem confœderati. Adverſuss tantos & tales quid poterit Eccleſia Cantuarienſis? Certè timendum eſt non ſolùm Cantuarienſis Eccleſiæ, ſed (quod Deus avertat) ne hujus rei occaſione ſedis Apoſtolicæ Autoritati in partibus Anglicanis derogetur. Quùm enim fundaretur Canonica illa, vox erat omnium, ſententia ſingulorum, ut ibi eſſent Epiſcopi, quaſi Cardinales; Archiepiſcopus ſederet quaſi Papa ; & ibi omnis* Reginaldi Ep. de temp. Baldwini p. 98. col. 1.

uls Appellatio subsisteret & querela. Hoc *quidem* Rex *Henricus machinabatur, approbant quamplures Episcopi; hâc de causâ (ut dictum est) ut possent de sub jugo sanctæ Romanæ Ecclesiæ colla excutere.* Now the building of the said Church is so forward, that there is ordain'd there a Dean, a Provost, and more than 40. Canons, founded of the Goods of the Church of Canterbury, by birth Noblemen, abounding in Wealth, Allies of the King, and of the Bishops. Some of them do adhere to the King; some have Offices in the Exchequer; all of them familiar Friends to the Bishops, and of a Confederacy with them. Against such and so great Persons, what is the Church of Canterbury able to do? Certainly it is to be feared, not only that the Church of Canterbury shall hereby be overthrown; but that upon this occasion, the Authority of the Apostolical See (which God forbid) shall in England be greatly diminish'd und prejudiced. For when this Canonry or Cathedral Church was founded, it was the common fame, and the opinion of every Man, that it was founded to this end, that Bishops should be there as it were Cardinals, and that the Archbishop should sit amongst them as Pope, and that there all Appeals and complaints should be determined. This assuredly was plotted by King Henry, and the same very many Bishops do allow, for this cause or end, that so they might deliver their Necks from under the Yoke of the Holy Church of Rome.

Again after the Death of *Celestin* the Fourth, the Cardinals being at so great a Dissention amongst themselves as that they could not agree for the space of a Year and nine Months, who should succeed him; both the Emperour and the *French* were greatly moved and offended therewith. The Emperour finding his advice unto them to hasten their Choice, to be despised and scorned, and how dishonestly some of them had broken their Promises and Oaths unto him made in that behalf; he gathered a great Host, and dealt sharply with them. And from *France* they received a Message, that

if

if they continued to dally, as they did, in prolonging the choice of a new Pope, they would utterly leave *Rome*, and choose to themselves a Pope of their own, to govern the Churches on this side the *Alps*. Hereof *Matthew Paris* writeth thus. " *Per idem tempus mise-* [Matt. Paris ad annum 1243.]
" *runt Franci folennes Nuncios ad Curiam Romanam; fig-*
" *nificantes perfuadendo præcisè, & efficaciter, ut ipfi Car-*
" *dinales Papam ritè eligentes Univerfali Ecclefiæ folatium*
" *Paſtora'e maturiùs providerent: vel ipfi Franci propter*
" *negligentiam eorum de fibi eligendo, & providendo fummo*
" *Pontifice citra Montes, cui obedire tenerentur, quantocyùs*
" *contrectarent.* About that time the State of France did send their solemn *Meſſengers* to the Court of Rome, ſignifying unto them, and perſwading them, precisely and effectually, that either the Cardinals ſhould more ſpeedily provide for the *Univerſal Church*, her *Paſtoral Comfort*, by their due choice of a new Pope: or elſe they themſelves (the French) becauſe of their negligence, would forthwith fall into deliberation of chooſing and providing for themſelves a Pope on this ſide the Mountains, whom they might be bound to obey. Thus the ſaid Hiſtory. Whereby, as alſo by the former words of the Monks of *Canterbury* it is very evident, that both *England* and *France*, was long ſince in deliberation to have abandon'd the Authority of the Biſhops of *Rome* out of both thoſe Kingdoms, as finding no neceſſity of the Univerſal overſwaying power of the *Roman* Papacy; and that the Churches within their ſeveral Countries and Territories, might receive as great benefit and comfort, by the Eccleſiaſtical Government of their own Archbiſhops, in every reſpect, as ever they had done from the Biſhops of *Rome*. For as it may truly be ſaid, not of one King to govern all the World, but of every particular King in his own Kingdom; ſo may it be truly affirmed, not of one Pope to govern the whole *Catholick Church*, but of every Archbiſhop, in any National Church and Province, to rule

rule and direct the same; that under the Government of one (*viz.* of Kings for temporal Causes, and of Archbishops for Ecclesiastical Causes) there is the best order, the greatest strength, the most stability for continuance, and the easiest manner and form of ruling.

We have spoken hitherto of the Government of the Church, especially as it was in the Apostles times and afterward, for the space of 300. years, when the civil Magistrates were Enemies unto it. Whereby we do infer, that if the particular Churches, setled then almost in every Country and Nation throughout the World, had so good success, when there were no Christian Magistrates, nor had any assistance of the temporal Sword, for the strengthning of their Ecclesiastical Government, but only Ministers, to teach and direct their Parishioners in the ways of Godliness; and Bishops over them in every Diocess, to oversee and rule, as well the Ministers, as the several People committed to their charge, that they taught no new Doctrine, or ran into Schisms; and Archbishops over them all, in every National Church and Province, for the moderating and appeasing of such oppositions and dissentions, as might otherwise have risen amongst the Bishops, and so consequently have wrought great distraction betwixt their *Diocesan* Churches: how much more then are the said particular Churches like to flourish and prosper, under such a Form of Ecclesiastical Government, wherein the Christian Magistrate is become to be, as the chief Member of the Church, so the chief Governour of it; to keep as well the said Archbishops within their bounds and limits, as all the rest of the Clergy, and Christians, Bishops, Ministers, and Parishioners, that every one, in their several places, may execute and discharge their distinct Offices and Duties which are committed unto them.

We shall have fit occasion hereafter to speak of the
Authority

Authority of Christian Princes in Causes Ecclesiastical: here we do only still prosecute the Government of the Church (when temporal Kings and Princes were her great and mortal Enemies) and the Folly, (if not the obstinacy) of our Adversaries, who either see it not, or will not acknowledge it, that peace and quietness may as well be preserved, in all the Churches in the World, by Archbishops and Bishops, without one Pope to govern them all ; as by Kings and Sovereign Princes in all the Kingdoms and temporal Governments in the World, without one temporal Monarch to rule and oversway them. For our Adversaries shall never be able to prove, that it may be ascribed (as we have before said) more to any want of discretion and due Providence in our Saviour Christ, that he hath not appointed the Pope to govern the *Catholick* Church, than that he hath not assigned the Government of the whole World to one King or Emperour. Rather it is to be attributed to their audacious temerity and presumption, that will either enforce our Saviour Christ to be contented with that Form of Government in his Church, which they think good to assign unto him, and so make him to divide stakes (as the Phrase is) with the Bishops of *Rome*; or else to be reputed amongst them for a Person of little Discretion and Providence, and to have dealt absurdly, in ordering and setling the external Government of his Church, as he had ordered and setled the external Government of his Universal Kingdom, over all the Kings and Princes in the World. Which profane, wicked, and blasphemous proceedings with Christ, will (no doubt) in short time, receive a heavy Judgment ; in that, although the Man of sin hath long wrought in a mystery, and taken upon him, for his time, and so every one of his Successors, during their Lives, to *sit in the Temple of God*, vaunting, that the said Temple, or Spiritual Kingdom

Kingdom of Chrift, is wholly at his Command; yet now he beginneth to be revealed and difclofed to be that Impoftor, that by the affiftance of Satan, hath with power, and figns, and lying wonders, in all deceiveablenefs and unrighteoufnefs, long abufed the Chriftian World, and is confequently to be confumed by our Saviour Chrift, with the Spirit of his mouth. In the mean while, and till this work be throughly effected, we are not to cenfure Chrift, either for his Difcretion, or Divine Providence, but indeed to admire and magnify them both; confidering, that by his Government, both of the Univerfal World, as he is the Son of God, and of his *Catholick Church*, as he is the Redeemer of it (in fuch manner and form as we have before expreffed, by feveral Kings and Priefts, within their Kingdoms, Provinces, and Dioceffes) he hath left unto them certain general rules and motives, which being diligently obferved, do tend to the univerfal good and prefervation, both of the one and the other; though they have no affiftance therein from the Bifhops of *Rome*. For as it is an apt and good reafon to perfwade all Kings and Kingdoms, to live quietly with their Neighbour Princes, and Nations, and to be at a firm League and Friendfhip with them, becaufe they have all but one Heavenly King, are Members and Subjects of one Univerfal Kingdom; have, or ought to have, but one moral Faith, one rule of Juftice, one fquare for Equity, one nature of Truth, one moral Law, one Kind, Form, and nature, of all the feveral Virtues, both Moral and Intellectual; one natural Inftinct, to know God, and to worfhip him, and one Form and Rule of mutual love and affection: So the particular Churches, difperfed over the World, when they had fmall Comfort from the civil Magiftrate, held themfelves bound to have a fpecial care one over another, that matters of Religion might proceed

ceed by one rule, with mutual Agreement and Uniformity, for avoiding of Schifms; in that they well knew, they had all but one Redeemer and Saviour, one Heavenly Spiritual King, or Archbifhop, were all of them Members of one myftical Body, whereof Chrift was the Head, had all of them but one Faith, one Baptifm, one Spiritual Food, one Hope, one Bond of Charity, one Redemption, and one Everlafting Inheritance in the Life to come. Which were fuch Arguments of mutual Confociation in thofe days, as when any great matters of importance did fall out in any one Country, through the willfulnefs and obftinacy of Hereticks and crafty Seducers of the People, which perhaps were countenanced with fome of ftrength and greater power than could eafily be withftood; their Neighbour Churches adjoining, did fometimes affift them, by their Letters, with the beft counfel they could give them; and fometimes did fend fome efpecial Learned Men unto them, for the better fuppreffing of thofe Evils; and fometimes (when occafions fell out thereunto moving) fundry Archbifhops and Bifhops of feveral Countries, with other learned Priefts, and Perfons of principal note, did as they might, for fear of danger, meet together, and upon due and mature deliberation, did fo order and determine of matters, as thereby Herefies and Contentions were ftill fuppreffed, and the Churches in thofe Countries received great comfort and quietnefs. And if in thofe troublefome times the peace of the Church were thus preferved; how much more, now under Chriftian Magiftrates, may it be ftrengthned, upheld, and maintain'd without the Pope; not only within their feveral Kingdoms, but likewife throughout (in effect) all thefe Weftern Parts of the World, if Chriftian Kings and Soveraign Princes would agree together for a general Council; to the end, that all thofe Herefies, Errours, Impoftures and Prefumptions,

wherewith

wherewith the Church of Chrift hath been long, and is now miferably fhaken, and difturbed, might be at the laft utterly fuppreffed and extinguifhed?

Many other means might here be alledged, to fhew how the ftate of Chriftian Religion is to be upheld and maintained, without any affiftance from the Bifhop of *Rome*. But our purpofe being in this place to refemble and compare the government of the *Catholick Church*, with the Univerfal Government of the Son of God, over the whole World; We hold it fufficient to obferve, That every National Church, may as well fubfift of her felf, without one Univerfal Bifhop, as every Kingdom may do without one general Monarch. Neverthelefs we acknowledge, that in this particular Tractate we have been very tedious; and it may be thought perhaps by fome, that our pains therein is altogether fuperfluous; becaufe many of our Adverfaries do (in effect) acknowledge, that there is the like neceffity of one Emperour to govern all the World, as there is of one Pope to have the overfight and ordering of the whole *Catholick Church*. Indeed, upon the fifting of the ufurped Authority of the Bifhops of *Rome*, our Adverfaries finding, that by their Arguments to bolfter up his faid Authority, the Erection of one Man to govern the World in temporal Caufes, is as neceffarily to be inforced, as of one Pope to govern the whole Church in Ecclefiaftical Caufes; they are grown to this moft admirable Infolency, and moft high prefumption, as that they dare affirm, and do take upon them, without all modefty, to maintain it, That the Pope is both the Monarch of the *Catholick Church*, and the Emperour of all the World. Which myftery of theirs is thus managed, and by piece-meal unfolded after this fort: *viz.* That to eafe the Pope, left he might be oppreffed with multitude of affairs, if he fhould take upon him, in his own Perfon, to govern the whole World,

as

as he doth direct the especial affairs of the *Catholick Church*; they do assign unto him Power and Authority to create and delegate under him, as his *Feudatary*, or Vassal, this one supposed Emperour, to whom (they say) he may commit the special Execution of his temporal Sword, to be drawn and put up, at his direction and commandment. And for this one base Emperour over all the World, many are now as busy, as others are, to maintain the Pope's Supremacy over the whole *Catholick Church*. Now to prove, that the Pope hath Universal Dominion over all the World *temporaliter*, temporally, and likewise sufficient Power to institute and appoint one Emperour under him, as his Substitute, to rule the whole World, they use this Argument. "*Summus Pontifex instituit, ac confirmat Imperatorem: sed Imperator habet Dominium universale temporaliter in toto Mundo: Ergo & Papa habet hoc idem Dominium temporaliter.* The *Bishop of* Rome *doth ordain, and confirm the Emperour: but the Emperour hath universal Dominion temporally in the whole World: therefore the Pope hath the very same temporal Dominion.* And about ten years since, one *Andrew Hoy*, the *Greek* Professor at *Doway*, made an Oration, *De novâ apud Europæos Monarchiæ pro tempore utilitate*; taking upon him to prove, that the King of *Spain* was the fittest Person of all the Kings and Princes in *Europe*, to be advanced unto this great Monarchy.

Dr. Marta de Jurisd. par. 1. c. 20. Carerius.

Marta ibid.

But what should we trouble our selves with this point? The King of *Spain* (we suppose) will greatly scorn to be the Pope's Vassal, and the Emperour that now is, or that shall succeed him hereafter, as likewise all the Kings and Princes in the World, may see most evidently, how grosly and shamefully they are abused, and how notably they neglect the greatness of their own Callings; especially they, who have been heretofore, or shall be hereafter Emperours, in that they do
intermeddle

intermeddle any thing at all with the Pope, or receive from him, either their Confirmation or Coronation; in that thereby he prefumeth moſt ridiculouſly, and without any ſhew of truth, to challenge them for his Servants and Vaſſals. It hath been before ſhewed, by the Judgment of the *Cardinalized Jeſuit*, That the Biſhops of *Rome* have no temporal Poſſeſſions at all; but ſuch as they have received from the Emperour, and other Kings and Soveraign Princes. In conſideration whereof, ſeeing, that now they inſult ſo notably over them all, both Princes, Kings, and Emperours, being ſo far from acknowledging themſelves to be the Emperour's Subjects, or to hold their ſaid Poſſeſſions, either of him, or of any King, that beſtowed them upon them: We do verily think, that the ſaid Princes, Kings, and Emperours, who have been ſo beneficial to the ſaid Biſhops, ſhall never ſhew themſelves to be of that Princely Magnanimity, and Proweſs, which their high places do require, nor free their Sceptres from the thraldom and baſe ſubjection to their uſurped Authority; until either they take from them, what before they gave them, or bring them to a more dutiful acknowledgment of their Duties unto them. And what we ſay of the Popes, we likewiſe do hold concerning all the Clergy beſides, in *Europe*, or elſewhere; that, if they ſhall either withdraw themſelves from their ſubjection unto their temporal Soveraigns, under whom they live, or deny to hold the Poſſeſſions of their ſeveral Churches of their ſaid Soveraigns, or to do them Homage for the ſame; they may lawfully, in our Judgments, not only reſume the ſaid Poſſeſſions into their own hands, but likewiſe proceed againſt them as Rebels and Traytors, according to the Form of their ſeveral Laws. But this is a Digreſſion. For in the beginning of this Chapter, we undertook to deal with thoſe only, who, though they maintain the

Pope's

Popes general Supremacy over the Catholick Church; yet they deny upon many weighty reasons, that God did ever ordain any one Emperour to govern all the World. But how long they will deny it, we know not; in that the principal *Jesuit* himself writeth thus: "*Utrum expediret omnes Provincias Mundi*, &c. *Whether it were expedient that all the Provinces in the World should be govern'd by one chief King in things Politick, although the same be not necessary, it may be a Question: Mihi tamen omnino expedire videtur, si possit eò perveniri sine injustitiâ, & bellicis cladibus: Yet it seemeth to me expedient, if such a Monarchical Government over all the World, might be gotten without Injustice, and such Calamities and Miseries as usually follow War.* What this *Jesuit* doth encline unto, it is hereby evident: But in that he confesseth, that such a Monarchical civil Government is not necessary, that is enough for our purpose, because hereby it likewise followeth, (as before we have shewed) that the Government of the Pope over the whole Church is, in every respect, as little necessary.

Bell. de Rom. Pont. l. 1. c. 9. §. Utrum.

CAN. X.

AND therefore if any Man shall affirm, under colour of any thing that is in the Scriptures, or that can be truly grounded upon natural Reason, or Philosophy, That our Saviour Christ should have shewed himself to have had no discretion, except he had left one chief Bishop to have govern'd all the Churches in the World: or, that except he appointed one to the said end, he should, as a Person void of Providence, have left his Faithful People in a miserable confusion, and without any Government at all: or, that any of all the Arguments, that may be deduced from Philosophy, and natural Reason, to prove, that one Man ought to have the Government of the Whole Catholick Church in spiritual Causes, are not as forcible to prove, that one King or Emperour ought to have the Rule and Government over the Whole World in Causes temporal: or, that any of the Philosophers ever meant to have their reasons (alledged by them to prove, that in every particular Country, the Monarchical

narchical Form of Temporal Government was the best) to be extended to prove, that there ought to be either one Bishop over all the Catholick Church (whereof they had no knowledge) or one Emperour over all the World: or, that, because all Men have their beginning from Adam, it doth not as well follow, that there ought to be one Emperour to govern all the World, as one Bishop over the whole Catholick Church: or, that Aaron was any more a Figure of St. Peter, and his Successors, that they severally, in their times, should govern the whole Church, than King David was of Augustus the Emperour, and his Successors, that they severally, in their times, should have committed unto them the Government of the whole World: or, that the resemblances in the Scriptures of the Church unto an Host well order'd, to a humane Body, to a Kingdom, to a Fold, to an House, to a Ship, may not fitly be applied as well to the Universal Kingdom of Christ over all the World, as unto the Church; and so consequently as well to our Saviour Christ, as he is the Governour of the whole World, that he is the General of that Host, the Head of that Body, the King of that Kingdom, the Shepherd of that Flock, the Housholder of that Family, and the Pilot of that Ship; as may these Titles be ascribed unto him, as he is the only Archbishop of the whole Church, viz. That he is the only General of this Host, the only Head of this Body, the only King of this Kingdom, the only Shepherd of this Flock, the only Housholder of this Family, and the only Pilot of this Ship: or, that the said Unities, concerning the Universal Kingdom of Christ, are not of as great validity to prove, that there ought to be one temporal King under him, to govern his Universal Kingdom over all the World; as are the other Unities, touching the Church, to prove, that there must be one Bishop under him, to govern all the particular Churches in the World: or that, because Kings, when they have occasion to be absent from their Kingdoms, do commonly appoint some Vice-Roy, to Rule their People until their return; it thereupon followeth, that Christ, supplying his corporal absence from his Spiritual Kingdom the Church, by the comfortable presence of the Holy Ghost, was

of

of necessity to leave one carnal Man to be his Vicar-General over his said Spiritual Kingdom: or, that seeing our Saviour Christ held it expedient for his Catholick Church, that he should deprive her of his corporal presence, that she might be ruled by the Holy Ghost; it is not to be thought great presumption for any Man to tell us, that his corporal presence is necessary for the Government of the said Catholick Church, as if he meant to put the Holy Ghost out of Possession: or, that either the said one Universal Kingdom of Christ (the King, and Creator of it) is otherwise visible upon the Earth, than by the particular Kingdoms, and several kinds of Governments in it (and perhaps in a sort, and by Representation, when some Neighbour Kings, either in Person, or by their Ambassadours, may be met together for the good of their several Kingdoms:) or, that the said one Catholick Church of Christ (as he is the chief Bishop over all) is otherwise visible on the Earth, than by the several, and particular Churches in it, and sometimes by general and free Councils lawfully assembled: or, that it is a better

consequent,

consequent, that if the Catholick Church have no visible Head, all other Bishops, Doctors, Pastors, and Ministers, are needless; than if one should say, because there is no one King to govern all the World, therefore there is no use of Emperours, Kings, and Soveraign Princes, or civil Magistrates: or, that it doth more follow, that Christ should have left his Faithful People in a confused Anarchy, except he had left St. Peter, and his Successors to govern the Whole Church; than it doth, that the Whole World hath been left by him in a Confusion, without any Government in it, in that he hath not left one Universal Emperour: or, that the intolerable Pride of the Bishop of Rome, for the time still being, through the advancement of himself, by many sleights, stratagems, and false Miracles, over the Catholick Church, (the Temple of God) as if he were God himself, doth not argue him plainly to be the Man of Sin, mentioned by the Apostle: or, that every National Church, planted according to the Apostle's Platform, may not by the means, which Christ hath ordained, as well sub-

sist

sist of it self, without one Universal Bishop, as every Kingdom may do under the Government of their several Kings, without one general Monarch; He doth greatly Erre.

The End of the Second Book.

LIB. III.

CAP. I.

IN purſuing our intended Courſe through the Old Teſtament, and until the deſtruction of *Jeruſalem*, we overſlipt, and paſſed by the fulneſs of that time, wherein the Son of God (the Maker and Governour of all the World) our Lord, and Saviour *Jeſus Chriſt*, was conceived by the Holy Ghoſt, and born of the Virgin *Mary*. So as now we are to return back, and proſecute our ſaid Courſe, as we find the true grounds thereof are laid down, confirmed, and practiſed in the New Teſtament. At our Entrance into which Courſe, We confeſs our ſelves to be indeed greatly aſtoniſhed, conſidering the ſtrange impediments, and mighty ſtumbling blocks, which through long practice, and incredible Ambition, are caſt in our way [in that we find the Eſtate of that Church (which would rule over all) to be degenerated in our days, as far in effect from her primary, and Apoſtolical Inſtitution and Rules; as we have ſhewed before, the Eſtate of the *Jewiſh* Church, to have ſwerved through the like Pride and Ambition, from that excellent Condition, wherein ſhe was firſt eſtabliſhed, and afterward preſerved, and beautified, by *Moſes*, and King *David*, with the reſt of his moſt worthy and godly Succeſſors.] For except we ſhould condemn the Old Teſtament (as many ancient Hereticks have done) and thereupon overthrow all which hitherto we have built; and not that only, but ſhould furthermore, either approve of their groſs Impiety, who read the Scriptures of the New Teſtament, as if they

Aug. de Hæreſ. c. 45.

they were falsified and corrupted, and by receiving and rejecting as much of them as they list, do prefer before them (as not containing in them all necessary Truth for Man's Salvation) certain obscure and *Apocryphal* Writings: Or should our selves impiously imagine, that the New Testament (as now we have it) was but a rough Draught, and a fit project compiled for the time by the Apostles, to be afterward better order'd, polished, and supplied with certain humane Traditions and Doctrines, by some of their Successors: We can see no sufficient Warrant, or probable reason, why the Bishop of *Rome*, should take upon him (as he doth) so eminent and supream Authority, over all the Kingdoms and Churches in the World, to rule them, direct them, bestow them, and chop and change them, under pretence of Religion, as he from time to time shall think fit. Sure we are, if the Scriptures may retain their ancient Authority, and continue to be true Rulers, and principal Directors to all Apostolical Bishops; that in them there will not be found any shadows, or steps, of those so high and lofty conceits. To the proof whereof, before we address our selves; We have thought it very expedient, for the carriage of our course more perspicuously and clearly; to make it apparent, by what degrees and practices the Bishops of *Rome* have proceeded in aspiring to that Soveraignty and Greatness which now they have attained.

Placet eis.

John Overall, Prolocutor.

CAP.

CAP. II.

AS it was said long since; *Religion brought forth Riches, and the Daughter devoured the Mother*: So may it very truly be said in these days, The *Empire begat the Papacy, and the Son hath devoured his Father*. For (as we suppose, by the Effects) no sooner did the Bishops of *Rome*, even in the first times of Persecution, get any rest and courage; but they began to think with themselves, That they were as able to govern all the Churches in the Empire, as the Emperours themselves were to govern all the Kingdoms and Nations, then subject unto them : and that *Rome* was as fit a Seat for such a Bishop, as it was for so great an Emperour. Some Seeds of this Ambition began to sprout there, when *Victor* presumed to threaten the *Greek* Churches, concerning the Feast of Easter : although *Irenæus*, then living, did greatly dislike it ; and the Bishops of *Asia*, little regarding him in that behalf, said, They nothing cared for such his threats. And it was not, we suppose, an idle conceit of one, who writing an abstract of the Bishops of *Rome*, and comparing those that were before *Victor*, with those that followed, saith thus, *In his Papis abundat Spiritus* ; *in posterioribus malesuada Caro* : *The Spirit abounded in the former Popes* ; *but in those that succeeded him, the seducing Flesh*.

Some more Light whereof, as also of the said undermining Ambition, brake out (little above 50. Years after *Victor*) in *Cornelius*, the 22th Bishop of *Rome*. Who notwithstanding the great trouble he had at home with his Fellow-Counter-Pope *Novatianus*, could find such leisure (under pretence of Importunity and threatnings) as to entertain a complaint against St. *Cyprian*, which was preferr'd unto him by one *Felicissimus*, a

Euseb. l. 5. c. 24. Id. ib. c. 23.

Geo. Vicelius Epit. Rom. Pontif.

Priest, sent to *Rome* from *Fortunatus*, an Usurping and Schismatical Bishop; whom together with *Felicissimus*, St. *Cyprian*, with other *African* Bishops, had lawfully excommunicated, for sundry their lewd and ungodly actions. With which injurious course, St. *Cyprian* being made acquainted, and somewhat moved, he writ to *Cornelius* an Epistle, wherein he justifieth his Proceedings, and disliketh those of his Adversaries. First, because there was a Decree amongst them, and that also Equal and Just, That *every Man's Cause should be there heard where the fault was committed*. Secondly, For that a Portion of the Flock was committed to several Bishops, which every one of them was to rule and govern, being to yield an account of his actions to God. Whereupon he inferreth thus; saying, " It doth not " become those, over whom we bear rule, to run gad-" ding about, nor by their crafty and deceitful rash-" ness, to break the united Concord of Bishops; but " there to plead their Cause, where they may have "both accusers and witness of their Crime: Unless " (saith he) the Authority of the Bishops of *Africk*, doth " seem unto a few desperate and outcast Persons, to be " less than the Authority of other Bishops.

It appeareth furthermore, that for the better Government of the Churches in those times of Persecution, it was thought fit, that there should be 4. *Patriarchs*, who were to take upon them the Inspection, and especial charge of all the Bishops, Priests, and Churches, that were severally assigned unto them. In which distribution the Bishops of *Rome* got the first place; it being then thought convenient to seat their chief Bishops in the principal Cities of the *Romans*, and to grant unto them Authority in Causes Ecclesiastical, much resembling the Prerogatives, which those Cities had in Causes Temporal. Of all the *Eastern* Lieutenantships, that of *Syria* was the Chief: and therefore *Antioch*, being the Principal City of that Province, was

made

Wolfgang. La-zius Comment. Reip. Rom. l. 2. Baron. t. 1. Ann. 39.

made alſo the Seat of one of the ſaid *Patriarchs*. Afterward likewiſe *Alexandria*, exceeding much in honour the City of *Antioch*, another *Patriarch* was there placed; who, according to the Dignity of that City, had the precedency of the Patriarch of *Antioch*. Whereby we judge, that the Patriarch, or Biſhop of *Rome*, had the firſt place amongſt the reſt of the Patriarchs; becauſe *Rome* was then the chiefeſt City in the World, and the Seat of the Empire. Which point is yet more manifeſt, by theſe words of the Council of *Chalcedon*: *Sedi Veteris Romæ Patres meritò dedèrunt Primatum, quòd illa Civitas aliis imperaret.* Howbeit (this Primacy, or Precedency notwithſtanding) the Biſhop of that See, before the Council of *Nice*, confirm'd by *Conſtantine* the Emperour, was little more reſpected, than any other of the *Patriarchs*: as a principal Perſon (afterward of that Rank) teſtifieth, ſaying, *Ante Concilium Nicæ-* Æneas Sylv *num ad Romanam Eccleſiam parvus habebatur reſpectus*: Ep. 288. *Before the Council of* Nice *there was little reſpect born to the Church of* Rome: Although, we doubt not by the premiſes, but that the Biſhops thereof endeavour'd what they could to equal the Primacy of that Patriarchſhip, to the honour and dignity of that Imperial City; as by their ſubſequent practices it will more plainly appear.

Placet eis.

John Overall.

CAP. III.

COnstantine the Emperour having received the Gospel, did in his Zeal greatly advance the Dignity of the Bishops of *Rome*, by endowing of that Bishoprick with great Honour and temporal Possessions. Besides, (whether it grew from the Cunning of those Bishops, and their especial Instruments, or through the Zeal of the People, or by both those Means) it is apparent, that within some 47. Years after *Constantine*'s Death, that Bishoprick was grown to so great Wealth, as when it was void, many Troubles, Garboiles, and Contentions arose for the obtaining of it. After the Death of *Liberius*, the second Bishop after *Constantine*, such were the Tumults in *Rome* betwixt *Damasus* and *Ursinus* in striving for that Place, as there were found in the Church of *Sicininus*, slain on both sides in one day 137. Persons, and great Labour was taken before the People could be appeas'd. " Whereat (saith " the Writer of that History) I do not marvel, and that " Men should be desirous of that Preferment : conside- " ring, that when they have got it, they may ever af- " terward be secure ; they are so enriched with the Ob- " lations of Matrons; they ride abroad in their Coaches " so curiously attir'd, and in their Diet are so delicate " and profuse ; *Ut eorum Convivia Regales superent Men-* " *sas , as their Feasts exceed the Fare of Kings.* Insomuch as a desperate Heathen Man was accustomed, in scorn to *Damasus,* after he had gotten the Victory against his Adversary, to cast out these Words *Facite me Romanæ Urbis Episcopum, & ero protinus Christianus,* *make me Bishop of Rome, and I will presently become a Christian.* Which alluring Plenty and Delicacy being added to the Primacy of that Place, and to the aspiring

Ammian. Marcellinus l. 27. Alphons. Chiaccon. in vit. Damas.

Hieron. ad Pammach.

Humours

Humours of those Bishops; their Ambition began to shew it self daily more and more. Insomuch as they hardly endured that any of the other *Patriarchs* should have any extraordinary Reputation, being ever most jealous of their own. The Fathers of the *Greek* Church, met together in the General Council at *Constantinople* about 40. Years after the Death of *Constantine*, finding themselves grieved (of likelyhood) with the Proceedings of the Bishops of *Rome*; and that the Bishops of *Constantinople*, were not so much regarded in *Rome*, as they ought to have been, *(Constantinople* being then the chief Seat of the Empire) did define with one Consent, " That " as Causes did arise in any Province, the same should " be determined in the Council of the same Province. And furthermore, they made this Canon; *Constantinopolitanæ Civitatis Episcopum habere oportet Primatûs honorem post Romanum Pontificem; proptereà quòd sit Nova Roma.* With these Proceedings, the Bishops of *Rome* were afterwards (as one noteth) much discontented; as fearing (we suppose) left by these Beginnings New *Rome* might in time more prejudice old *Rome*, than they could well brook or endure. But that all Causes should be tried in the Provinces, where they did arise, it was no marvel, though they disliked it. Therefore to meet with that Inconvenience (as they might) after some distance of time, one *Apiarius* being excommunicated in *Africk*, and thereupon appealing to *Rome*, *Zosimus* the Bishop there, did very readily embrace his Cause, and without hearing of the other side, pronounced him innocent, and so absolved him. Which Fact of his was afterward approved by *Boniface* the first, and *Cælestinus* the first; pretending, as it seemeth, that as in all Civil Causes for these *Western* parts, there lay Appeals to the City of *Rome*; so in all Ecclesiastical Causes, when Men received (as they thought) Injury under any of the Patriarchs or other Bishops, they might, if they would, appeal to the Bishop of that See. And to justi-

Tripart. Hist. l. 9. c. 13.
Conc. Constant. 1. Can. 1.

Annot. in cap 5. Concil. C. P. edit. Venetiis, 1585. Surius in Concil. Chalced. Can. 28.

fie

fic that their ambitious Challenge, they forged a Canon of the Council of *Nice*, as it was directly proved in the *African* Council, holden at *Hippo*, about the Year 423. Whereupon the Bishops of the said Council (in which number St. *Augustin* was one) perceiving what the Bishops of *Rome* meant by that sleight, *viz.* that if once they might obtain a Power to receive Appeals from all the Churches within the Empire, they would shortly after grow to challenge some Universal Authority over all the said Churches: did, to prevent the same, make two Decrees; "That if any Clergyman would appeal "from their Bishops, they should not appeal but to the "*African* Councils, or to the Primates of their Province: "adding this Penalty, That if any did appeal to the "transmarine Parts, *à nullo intra Africam in Communionem suscipiatur*. And their second Decree is thus set down by *Gratian*, *Primæ sedis Episcopus non appelletur Princeps Sacerdotum, vel summus Sacerdos, aut aliquid hujusmodi; Sed tantùm primæ sedis Episcopus: Vniversalis autem, nec etiam Romanus Pontifex appelletur*. It is strange to consider, how the Bishops of *Rome* were vexed with this Council; and how from time to time they sought to discredit it: as also what Shifts and Devices their late Proctors have found out to the same Purpose; but all in vain: For the Truth of that whole Action is so manifest, as it cannot be suppressed by any such Shifts or Practices whatsoever.

Concil. Afric. per Surium. cap. 101.

Conc. Afric. Can. 92.

Distinct. 99. primæ.

Præfat. in Con. Afric. vel Carthag. 6. in Con. editis Venetiis. 1585. Sander. de Visib. Monarch. l. 7. Turrian. l. 3. pro Epistolis Pontif.

Placet eis.

John Overall.

CAP.

CAP. IV.

Although the said Council of *Africk* troubled the Bishops of *Rome*, as is abovementioned: Yet, shortly after, some other new Occasions happen'd, which stung them more sharply. For about the Year 451. when the City of *Constantinople* was grown to be in very great Honour; it seem'd good to the Fathers of the *Greek* Church, and others assembled in the General Council, holden at *Chalcedon*, to make this Canon following, " The ancient Fathers did justly grant Priviledges to the Throne of *Old Rome*, because that City bare then the chief sway: and with the same Reason " 150. godly Bishops being moved, did grant equal Priviledges to the Throne of *New Rome*, rightly judging, that the City of *Constantinople*, which was then " honoured with the Empire and Senate, should enjoy " equal Priviledges with *Old Rome*; and, that in matters " Ecclesiastical, she ought to be extolled and magnified as " well as *Rome*, being the next after her. Against this Canon Pope *Leo* stormed exceedingly; and the whole Council it self, in respect of the said Canon, is of later Years sought to be discredited. Concil. Chalced. per Surium Can. 28.

Surius in Cap. 28. Concil. Chalced.

But the great and main quarrel betwixt *New Rome* and *Old Rome*, began about the Year 586. when *John* the Patriarch of *Constantinople*, not contenting himself to have equal Priviledges with the Bishops of *Rome*, would needs be accounted the *Universal Bishop*. Which Challenge did the rather move the Bishops of *Rome*, because they found, that *Mauricius* the Emperour inclined greatly to his desire. Whereupon *Pelagius* the second, and after him *Gregorius* the first, as fearing the Issue that might ensue of that Contention, to the great prejudice of the Church of *Rome*; they blew successively both

both of them a hasty Retreat, and pretended very earnestly, that it was utterly unlawful for any Bishop to seek so great an Authority over all other Bishops and Churches. And first *Pelagius*, opposing himself against the said *John*, Patriarch of *Constantinople*, wrote

1.Epist. Pelag.
2. Tom. 2. Concil.

thus to certain Bishops: *Let none of the Patriarchs ever use this so prophane a word: For if the chief Patriarch be called Universal, the name of the other Patriarchs is derogated from them: but far be it from the mind of every faithful Man, so much as to have a Will to challenge that to himself, whereby he may seem, in any respect, how little soever, to diminish the honour of the rest of his Brethren.*

Greg. l. 4. Epist. 32. Ibid. Ep. 36. 38.

But *Gregory* in this point exceedeth. He telleth *Mauricius* the Emperour, and others, in sundry of his Epistles, *That it is against the Statutes of the Gospel, for any Man to take upon him to be called Universal Bishop: That no Bishop of* Rome *did ever admit of that name of singularity, and profane Title. That* John, *his endeavour therein,*

Ibid. Ep. 34.
Ibid. Ep. 38.

was an Argument, that the times of Antichrist drew near: That the King of Pride was at hand, and that an Army of Priests was prepared for him: and thus he concludeth, *I*

Id. l.6.Ep.30. ad Mauricium.

confidently affirm, that whosoever calleth himself Universal Bishop, or desireth so to be called, he doth in his Pride make way for Antichrist. After *Gregory* succeeded *Sabinianus*: who had so hard a conceit of *Gregory*, his Predecessor, that he was purposed to have burnt his Books, rather (as we suppose) because he had written so much against the Title of Universal Bishop, than for

Plat. in vit. Sabin. 1.

either of the Conjectures, which *Platina* mentioneth. But the Issue of the said Contention was this: *Mauricius* the Emperour being slain by *Phocas*, his Servant,

Plat. de Bonifac. 3.

and *Phocas* himself having gotten the Empire; *Boniface* the third prevail'd so far with him, after much and great Opposition, as the Emperour gave Order, that the Church of *Rome* should be called, and accounted,

Genebr. Chronol. de Bonifac. 3.

Caput omnium Ecclesiarum. Which another Man of great account amongst them in these days, reporteth after

this

this fort. *The Contention betwixt the Patriarch of* Constantinople, *and the Bishop of* Rome; *for the Primacy was again determined by* Phocas *the Emperour, pronouncing out of the old Councils and Fathers, that the Church of* Rome *should be the Head of all Churches.* For his [Again] he might well have left it out; as also his Phrases of *Councils* and *Fathers*; and therefore we prefer in this point *Platina* before him; who making neither *mention* of *Councils,* nor *Fathers,* dealeth more truly, and saith, That the Church of *Constantinople sibi vendicare conabatur,* that place, which *Boniface* obtained from the Emperour *Phocas:* and that the same was obtained upon these grounds, *viz. That whereas the Bishop of* Constantinople *insisted, eò loci primam sedem esse debere, ubi Imperii Caput esset;* It is answered by the Bishop of Rome, and his Agents, that Constantinople *was but a Colony, deduced out of the City of* Rome; *and therefore, that the City of* Rome *ought still to be accounted Caput Imperii: That the Grecians themselves, in their Letters, termed their Prince the Emperour of the Romans; and that the Citizens of* Constantinople, *were called not Grecians, but Romans.* Indeed *Platina* further saith (being peradventure of our mind) that he will omit, how the Keys of the Kingdom of Heaven were given to St. *Peter,* and so to the Roman Bishops, his Successors, and not to the Bishops of *Constantinople:* and we likewise, following his Example, as a thing impertinent to our purpose, will here omit the same. Only we do observe, that the contention betwixt the Bishop of *Rome,* and the Bishop of *Constantinople,* was *de Primatu*; and that the Bishop of *Rome* obtain'd that place by *Phocas* his means, which the Bishop of *Constantinople* did challenge to himself. Whereupon we offer to Mens Considerations, these two Arguments. Whosoever taketh upon him that Primacy, or place in the Church, which *John*, Bishop of *Constantinople,* did challenge to himself, is the forerunner of *Antichrist*: but

Plat. in Bonifac. 3.

the Bishops of *Rome* do take upon them that Primacy and place: *Ergo.* Again; Those Priests, which do adhere unto him, that taketh upon him that place and Primacy, which *John,* the Bishop of *Constantinople* did challenge to himself, are an Host prepared for the King of Pride: but all the Priests, that do adhere to the Bishop of *Rome,* do adhere unto him, that taketh upon him that Primacy and place, which *John,* the Bishop of *Constantinople,* did challenge to himself: *Ergo.* But our purpose is not to dispute: only this we add, that till this time, that the Bishop of *Rome* had prevailed so far with *Phocas,* as is aforementioned, his Predecessors, notwithstanding their great Authority, after *Constantine*'s Reign and favour with the Emperours succeeding, they behaved themselves dutifully toward them, and acknowledged them to be their Lords and Masters. But afterward, in short time, they left those Phrases, and began to call the Emperours their Sons. To which alteration, a very worthy Man taking exception; he is answered by another of many good parts (it must be confessed) after this sort. St. *Gregory* might call *Mauricius* his Lord, either of Courtesie, or of Custom; and yet our holy Father, *Pius* the Fourth, shall not be bound to do the like; in consideration, that the Custom hath long since been discontinued.

Innocent. 3. Epistc. Atinacensi in l. 5. Decret. Constitut. Bishop *Jewel*'s Defence of his Apol. Part 4. Dr. *Harding* ibid.

Placet eis.

Jo. Overall.

CAP.

CAP. V.

ALthough when the Bishops of *Rome*, after much opposition, had obtain'd their desires for their Primacy beforementioned, they might well enough (as we suppose) have been contented: Yet forasmuch as still they remain'd in greater subjection to the Emperours, than they thought was agreeable with their greatness, their aspiring mind rested not there; but began shortly after to cast about, how they might in their places be independent and absolute. For the compassing whereof they took hold of every occasion, that might serve, or be wrested, and drawn to that purpose. At the first receiving of the Gospel, Men are ever, for the most part, very zealous, and great Favourers of the Ministry. In the Apostles times they *sold their lands and possessions, and laid the price of them at the Apostles feet.* St. *Paul* was received by the *Galatians,* as *an Angel of God;* yea, as *Jesus Christ:* and such was their love toward him, that to *have done him good they would have plucked out their Eyes, and given them unto him.* When the Emperours of *Rome* became Christians, they did exceed in this behalf; especially towards the Bishops of that See: bestowing upon them very great riches and ample possessions. Of all which zealous Dispositions, benefits and favours they ever made, above all other Bishops, their greatest advantage, by imploying the same to the advancement of their greatness. Wherein they were furthermore very much helped, and further'd by the Authority which the Emperours gave unto them in temporal Causes: holding them for their Gravity, Learning and Discretion very meet, and fit Persons in their own absence from *Rome,* to do them that way very great service.

Act. 4. 34.
Gal. 4. 14, 15.

Besides,

Besides, if we shall deal sincerely and truly (as we hold our selves always bound, and more strictly in a cause of this Importance;) we must needs confess, that it hath been the manner of Divines, from the Apostles times almost, to magnify and extol the worthiness and excellency of their own calling: which was a very commendable and necessary course in many (the ordinary contempt of the Ministry consider'd) and had been so in all of them, if they had not therewith depressed too much the Dignity and preheminence of Kings and Princes. Comparisons in such Cases were ever worthily held to be odious. Bishops and Priests, might without any just reprehension, have been resembled to Gold, to the Sun, and to what else is excellent; without comparing the highest Magistrates, under God, in respect of themselves, to the Moon, to Lead, and to some other things of such like base Estimation. And we doubt not, but that they would have refrain'd from such Comparisons, if they could have foreseen, how the Bishops of *Rome* would to the disgrace and dishonour of civil Authority, have wrested and perverted them: notwithstanding, that their Inferences thereupon have ever had more shew and probability, than substance and truth; except we shall say, that the Callings of Schoolmasters and Physicians, are in Dignity to be preferr'd before all other Temporal Callings, because the end of the one is the instructing of Mens understandings, and of the other, Health; which either are, or ought to be, both of them in their kinds, of greater Estimation, than any other things whatsoever.

We shall not need to trouble our selves with the citing of any Authorities, to prove how eagerly the Bishops of *Rome* (especially after *Boniface* the Third had obtained of *Phocas* the said Supremacy) have pressed the same Comparisons; It is so evident, both in their own Writings, and likewise generally in all their Treatises,

tises, who from time to time, have laboured with all their force and might, to advance, above all other Authority upon Earth, the Soveraignty of that See.

Placet eis.

John Overall.

CAP. VI.

ALbeit the former occasions (as they were handled) and particularly the device last before specified, wrought very much in the hearts of the simpler sort, to the debasing of the Imperial and Regal Authority, in respect of the Spiritual; and that it was therefore prosecuted and amplified, with all the skill and rhetorick that could be: Yet there was another matter, which troubled the Bishops of *Rome* exceedingly, and never gave them rest until they had prevailed in it; as if without it they had gained little by their *Primacy*. It seemeth, that *Constantine* the Great, when he left *Rome*, notwithstanding his especial benefits and favours to the Bishops of that See, did in his wisdom think it fit, that none should be advanced to that Bishoprick without the Emperour's consent. For the better manifestation whereof, it is to be observed, that whilst the Bishops of *Rome* were labouring so earnestly for their Supremacy, till *Phocas*'s time, the City of *Rome* had been four times surprised by divers barbarous Nations, *An.* 413. by *Alaricus*, the second King of the *Goths, Innocentius* the First being then Bishop, *An.* 457. by *Gensericus*, the Leader of the *Vandalls, Leo* the First being then Bishop, *An.* 470. or thereabouts, by *Odoacer, Simplicius* being then Bishop, *An.* 493. or thereabouts, by *Theodoricus*, and the *East Goths, Gelasius* the First being then Bishop; and was again, by *Belisarius*,

Genebr. Chronol.

the

the Captain of *Justinian* the Emperour, recover'd out of their hands, about the year 537. *Sylverius* being then Bishop. By all which attempts of the said barbarous Nations, although the Empire received great detriment; yet the Bishops of *Rome* had leisure to contend for Superiority; because the said barbarous Nations, being Christians, and very superstitious, did sometimes greatly honour them, and rather admired their Pomp and State, than sought any ways to impeach it. Which caused, as it seemeth, that the Bishops of *Rome*, at the last, began to favour them more than they did their Emperours. Insomuch, as *An.* 536. the said *Sylverius* obtained that Bishoprick (as one noteth) *Theodohato Gothorum Rege jubente; cùm anteà non Regum, sed Imperatorum autoritas soleret intervenire: by the Commandment of* Theodohatus, *whereas before, in the choice of the Bishops of* Rome, *the Authority of the Emperours, and not of those Kings, had been usually obtained.* Whereupon when *Belisarius* had recovered the City from the *Goths*, and was inform'd by certain sworn Witnesses, that the said *Sylverius* was plotting, how he might render it again unto the *Goths*; he the said *Belisarius* removed him from that See, and placed *Vigilius* in his room. Whereof the Emperour being advertised, did approve greatly that which *Belisarius* had done; and took a strict Order with *Vigilius*, that no Bishop of *Rome* should thenceforward be consecrated, until the Emperour had approved of him, and confirmed his Election: So as thereby the Emperours, (having then their Residence at *Constantinople*) might be always assured of the Qualities and Dispositions of the new Bishops, whose Authority then began to be great: Lest otherwise some factious Person, or Enemy of the Emperours, being advanced to that See, the City of *Rome*, and *Italy* it self, might perhaps by his means, revolt from the East Empire; as a great Friend to *Rome* hath very well observed: Who furthermore addeth thereunto,

Marginalia:
Alphonf. Ciacc. de vit. & Geft. Roman. in vit. Sylverii.

Id. ibid. ex Anaftaf. Procop. de bell. Goth. l. 1.
Evagr. l. 4. c. 18.
Onuphr. in vit. Pelagii 11.

unto, that this Custom did afterward continue, until the time of *Benedict* the Second, that is, for 150. years: in which space *Gregory* the Great, and *Boniface* the Third (who had prevail'd with *Phocas* for the Supremacy of *Rome*) and 18 Bishops more successively enjoyed that Bishoprick.

Onuph. ubi supra.

It was but touched before, how in the time of *Sylverius* the Authority of the Bishops of *Rome* was grown great; whilst by the Incursions of the said Barbarous Nations into *Italy*, the Power of the Emperours in this West part of the world was greatly decayed. And although *Justinian* the Emperour recovered in some good sort the former Estate of the Empire, in these Parts: Yet not many Years after the *Lombards* setting Foot into *Italy* did greatly impair the same. But the utter ruin of it did principally proceed (for ought we find to the contrary) from the Bishops of *Rome*. For when about the Year 686. the Emperour *Constantine* the Fourth, greatly favouring *Benedict* the Second, gave the Clergy and People of *Rome* licence to choose and admit from that time forward their Bishops, without any further expectation of the Emperour's Authority to approve and confirm the same (little remembring the Wisdom and Providence of *Justinian*) they, the said Bishops, grew to great Presumption and Boldness against their succeeding Emperours; until by their means, *Rome*, *Italy*, and the *Western* Parts of the Empire were utterly cut off from the *East* Empire: which *Justinian*, and his Successors by keeping the Bishops of *Rome* in some due Subjection, through their Authority in their Preferments to that See, did seek to have prevented. No sooner had the same Emperour given the Bishops of *Rome* this Immunity, and Freedom; but, to omit what dangerous Quarrels arose amongst the Citizens of *Rome* in the choice of their Bishops, scarce 20. Years were passed, before they began to insult greatly over the Emperours. It is noted for a great Commendation

Platin. in vitâ Benedict. 2.

Onuphr.in vitâ Conſtantin. 1. mendation in Pope *Conſtantine* the firſt, becauſe he was the firſt that durſt take upon him, openly to reſiſt *Philippicus*, the next Emperour after the ſaid *Juſtinian, in Os, to his Face.* But the Oppoſition which *Gregory* the ſecond made againſt *Leo* the third (the next but one to the ſaid *Philippicus*) is indeed very memorable. He proceeded ſo far againſt him, for giving Commandment throughout all his Empire, that, for the avoiding of Idolatry, Images ſhould be removed out of all *Sabellicus Ennead. 8. l. 7.* Churches; as by his Letters ſent abroad, far and near, he procured ſuch paſſing hatred againſt *Leo*, eſpecially amongſt the *Italians*, as they brake out in divers places *Blondus Decad. 1. l. 10.* into open Rebellion. Wherein they went ſo far, that every City and Town rejected the Magiſtrates appointed by the Emperour's Authority, and created Magiſtrates of their own, whom they called *Dukes*; entring into a courſe to have abrogated the Empire of *Conſtantinople*, and to have ſet a new Emperour in *Italy*. *Papir. Maſſon. l. 3. in vit. Greg. 2.* From which Courſe, although the *Pope* diſſwaded them, as diſliking (we ſuppoſe) to have an Emperour ſo near him: Yet he took ſuch Order, as both *Rome*, and the reſt *Blondus ibid.* of the *Italians* withdrew, from that time forward, their Cuſtoms, and Tributes, which had, beforetimes, been paid to the Emperour: And their Rebellion ſo increaſed every day againſt him, that the Romans forſook him, and *Alphonſ. Ciaccon. in vit.Gregor. 2.* ſubmitted themſelves, by an Oath, to the ſaid *Gregory* the ſecond, to be order'd and govern'd by him in all things. Whereby, *Rome*, and the *Dukedom* thereof, was violently taken from the Emperour of *Conſtantinople*, and beſtow'd upon the Biſhop of *Rome*. In reſpect of which moſt irreligious and un-biſhop-like Proceedings, the Patrons of that See do greatly commend *Papir. Maſſon. in vit. Gregor. 2.* him. One of them ſaith, "That the Biſhops of *Rome* "are either beholding to him, or to none, for their Prin- "cipality. For (as he in the ſame Place further affirm- "eth) he made his Succeſſours great Princes: the Be- "ginning whereof was hard, the Progreſs more eaſy, "and

"and the Event profperous and happy: *Tantæ molis e-*
"*rat Romanam condere Gentem*; It was a matter of fo
"great difficulty to erect the Papacy. Indeed it is behoveful for them to meafure the *Pope*'s dealings, by their Succefs and Events; for otherwife, they were in themfelves very abominable: Every *Pope* growing ftill one more infolent than another, as appeared by the practices of *Gregory* the Third, perfifting in his Predeceffors fteps, againft the faid Emperour; and of *Stephen* the Second, againft *Conftantine* the Son of *Leo*.

Now whilft thefe famous Popes were playing their parts on the one fide (as we have fhewed) againft the Emperour, to withdraw the hearts of the *Italians* from him: the *Saracens* were as bufy againft him on the other fide. Which might have moved their Holinefs (if they had had the fear of God before their Eyes) rather to have procured fome Affiftance from the *Italians* to the Emperour, in a Cafe of that Nature, than to have drawn his own Subjects from him. But their courfe was bent another way. For the *Lombards* beginning to trouble *Rome*, and they being afham'd to crave Aid from the faid Emperour, whom they had fo abufed: they left their own Soveraigns, under pretence, that in regard of their Wars with the *Saracens*, they were not able to affift them; and procured affiftance from *France*: Firft by *Carolus Martellus*, and then by *Pepin* his Son: the faid *Stephen* the Second, having bound the faid *Pepin* (as it feemeth) by an Oath, that if he overcame the *Lombards*, all that appertained to the Exarchate of *Ravenna*, which had lately been the Emperours, might be annexed to the Bifhoprick of *Rome*: which was afterward, by him, performed accordingly.

Platin. in vit. Steph. 2.

Alphonf. Ciac. con. in vit. Steph. 2.

Suitable hereunto were the proceedings of Pope *Adrian* the Firft. Who being again troubled with the *Lombards*, obtain'd help from *Carolus Magnus*; by whofe coming into *Italy*, the *Lombards* were fhortly fubdued,

Marianus Scotus.
Hermanus Contractus.
Plat. in Adrian. 1.

subdued, and the *Pope's* Eſtate greatly advanced; but the *Emperour's* was in effect utterly overthrown, concerning his Intereſt and Authority, which he had before in thoſe Parts. For the ſaid *Carolus* having vanquiſhed the *Lombards*, and none elſe there being able to reſiſt him, he cauſed the ſaid *Pope* to Anoint his Son *Pepin* King of *Italy*, and ſo returned into *France*. But above Four Years after, *Leo* the Third being *Pope*, and afterward faln into ſo great Hatred amongſt the *Romans*, as he hardly eſcaped them with his Life: He the ſaid *Leo* uſed ſuch means, as that he brought the ſaid *Charles* again to *Rome*; before whom *Leo* purged himſelf by his Oath from thoſe Accuſations, wherewith the *Romans* charged him. In Requital whereof, and the rather, becauſe at that time *Irene* the Empreſs, and Wife of *Leo* the Fourth, Raign'd at *Conſtantinople* after her Huſband's Death, (which the *Romans* diſliked;) the ſaid *Charles* was in *Rome* created *Emperour* over the *Weſtern Parts*, which belonged before to the ancient *Empire*. Touching which Point, an ancient *Hiſtoriographer* writeth in this ſort: The Romans, *who were in Heart long before faln from the Emperour of* Conſtantinople, *taking this occaſion and opportunity, that a Woman had gotten the Dominion over them, did with one general Conſent proclaim King* Charles *for their Emperour, and Crowning him by the Hands of* Leo *the Third, Saluted him as* Cæſar *and Emperour of* Rome. And this was the fruit of the Exemption which was granted to the Biſhops of *Rome*, by the Emperour *Conſtantine* the Fourth, for their Preferment to that *See*, without the Emperour's Approbation; *Rome* and *Italy* are cut off from the ancient Empire, a new Empire is erected by the Practices and Treacheries principally of the Biſhops of *Rome*, it being in a ſort neceſſary, that ſo notable a Treaſon againſt the ſaid ancient Empire, ſhould be eſpecially effected by ſuch notorious Inſtruments.

Placet eis. **JO. OVERAL.**
 CAP.

Sigibert. Ann. 781.
Otho Friſing. lib. 5. cap. 28.
Sigibert. Ann. 800.
Otho Friſing. lib. 5 cap. 30.
Platin. in Leon. 3.
Sigibert. Ann. 801.

CAP. VII.

CHARLES *the Great* having poſſeſſed himſelf *Jure Belli* of the greateſt part of *Italy*, and made his Son King thereof, although he beſtowed much upon the *Church* of *Rome*, and uſed *Pope Urban* very honourably; yet, he being a wiſe and a very provident Prince, could not be ignorant how inſolently the Biſhops of *Rome* had behaved themſelves toward their former Emperours; and how traiterouſly they had long ſought to make them odious in *Italy*, after they had gotten themſelves to be releaſed from the Emperour's Authority in their Advancement to that *See*. That he might therefore prevent the like dangers for the time to come, and ſecure both himſelf and his Poſterity, in that behalf; He ſo uſed the matter with the ſaid *Urban*, as he brought the *Popes* to their former Subjection. The Relation whereof is thus recorded by a principal Upholder of that *See*. Carolus *being returned to* Rome (ſaith he) *appointed a Synod there with Pope* Adrian *in the Patriarchal Palace of* Lateran: *Which Synod was Celebrated by One hundred and fifty three religious Biſhops and Abbots. At what time* Adrian *the Pope, with the whole Synod, deliver'd or yielded to* Charles's *Intereſt and Power of chooſing the Biſhop of* Rome, *and of ordering the* Apoſtolical See. *Moreover, He the ſaid* Adrian *defined, that all the Archbiſhops and Biſhops through all particular* Provinces *ſhould receive from the ſaid* Charles *their Inveſtiture; and that none ſhould be Conſecrated by any, except he were firſt commended, and inveſted Biſhop by the King, under pain of Excommunication.* Diſtinct.63. Adrianus.

Howbeit, when *Charles* being dead, his Son *Ludovicus* was (as it ſeemeth) ſo wrought upon through the ſoftneſs of his Nature, as he was contented, that the *Romans* Platin. in v.s. Paſchal. 1.

Romans according to their own Judgment, should Create and Consecrate their new Bishop, so it were done without Tumult, or Bribery; always provided, that the new Bishop should advertise him by his Legats, as touching his Consecration, and conclude a Peace with him; Or, as another saith, That Legats should be directed unto the Emperour, and to his Successors Kings of *France*, to make a League of Friendship, Love and Peace betwixt them, and the Bishops of that *See*. With this Order, though it tended much to the prejudice of the Empire, the Bishops of *Rome* were not long satisfied, as brooking no shew of any Superiority over them, but were still shifting, as they might, to cast off likewise that Yoak: Which *Otho* the First well perceiving, when he came to the Empire, sought to reform (as knowing how dangerous their ambitious Humours were to his Estate) by causing *Leo* the Eighth, with all the Clergy and people of *Rome*, to decree in a *Synod* about the Year 964. "That he (the Emperour) and "his Successors, should have the power of Ordaining "the Bishops of *Rome*; that if any should attempt any "thing against this Rule, he should be subject to Ex- "communication; and that if he repented not, then "he should be punished with irrevocable Banishment, "or be put to Death. Afterward, also about the Year 1046. *Henry* the Third, finding those Bishops still to persist in their said aspiring Course of exempting themselves from the Emperour's Authority, and that thereby there grew divers *Schisms* and *Quarrels* in their Elections; he held a Council at *Sutrium*, not far from *Rome*, wherein it was determined, that the *Romans* should no more intermeddle with the Choice of their Bishops; but that the same should always be referred to the *Emperour*. At what time also, the *Emperour* made the *Romans* to swear, that from thence-forward they would neither Choose, nor Consecrate any *Pope*, but such a One as he should tender unto them.

By

[299]

By thefe and fuch like other means, from the time of *Charles the Great* hitherto, for about the fpace of 236 Years, the Emperours kept the Bifhops of *Rome* in fome reafonable good Obedience towards them; but not without their own great trouble, and much kicking and repining by thofe Bifhops at it, as growing daily worfe and worfe: Infomuch, as there being Sixty of them, if not more, who fucceeded in that *See*, within the compafs of the Years before-mention'd; about Fifty of them did fo degenerate from the Vertues of their Predeceffors (as a great Friend in his time to the *Papacy*, reporteth;) That they rather deferv'd to be termed *Apotactaci, Apoflaticive potiùs quàm Apoflolici*; *Unruly, or Runnegates, than Apoflolical Bifhops*. The laft of which number was *Leo* the Ninth, who within five or fix years after the faid Council of *Sutrium*, renounced the Emperour's Favour, whereby he was prefer'd to the *Papacy*, being perfwaded by one *Hildebrand*, That it was unlawful *per manum Laicam*, to take upon him that Government, and was thereupon again chofen and admitted Pope by the *Romans*, contrary to their former Oath, and to the Decree of the faid Council. This *Hildebrand* being a man both of a great Wit and Courage, and having an Eye himfelf unto the *Papacy*, made his way in that behalf, by thrufting five or fix Bifhops fucceffively into Oppofition againft the Emperour; of purpofe, that if it were his Fortune to come to that Place, he might find the Ice broken by them to his own Rebellion, and moft traiterous Defignments. The faid *Leo* became a Warriour and General of the Field againft fome troublefom Perfons in *Italy*, called *Normans*, by *Hildebrand*'s means (as it feemeth) *Cujus Confiliis, & nutu Pontificatús munus perpetuò adminiflravit*. The like Sway he alfo bare with Pope *Nicholas* the Second, who made him *Archdeacon* of *Rome*, in requital for his helping of him to the *Popedom*; and by whofe Advice the faid *Nicholas* held a Council in the

Genebr. Chronol. sæculo 10.

Otho Frifing. lib. 6. cap. 33. Plat. in Leon. 9.

Alphonf. Ciaccon. in vit. Leon. 9.

the Church of *Lateran*, wherein it was Ordain'd, *That from thenceforth the Bishops of* Rome *should be chosen by the Cardinals, with Approbation of the Clergy and People of* Rome. Also the said *Hildebrand* opposed himself against the *Emperour*, and prevail'd therein for *Alexander* the Second; the *Emperour* having appointed *Honorius* the Second to that Place: Which *Alexander* so advanced, made a Decree, *That no man should in time to come receive any Ecclesiastical Living or Benefice from a Layman, because it was then called* Symony *so to do*. And thus these *Popes* by *Hildebrand*'s Instigation decreed, and did what they list, to the great prejudice of the *Emperour*, and of his Authority; the same being now, in respect of former times, almost at the last cast.

Alphonf. Ciaccon. in vit. Nicol. 2.
Genebr. Chronol.
Alphonf. Ciaccon. in vit. Alexand. 2.
Genebr. Chronol.

Placet eis.

John Overall.

CAP.

C A P. VIII.

IT was great Policy in the *Emperours* (as we have shewed) to do what they could for the Maintenance of their Authority in placing of the Bishops of *Rome*, and in bestowing of other Bishopricks and Abbacies within their Dominions: But such was the Ignorance, Hypocrisie and Superstition of those Times, so far spread by the inferiour Bishops and Priests, and so rooted every where in men's Hearts by the Bishops of that *See*, under colour of Religion, and of their pretended Supremacy, derived by them from St. *Peter*, as they feared not to attempt any thing against any whosoever, so the same might tend to the Advancement of their own Authority. Again, it was a great Oversight in *Charles the Great*, considering his Wisdom, and that he well knew the proud and aspiring Minds of those Bishops, that after his own Coronation at *Rome* by *Leo* the Third, he did not provide for the benefit of his Successors, that none of them after that time should ever be Crowned there, or by the Bishop of that Place. For that Slip and Omission, being not well look'd to, and Reform'd by any that did succeed him, became at the last the great Bane of the *Empire*. Besides, the State of the *Emperours* shortly after the Days of the said *Charles*, did very greatly decay; Insomuch, as within about Sixty Years, *Ludovicus* the Second had but the Ninth part of the *Empire*, the rest being diversly and by sundry Distractions and Divisions, rent and drawn from it. *Otho Frising. l. 6, c. 1. Gotefrid. Viterbiens. Chron. part. 17.*

Which Weakness of the *Empire* being throughly known to the Bishops of *Rome*, and *it* discern'd by them to decrease more and more; they grew more insolent than ever they were, and began to insist upon their

their Preheminence and great Superiority over the *Emperours*; becaufe forfooth they received at their hands the *Diadem* and *Crown Imperial*. Thefe things will appear manifeftly by the Proceedings of thofe fucceeding *Bifhops*, if we fhall begin with *Hildebrand* before mention'd; who after he had procured Six *Bifhops* of *Rome* to be poyfon'd by one *Brazutus* (as many thought) was upon the Death of *Alexander* II. *Ann*. 1073, or thereabout, made *Pope* himfelf, and termed *Gregory* the Seventh, with the Confent of *Henry* the Fourth then *Emperour*, as fome fay; without it, fay others: But whether with it, or without it, when he had gotten that Place, fo long by him expected, he ruffl'd and beftir'd himfelf very notably in it.

<small>Eenno Cardin. in vit. Hildebr. Balæus in Greg. 7. Functius in Comment. Ch:onolog. l. 10 Platin. in Greg. 7. Lamb. Schafnaburg. de Reb. German.</small>

About that time there was a great Rebellion againft the *Emperour* in *Germany* by the *Saxons*; who very well knowing the Pride and violent Difpofition of the *Pope* againft the *Emperour*, and how apt he would be to take any Occafion that might tend to his own Glory, and to the Honour of his Place, defired his Affiftance, deprived the Emperour very fhamefully; and the rather to allure the Pope unto them, told him by their Agents, that the Empire was but *Beneficium Urbis*; and thereupon moved him, that He and the People of *Rome* would together with them adminifter the Empire, and take Order by a Decree of Council, and Agreement of Princes, who fhould be Emperour: *Grata admodùm* Gregorio *ifthæc fuere*; *Thefe things pleafed* Gregory *exceedingly*, as a Friend to *Rome* affirmeth. He thought, that in fuch a whirling of things he was not to fit idle; as being perfwaded, that a fit time was come when he might free the Bifhops of *Rome* from Servitude, fhake off the Yoak of the Emperour (his Abilities being diminifhed) abrogate his Authority, lawfully tranflate the whole Power to himfelf, and fo eftablifh the Pontifical Principality. And nothing feemed more Glorious for him, than (Fear being taken away)

<small>Aventin. Anal. l. 5.</small>

way) to stand in dread of no mortal man, and to enjoy the Liberty of the Church as he list himself; there being an Emperour whose Arms and Force were not to be feared, as who did Reign but at the pleasure of the Bishop of *Rome*. Which Points thus debated with himself, and probably resolved, he joyned Friendship with the said Rebels and Traytors, promising them his best Assistance, agreeably to their own Desires; and thereupon being furthermore strengthned by the Amity, which he likewise had entertained with certain other Rebels in *Italy*, and by the Purse of a great Lady in that Country, one *Machtilda*, his Concubine, as it was supposed; he following the traiterous Humours stirred up by himself, and maintain'd a long time in sundry of his Predecessors, did prosecute the Emperour with admirable Malice, Pride and Contempt, because he opposed himself in his own Right, and for his own Defence against him. Which the Pope took in such Scorn, as he Cursed him by his Excommunication, releas'd his Subjects from their Oaths of Allegiance, and stir'd them up by all the means he could to take Arms, and to enter into any wicked Practices that might tend to the Emperour's Overthrow. *Noluit enim, &c. For he would not endure it*, (as One saith) *that his Consent should be required in the* Election *of the Bishop of* Rome; *nor that the* Emperour *according to his will should have the bestowing of the Bishopricks, that were included within the limits of the* Empire.

Surely, it might have pleased him to have endur'd both the one and the other, as sundry Popes, his Equals, had done before him. And howsoever, this Attempt of *Gregory*, is eagerly maintain'd in these days, and held to be Apostolical; yet then it seem'd very strange to many. Therefore an ancient Historiographer writeth in this sort. *Lego & relego Romanorum Regum, & Imperatorum Gesta*, &c. *I read over and over again, the Acts of the Roman Kings and Emperours; but can find in*

Lamb. Schafna-
burg. *An.* 1077.

Platin. in Greg. 7. Abbas Urspergens.

Genebr. Chronol.

Otho Frising.
l. 6. c. 35.

no place, that any of them before Henry *the Fourth*, *was excommunicated by the Bishop of* Rome, *or deprived of his*

Id. de Gestis Fred. l. 1. c. 1.

Kingdom. And again, *the Empire was the more vehemently moved with Indignation, through the Novelty of this Attempt; because such a Sentence against the Emperour*

Sigibert. Ann. 1088.
Vincent. in spec. hist. l. 25. c. 24.

of Rome, *was never heard of before those times.* And another more ancient than the former, and almost of 500. Years standing, doth not only term the said Fact of the *Pope*, *a Novelty*; but saith in Effect, that it was an *Heresy*. These are his words: *Surely this Novelty (I will not call it Heresy) was never before heard of in the World*, viz. *That Priests should teach the People, that they owe no Subjection unto Evil Kings; and that notwithstanding they have taken an Oath of Fidelity unto them, yet they owe them no Fidelity, nor are to be acounted perjur'd, that violate the said Oath: Nay, that if any obey their King in that Case, he shall be held for an excommunicate Person: and he that attempteth any thing against such a King, shall be absolved both from the Offence of Injustice, and of Perjury.*

Abbas Uspergens.
Lamb. Schafnaburg.
An. 1077.
Platin. in Greg. 7.

To this Heretical Novelty, and most insolent Attempt (which since hath had many false Colours cast over it, to cover the Lewdness and Deformity of it) we might add the said Pope's very admirable Pride, in permitting the said Emperour, when he came unto him, to be absolved from the said Excommunication, to stand bare-footed, in the Frost and Snow, Three days at his Gates. But that which ensued this Novelty, or Heresie, this Unpriestly and Inhumane dealing, with so great a Person, is most remarkable above all the rest: viz. How he wound himself, like a cunning Serpent, into the Interest of the Empire, and upon a sleight Occasion. The said Rebels of *Germany*, in their Fury against the Emperour, having suggested

Aventin. Annal. l. 5.

unto him, That the Empire was a Benefit belonging to the City of *Rome*, to be bestowed where she thought fit; although they added therewith, that the same was

was to be done by the Bishop, and by the People of *Rome*, with the Consent of other Princes: Yet he, finding what would serve his turn, and was most available to his own Designment, did afterward, of himself, and by his own Authority, take upon him to dispose of the Empire (as being void by Virtue of a second Excommunication) and did accordingly send a Crown of Gold to *Rodulphus* Duke of *Suevia* (now also grown a Traytour) with this Inscription;   Aventin. l. 5. Matth. Paris in Gulielmo 1. Paul Langius, An. 1078.

Petra dedit Petro; Petrus Diadema Rodulpho:

Christ gave St. *Peter* Authority to make Emperours; and I, his Successor, do thereupon send you this Crown, and by my Authority, from St. *Peter*, do give you the Empire.

It is plain and evident, that many Emperours, in former Ages, bestowed the Papacy; and sometimes took it from one, and gave it to another: but that ever Pope there, before this Man, did so dispose of the Empire, we do not find it in any approved Author. Neither can we conceive, or easily believe, that Christ ever gave St. *Peter* any such Authority, as is here dreamed of. Only we observe, by the Report of One (no Protestant) "That *Gregory*, to justifie and colour his   Aventin. Annal. l. 5.
"said Presumption, bragged above measure, that the
"West Empire was his; that he was both Bishop and
"Emperour, Christ having imposed upon him those
"two Persons; that he had no Equal, and much less
"any Superiour; that he might take all Right and
"Honour, from other Men, and transfer the same un-
"to himself; and do much more than here we will
mention: But touching any Proof for all these great Prerogatives, we find none; Except this will serve his turn, That St. *Peter received power to bind and loose*; which we hold insufficient, notwithstanding that the Papists now-a-days do allow them all, and admire him for it. It

It hath been a usual Custom, for the Pope's Friends, to extol those Bishops of *Rome* most, who shewed themselves, whilst they lived, the greatest Practitioners, and Traytors against the Emperours. Agreeably whereunto One saith of him, " That he was a " Man worthy of the Pontificalship, because he de- " pressed the Insolency of Politicks, terrified Monarchs " with the Glory of his Name and Zeal, and deliver- " ed the Church from the Captivity and Servitude, " which it endured under Princes ; and that, of all the " Bishops of *Rome*, he was One of chief Zeal and Au- " thority, and a Man *verè Apostolicus, truly Apostolical*, " and most to be praised. *Proceres & Populum sacra-* " *mento præstito sanctè solvit, & ut Rodolpho adhæreant,* " *sanctius imperat :* he did godly absolve the Noblemen, " and People from their Oath of Allegiance to the Empe- " rour, and did more holily command them not to obey him. What was thought long since of these so Godly and Holy Practices, we have above touched : and we must also of necessity confess that to be true, which this Authour, and his Fellows do write, of *Gregory's* Greatness. For it is further recorded of him, that he did first erect *Imperium Pontificium*, the *Papal Empire*. But touching his Vertues (if an ancient *Cardinal*, that wrote his Life, did know him) there is no cause why any Man should be in love with them. And as concerning this new, and before unheard of Pontifical Empire, (if we may believe another of their own Authors) it brought with it, into the West Empire, Wars, Bloodshed, Homicide, Parricide, Hatred, Whoredome, Theft, Sacriledge, Dissention and Sedition, both Civil and Domestical, Corruption of the Scriptures, false and sycophantical Interpretations, with many more Mischiefs, there by him mentioned : and yet (saith he) *Gregory's* Successours did uphold it by the space of 450. Years, *invita Mundo, invitis Imperatoribus, in spite of the World, and of the Emperours*, and thereby

Genebr. Chronol.

Aventin. Annal. l. 5. Benno Cardinalis.

Aventin. ubi supra.

thereby drew both Heaven and Hell into their Subjecti
on, and Servitude: Again, "In former times, God, as a   Id. ubi supra.
"most indulgent Father, did often chastise the We-
"stern Christians, by *Saxons*, *Hunns*, *Normans*, *Venetians*,
"*Lombards* and *Hungarians*, Men differing from us in
"Religion: but now (as if God were become an an-
"gry Father towards us, and we were neglected, and
"dis-inherited by him) we have, for above 400. Years,
"tyranniz'd amongst our selves, worse than *Turks*:
"We deceive, we circumvent, we kill, we turn our
"Weapons into our own Bowels; we are left to our own
"Lust, we live as we list, we behave our selves proud-
"ly, covetously, without Punishment, and we are
"not ashamed to give God the lie.

Placet eis.

John Overall.

C A P.

CAP. IX.

IT were impertinent, to our Purpofe, to enter into any particular Relation of the great Stirrs, and Troubles, which, through the Pride of the Bifhops of *Rome*, after *Gregory* the *Seventh*'s time, were moved throughout all Chriftendom, during the faid Term above mentioned, of 450. Years; whilft the Emperors, with their Adherents, endeavoured ftill to have retained their ancient Authority; both in the Choice of the faid Bifhops, and of beftowing of other Ecclefiaftical Peferments in the Empire: which the Popes, with their Friends, did withftand with all their Mights, and poffible Means and Practices, that they could devife, and put in execution by their Excommunications, and ftirring up the Emperours Subjects to rebel againft them. In which Garboils and bloody Oppofitions, when the Emperours prevailed, the Popes were depofed, and others fet up in their Rooms: betwixt whom (the Parties difplaced) to recover their Dignity, and the others, poffeffed of it, to retain it, no Cruelty or cunning Stratagems were omitted. And, on the other fide, when the Popes got the upper hand of the Emperours (for the moft part by Treafon and Rebellion, and always by Conftraint and violent Ufurpation) they did not fpare to ufe them moft difhonourably, and with all the Reproach and Contempt, that might be well devifed. Some Examples whereof may be thefe.

Whereas before Pope *Pafchal* the Second's time, the former Bifhops of *Rome* were accuftom'd to add the Years of the Emperours to their Bulls, Epiftles, and Libels; He the faid *Pafchal*, a little after *Gregory* the Seventh's Days, alter'd that courfe, and withdrawing the

Aventin. l. 6.

the Years of the Emperour *Henry* the Fifth, whom he had otherwise greatly vexed, added the number of his own Papacy : which was a very insolent and proud attempt, and yet ever since (for ought we remember) the same hath still been continued by all his Successours. *Innocentius* the Second having brought *Lotharius* the Emperour to some dishonourable Compacts and Conditions, before he would crown him, caused the story thereof, not without a great Blemish to the Imperial Majesty, to be painted on the Wall of his Palace, with these two reproachful Verses under it ;

<small>Badevicus de Gestis Feder. l. 1. c. 10. Alphons. Ciaccon. in vit. Innocent. 2.</small>

Rex venit ante fores, jurans priùs Urbis Honores :
Post homo fit Papæ ; sumit, quo dante, Coronam.

Alexander the Third, when *Frederick* the Emperour was driven, through Rebellion of his Subjects, to come unto him for his Absolution, set his Foot upon his Neck, and applied these Words of the Psalm unto himself : *Super Aspidem & Basiliscum ambulabis ; & conculcabis Leonem, & Draconem.* It is reported of *Cælestinus* the Third, that with his Feet he set the Crown upon the Head of *Henry* the Sixth, and with one of them struck it off again ; shewing thereby, That he could make and unmake Emperours at his Pleasure. But we will omit these insolent Facts ; as also the great and dishonourable Servitude, whereunto by Extremity they brought the Emperours, " and whereof the Pope's Re- " cords and Books do make mention ; as of carrying " up their first Dish, giving of them Water, bearing up " their Trains, leading their Horses, holding their Stir- " rup, and kissing their Feet : and will apply our selves to the consideration of their Divinity, how they have dealt with the Scriptures to uphold these Presumptions, and Apostatical, and no way Apostolical, Seditions, Rebellions, Murders, and Treasons, One of their own Friends observing, how shortly after *Gregory* the Seventh's time,

<small>Carion Chron. l. 4. Alphons. Ciaccon. in vit. Alexand. 3. Genebr. Chronol. Ranulphus in Polychron. l. 7.</small>

<small>Pontif. Roman. Greg. 13. par. 1. Ceremoniale Rom. l. 1.</small>

his Succeſſours, by his Example, behaved themſelves,
in this behalf, writeth thus : *The moſt Holy Philoſophy,
delivered from Heaven by the Holy Ghoſt, they make apt or
fit to their own Conditions, by their Interpretations, they
compel it to ſerve their Ambition : the Determinations and
Decrees of Chriſt they will not keep, but make them to ſerve
their own Humours.* We have ſhewed before, how by
ſundry Councils it was decreed, That the Emperours
ſhould have the inveſting of Biſhops within their own
Dominions : and *Paſchal* the Second himſelf yielded as
much to *Henry* the Fifth, being then preſent; but after
his departure from *Rome*, the Caſe was alter'd: For then
he could affirm with ſhew of great Devotion, that ſuch
a Priviledge was againſt the Holy Ghoſt. And another
Biſhop (as it were, to uphold him therein) affirmed,
that it contained Wickedneſs and Hereſy. To which
purpoſe, we ſuppoſe, ſome Places of the Scriptures
were notably perverted. In which Courſe, *Hadrian*
the Fourth preſumed very far, when he durſt write
thus ; *Whence hath the Emperour his Empire, but from Us ?
By the Election of Princes he hath the Name of King ; by
our Conſecration he hath the Name of Emperour,* Auguſtus,
and Cæſar. Ergo *per Nos imperat ; therefore he raigneth by
Us, and that which he hath, he hath from Us. Behold, it is in
our Power to beſtow the Empire on whom we liſt.* And how
doth he prove all this? By the words of the Lord, to
the Prophet *Jeremy : propterea conſtituti à Deo,* &c. *We
are, to that End,* (ſaith he) *placed by God over Nations
and Kingdoms, that we may deſtroy, and pull up, and build,
and plant.* Herein *Innocentius* the Third, likewiſe, had
an eſpecial Gift : For, ſpeaking of *Sylveſter*, he ſaith,
he was both a Biſhop and King ; relying not only upon
the Scriptures, where Chriſt is called *King of kings,
and Lord of lords* ; but upon another place of St. *Peter*,
You are a Choſen Generation, and Royal Prieſthood ;
in which words, he affirmeth, may be ſpiritually underſtood
of *Sylveſter*'s Succeſſours ; becauſe, ſaith he, *the Lord hath
choſen*

chosen them to be both Priests and Kings. And to prevent an Objection, left any Man should ask, where it might be found that the Lord had so chosen them to both those great Dignities; he telleth us, that *Constantine*, by a Divine Revelation, gave unto *Sylvester*, with a Crown of Gold, the whole Kingdom of the *West*. But yet he hath some better proofs to this purpose. For whereas Christ said unto S. *Peter, Duc in altum, launch out into the Deep*; this Deep, saith *Innocentius*, is *Rome*; which had then the Primacy and Principality over all the World; and therefore, where the Lord saith, *Launch out into the Deep*, it is as though he should have said, *Vade Romam, go to* Rome, the Seat both of the Priesthood and the Empire. Again, expounding these words, *Who is a faithful Servant and wise, whom his Master hath made Ruler over his House?* he applieth them to St. *Peter*; and therefore thus testifieth of himself, OF truth, I am appointed over this Family; but who am I, to sit higher than Kings, and to hold the Throne of Glory? *Mihi namq; dicitur in Prophetâ,* &c. For to me it is said in the Prophet, *I have appointed thee over Nations and Kingdoms, that thou mayst pluck up, and root out, and destroy, and throw down, and build, and plant.* And a little after; *You see, who is this servant, even the Vicar of Christ*; the Successour of Peter; *the Christ of the Lord*; *the God of* Pharaoh; *one plac'd in the midst betwixt God and Man*; *short of God, but beyond Man*; *less than God, but greater than Man.* Likewise from St. *Peter's* walking on the Water, he maketh this Inference. *Forasmuch* (saith he) *as many Waters are many People, and the Congregations of Waters are the Sea*; *in that St.* Peter *did walk upon the Waters of the Sea, he did demonstrate his Power over all the World.*

Further this *Innocentius* having written a malapert Letter to the Emperour of *Constantinople*, his Majesty, in answer of it, putteth him in Mind, how St. *Peter commandeth all Men to be subject to Kings*: whereunto the Pope replyed, saying, that St. *Peter wrote so to his*

Luc. 5. 4.
In Fest. S. Petri & Pauli, serm. 2.

Matth. 24. 45.

In Consecrat. Rom. Pontif. serm. 2.

Jer. 1. 10.

Innocent. Patriar. h. C. P. Epist. Decret. l. 2.

Innocent. Imperator. C. P.

own Subjects, and did not therein include himself: and that moreover he might not only have remember'd, that it was not said to any King, but to a Priest, *Behold I have placed thee over Nations and Kingdoms,* (and so followeth the words of the Text:) but likewise, that *as God made two lights in the Firmament of Heaven, a greater and a less, the one for the Day, the other for the Night*; so for the Firmament of the Universal Church he made two dignities, the Pontifical and the Regal; the Pontifical resembling the Sun, which is the great Light, and the Regal the Moon, which is the less Light: to the end, that thereby it might be known, that there is a great difference betwixt Pontifical Bishops and Kings, as there is betwixt the Sun and the Moon.

<small>Matt. Paris in Johan.</small>

But here we must a little digress, to observe, that this Pope, being swoln as big as the Sun, cast his Beams, not only into *England*, and scorched King *John* exceedingly about the Year 1212. by thundering against him, and interdicting the Kingdom, and by exciting his Subjects to Rebellion and Treason (the Weapons of those Bishops) but likewise fired *Otho* the Emperour out of the Empire, by raising up against him *Frederick* the *Second*. And when he had played these two Feats, amongst many other, he held a Council at *Lateran, Anno* 1215. wherein, to strengthen such Traiterous Proceedings, he caused it to be ordained,

<small>Abbas Uspergensi. Genebr. Chronol. Plat. in Innoc. 3.</small>

<small>Concil. Lateran. c. 3. Oper. Innoc. Tom. 1.</small>

(as it is pretended) "That if any Temporal Lord, "being admonished by the Church, should not purge "his Countrey from Heresie, the Metropolitan, "and other Comprovincial Bishops should excommu- "nicate him; and if within a Year he did not give sa- "tisfaction in that behalf, the same should be signified "to the Bishop of *Rome*; that so he, from thence for- "ward, might denounce his Vassals absolved from "their Fidelity to him, and expose his Land to Catho- "licks, to be, without Contradiction, by them pos- "sessed. Upon this Canon, many, in these days, do
much

much rely: although indeed it was but a Project, amongst many other, to have been concluded in that Assembly; wherein nothing could be clearly determined (saith one of their Writers) because by Wars it was broken off; which the Pope labouring to suppress, died in that Journey. *Platin. in Innoc. 3.*

And now we return from whence we digressed; and leaving *Innocentius*, do address our selves to *Boniface* the *Eighth*, who had as great dexterity, as his said Predecessour, in expounding of the Scriptures. For whereas the Apostles, upon a mistaking of Christ's meaning, where he bad them to *provide bags, and scrips for themselves, and that he who wanted a sword, should sell his Coat, and buy one*; they answered, saying, Lord, *we have two swords:* This Pope inferreth, *there is, in the Church, a Spiritual Sword, and a Temporal*; and that consequently they are both at the Commandment of the Bishops of *Rome*. Also to make the matter more clear, touching the temporal Sword, which should rule the World in all temporal Causes; he (saith *Boniface*) that shall deny, that St. *Peter* had this temporal Sword, doth not well understand Christ's Words, when he bad St. *Peter* (after he had cut off *Malchus*'s Ear) that he should put up his Sword. Again; whereas the Apostle doth teach us, that *the spiritual Man judgeth all things, but is judged by none*; this good Bishop doth ingross these words to the only Use of the Popes; and thereupon concludeth, that they have Power to judge and censure all Earthly Powers and Authorities; but are themselves exempted from the Checks and Censures of any, as being only subject to God, and to his judgment. And again, that the Spiritual Authority may institute and judge the Terrestrial, it is verified by the Prophecy of *Jeremy*, *Behold, I have placed thee this day over Nations and Kingdoms*: for the perverting of which Portion of Scripture, both this Pope, and *Innocentius* the *Third*, with all the Popes that since have followed,

Extrav. de major. & Obed. Unam sanctam. Luc. 22. 36, 38.

1 Cor. 2. 15.

followed, were, and are much beholding to *Adrian* the *Fourth*; he being the first, for ought we find, that so did overstrain it. Lastly, That he might imitate (as he seemeth) the Governour of the Feast in the Gospel, that *brought forth his best wine in the end of the feast*; and likewise such skilful Rhetoricians, as commonly build their principal Conclusions upon their most pinching Arguments: His *Holiness* relying upon the Scriptures, because it is not said, *In the beginnings*; but, *In the beginning God made Heaven and Earth:* Therefore except we will say with the *Manichees*, That God did not Himself make all Things, but that there was also another Creator as well as he: It must needs be confessed, that there is but One, *viz.* St. *Peter's* Successor, that is the chief and principal Ruler of all the World; and so he cometh to his irrefragable Conclusion; *We declare, we define, and we pronounce, that it is of the Necessity of Salvation for all humane Creatures to be subject to the Bishop of* Rome.

We may not therefore marvel, that having thus notably made perfect the rough Platform (drawn out by *Gregory* the VIIth. rubbed over by *Hadrian* the IVth. and amended by *Innocentius* the IIId.) of so infinite a Soveraignty; if He the said *Boniface*, to make the Honour and Glory more conspicuous and memorable to all Posterity, (after He had thrice refused to yield the Crown of the *Empire* to *Albertus Austriacus*) came forth one day amongst the people to be admired of them with a Sword by his Side, and a Crown upon his Head; saying, That He, and none but He was *Cæsar, Augustus, Emperour,* and *Lord of the World*. It had been plain dealing, if for the better strengthning of this his Greatness, He had alledged the Words in the Gospel, for the Honour of his Lord Paramount; *All these will I give thee*, because He did so worthily by his said Proceedings magnifie his Name and Authority.

Placet eis. John Overall.

CAP.

Aventin. l.6.

John 2.

Gen.1.1.

Joan.Marius de Schism. part.2. cap.18.

Matth. 4.5.

CAP. X.

WE have hitherto followed the Bishops of *Rome* through many Windings, from their mean and militant Condition, like to their Brethren, unto their Glorious Estate, and (as we may say) Triumphant: We found them at the first little better than their Master; *Who had not a place where to lay his head.* But now they are (as we see) become *Cæsars*, *Emperours*, and *Lords* of all the World: It was long since said by a good Friend of that See, *Excellentia Romani Imperii extulit Papatum Romani Pontificis supra alias Ecclesias*; *The Excellency of the Roman Empire did lift up the Papacy above other Churches.* Which Exaltation and Advancement of those Bishops (He might well have added) hath been (as elsewhere we have said) the very Bane and Cankerworm of the *Empire* it self, by their sucking out of it for the strengthning of themselves, the Juice, and those Vital Spirits, whereby formerly the Vigour and Glory of it did subsist, and all by Rebellion and Treason, under the pretence of Religion; and through their false Glosses, Applications, and violent Inforcements to a wrong Sense of the Sacred Scriptures: Wherein altho' they had an especial Faculty; yet they could never have so greatly prevail'd as they did, against such an Estate as the *Empire* was, nor against so many great *Kings*, and other *Princes* that were not subject unto it, if they had not been upheld in all their said wicked Courses by sundry their Flatterers and Parasites, who imitating their Examples in perverting and wresting the Scriptures, did take upon them to make good, and to justifie whatsoever the said *Popes* had either done, or said, were it never so Impious, Treache-

Gabr. Biel. Ex- pof. Can. Miss. Lect. 23. ex Eufebio.

rous, or Traiterous; as by that which followeth, it will plainly appear.

Genebr. Chronol.   About the Year 1140, which was upon the point of Fifty eight years after *Gregory* the Seventh's Death, *Theologia Scholastica, five Disputatrix,* The *Scholastical, or brabling Divinity* (as One calleth it) began to peep into the World, when *Peter Lombard* writ his Books of *Distinctions*; and did not only himself there-

Aventin.l.5.   by trouble the Truth (as Another saith) with the Mudd of Questions, and Streams of Opinions; but also set many men after him on work in writing long Commentaries upon his said *Distinctions,* to the hatching of infinite Oppositions and difficult Perplexities. In which number *Thomas of Aquine* bare the greatest sway; who entring into this Course about Forty years after *Innocentius* the Third's days, and finding how *Gregory* the Seventh, *Paschal* the Second, *Innocentius* the Second, *Adrian* the Fourth, *Alexander* the Third, and the said *Innocentius* the Third, with divers other Popes had ruffled with the Emperours, and what a hand they had gotten over the *Scriptures,* became the chiefest Champion of a Schoolman that *Rome* ever had.   Out of these

John 1. 15.
Tho.Aquin. de
Regin. Princ.
l.3. c. 10.
 words, *Of his fulness we have all received,* he was able to collect, that there is in the Bishop of *Rome* the Fulness of all Graces.   Again, because *Christ* (whom he maketh Bishop of *Rome*) may be called (as He saith) *A King,* and a *Priest*; He therefore inferreth it, not to be inconvenient, that his Successors should be so styled. Also we know not how, but He hath found it out, that when God said to *Jeremy, I have set thee over Nations*

Id. ib. c. 19. *and Kingdoms;* He spoke so unto him, *In personâ Vicarii Christi, In the person of Christ's Vicar.*   Furthermore, in that *Aristotle* saith, *That the Body hath his Vertue and Operation by the Soul*; He supposeth it must needs follow, that the Jurisdiction of Princes hath her Being, Vertue and Operation from St. *Peter* and his Successors.   For further Proof whereof, (as fearing it would be thought

insuffiinfufficient, that he had faid before) he buckleth himself to certain Facts of the Popes and Emperours; faying, That *Constantine* did give the Empire to *Sylvester*; that Pope *Adrian* made *Charles the Great* Emperour; and that likewife *Otho* the Firſt was created Emperour by Pope *Leo*: But at the laſt, He ſtriketh this Point dead; becauſe (faith He) it is manifeſt that. Pope *Zachary* depoſed the King of *France*, and abſolved all his Barons from their Oath of Fidelity; that *Innocentius* the Third took the Empire from *Otho* the IVth, and that *Honorius* (his next Succeſſor) dealt in like fort with *Frederick* the Second: And as it were to make up all, ſpeaking of the Emperour's Crowns, and the Cuſtom (as it ſeemeth) then in uſe; He ſaith, That the Emperour did receive a Crown of Gold from the Biſhop of *Rome*, and that the Pope deliver'd it to him with his Foot, *In ſignum ſubjectionis ſuæ, & fidelitatis ad Romanam Eccleſiam; Thereby to teach him his Subjection and Loyalty to the Church of* Rome. Ibidem c. 20:

But hitherto we have heard this great Schoolman by way of Diſcourſe, wherein peradventure he is more remiſs and diſſolute, than when he preſſeth his Points Logically, as the manner is in the Schools: We will therefore trace him a little in that Path; if firſt we ſhall obſerve, that it is his cuſtom, when He handleth a Queſtion that doth concern the Church of *Rome*, as ſoon as He hath propounded it, He firſt proceedeth with his *Videtur quòd non*, and bringeth ſometimes both Scriptures and Fathers for the Negative part; his purpoſe ſtill being to encounter them with his, *Sed contrà eſt*; but, *ſuch or ſuch a Pope holdeth the contrary*: And then He cometh in firſt with his Concluſion, and ſecondly with his *Dicendum eſt*; wherein He ſo laboureth and beſtirreth himſelf, as that always the ſaid Scriptures and Fathers are wrung and enforced to yield to the *Pope*: As for example, Having propounded this Queſtion, *Whether for Apoſtaſie from the Faith a Prince doth*

T t *loſe*

22. 2x. Quæst. 12. art. 2.

Card. Toledo.
Card. Alanus.

lose his Dominion over his Subjects ; *and so consequently, if he be Excommunicated,* (there being the same Reason for the one, as there is for the other, as two great Cardinals do affirm) He falleth upon his *Videtur,* saying, *It seemeth that a Prince for Apostasie from the Faith doth not lose his Dominion over his Subjects, but that they are still bound to obey him:* For St. *Ambrose* saith, That *Julian* the Emperour though he were an *Apostata,* yet had under him Christian Soldiers; to whom when he said, Bring forth your Army for Defence of the Commonwealth, they obeyed him. Therefore for the Apostasie of the Prince, their Subjects are not absolved from his Dominion. Moreover, an *Apostata* from the Faith is an Infidel : but some holy men are found faithfully to have served Infidel-Masters, as *Joseph* did *Pharaoh, Daniel Nebuchadnezzar,* and *Mardochee Assuerus*; Therefore for Apostasie from the Faith, it is not to be yielded, but that such a Prince must be obeyed by his Subjects. *Sed contra est, quod* Gregorius *septimus dicit* ; *But* Gregory *the Seventh is of a contrary Opinion,* where he saith, *We keeping the Statutes of our holy Predecessors, do by our Apostolick Authority absolve from their Oath those who are bound to excommunicate persons by Fealty, or the Sacrament of an Oath* ; *and do by all means prohibit them, that they keep not their Fidelity unto them, until they come to satisfaction.* Whereupon *Thomas* concludeth, *That all* Apostata's *are Excommunicated, sicut & Hæretici, As all Hereticks are* ; *and that therefore their Subjects are delivered from their Obedience and Oaths of Fidelity unto such Lords and Princes* ; and so addeth his *Dicendum est :* "Where dallying and
" shifting with his Distinctions, the Answer which he
" maketh to the Words of St. *Ambrose*, is this ; at that
' time the Church being in Her minority, had not the
" power to bridle Princes ; and that therefore she
" suffered the Faithful to obey *Julian* the *Apostata* in
" those things, *Quæ nondum erant contra Fidem, Which
" were not then against Faith* ; *Ut majus periculum Fidei*
"*vi-*

"*vitaretur*, That the greater danger of Faith might be *ef-*
"*chewed*. And the second Objection He more slightly
"passeth over, saying, That there is not the like Reason
"of *Infidels* and *Apostata's*. And thus this great Schoolman relying upon the Authority of *Gregory* the Seventh, had adventur'd to oppose himself against the
Examples alledged out of the Old Testament, against
the Practice of the Primitive Church, and against the
Judgment of St. *Ambrose*, not caring how many Thousands by this Rebellious Doctrine might come to Destruction, so as the Bishops of *Rome* might have the
World at their commandment. We here omit, how
as *Thomas*, and divers others writ many large Volumes
upon *Peter Lombard* the *Master of the Sentences*, his *Distinctions*; so afterward, and especially of later Times,
Books upon Books have been published upon his (the
said *Thomas*'s) Works; all of them pursuing, as
they come unto it, this seditious and trayterous Doctrine so Clerk-like handled by their Master: Only we
observe this great Schoolman's Conscience, how in labouring to shift off the Truth maintain'd by St. *Ambrose*, he could pass over a Lye in *Gregory* the Seventh,
where he saith, *That in absolving of Subjects from their
Oath of Obedience, and in prohibiting them from performing
their Duties and Fidelity towards their Soveraigns*; *He followed the Statutes of his holy Predecessors*: Being himself
the first that ever durst be so desperate: As also that
he confesseth, it was not in St. *Ambrose* his time, *contra
fidem* for Subjects to obey their Soveraigns, though they
were either *Infidels*, or Excommunicate; and likewise
how thankfully the Bishops of *Rome* accepted and approved this Man's Travels, so resolutely undertaken on
their behalf. *Urbanus* the Fourth did so admire him,
as he reputed his Doctrine *Veluti cœlitus delapsam*, *As to* Aug. Hunn. E-
have fallen from Heaven. *Innocentius* so admired both pist. ad Pium
Him and his great Learning, *Ut ei primum post Canoni-
cam Scripturam locum tribuere non dubitaverat*; As he
     T t 2   *doubteth*

doubteth not to give unto Him and to his *Works* the next place after the *Canonical Scriptures*: And *John* 22th. made him a Saint in the Year 1329, about forty nine years after his Death: He was born during the Reign of *Henry* the Third, King of *England*; died about the second Year of King *Edward* the First, and was Canonized a Saint in the time of King *Edward* the Second: so ancient is this Chief Pillar of Popery.

<small>Surius de Sanctorum Histor. tom. 2. Martii 7.</small>

Placet eis.

John Overall.

CAP. XI.

<small>Genebr. Chronol.</small>

Justinian the Emperour, about the Year 533. did so contract the Civil Law, as he brought it from almost 2000 Books into 50; besides some others, which he added of his own. Howbeit shortly after it grew out of Use, in *Italy*, by reason of the Incursions of sundry barbarous Nations, who, neglecting the Imperial Laws, did practise their own: till after almost 600 Years, that *Lotharius Saxo*, the Emperour, about the Year 1136 did revive again in that Countrey, and in other places also, the ancient Use and Authority of it. Which Course of the Emperour did not much content (as it seemeth) the Bishops of *Rome*; because it revived the Memory of the ancient Honour and Dignity of the Empire. Whereupon, very shortly after, *Eugenius* the Third set *Gratian* in hand to compile a Body of Canon-Law, by contracting, into one Book, the ancient Constitutions Ecclesiastical, and Canons of Councils; that the State of the Papacy might not, in that behalf, be inferiour to the Empire. Which Work the said *Gratian* performed, and published in the days of *Stephen*, King of *England*, about the Year 1151.

<small>Abbas Urfperg. Curion. Chron.</small>

<small>Petr. Greg. Partition. Juris Canon. l.1.c.1.</small>

terming

terming the same *Concordia discordantium Canonum, a Concord of disagreeing Canons.* Of whose great pains therein, so by him taken, a Learned Man saith thus; *Gratianus ille Jus Pontificale dilaniavit, atq; confudit;* that fellow, Gratian, *did tear in pieces the Pontifical Law, and confound it*; *the same being, in our Libraries, sincere and perfect.* But (this Testimony, or any thing else to the contrary, that might truly be objected against that Book notwithstanding) the Author's chief Purpose being to magnifie and extol the Court of *Rome*; his said Book got (we know not how) this glorious Title) *Decretum aureum Divi Gratiani,* The Golden Decree of S. *Gratian*; and he himself (as it appeareth) became, for the time, a Saint for his Pains. [Aventin. l. 5.] [Decret. Grati impress. Parif. 1510.]

Indeed he brake the Ice to those that came after him, by devising the Method, which since hath been pursued, for the enlarging, and growth of the said Body, by some of the Popes themselves. *Gregory* the Ninth, about the Year 1236. and in the time of King *Henry* the Third, after sundry Draughts made by *Innocentius* the Third, and others, of a second Volume of the Canon-Law, caused the same to be perused, enlarged, and by his Authority to be published; and being divided into 5 Books, it is Entituled, *The Decretals of Gregory the Ninth.* *Boniface* the Eighth, the great *Augustus* (as before we have shewed) commanded likewise another Collection to be made of such Constitutions and Decrees, as had either been omitted by *Gregory,* or were made afterward, by other succeeding Bishops and Councils; and this Collection is called, *Sextus Liber Decretalium,* the *Sixth Book of the Decretals*; and was set out to the World in the Year 1298. in the Reign of K. *Edward* the First. *Clement* the Fifth, in like manner, having bestowed great Travel upon a Fourth Work, comprehending 5 Books, died before he could finish it: but his Successour, *John* the 22th. did, in the Year 1317. and in the time of King *Edward* the Second, [Petr. Greg. ib.] [Genebr. Chronol.] [Proœm. Clementin.]

make

make perfect, and publish the same Work of *Clement*, and gave it the Name of *The Clementines*. Afterward also came out another Volume, termed *The Extravagants*; because it did not only comprehend certain Decrees of the said *John* the 22*th*. but likewise sundry other Constitutions, made by other Popes, both before and after him; which flew abroad uncertainly in many Mens hands, and were therefore swept up, and put together after the Year 1478. into one Bundle, called *Extravagant Decretals*, which came to light *post sextum*, *after the sixth*. By which Title the Compiler of this Work, would gladly (as it seemeth) have had it accounted the *seventh Book of the Decretals*: but it never attaining that Credit, the same by *Sixtus Quintus*'s Assent is attributed to a Collection of certain other Constitutions, made by *Peter Matthew*, of divers Popes, from the time of *Sixtus* the Fourth, who died in the Year 1484. To all these Books mentioned, there have been lately added Three great Volumes of *Decretal Epistles*, from St. *Clement* to *Gregory* the Seventh's days; also a huge Heap of the *Pope's Bulls*, from the said *Gregory*'s time to *Pius Quintus*; and lastly no short summ of *Papal Constitutions*, set forth a little before the said 7*th*. Book of the *Decretals*. So as all these Volumes being put together, they exceed as far the Body of the Civil Law, as the usurped Dignity of the Papacy exceedeth the mean Estate of the Empire.

Placet eis.

John Overall.

CAP.

WE have in the former Chapter made mention of the new and later sort of *Decretals*, *Bulls*, and *Constitutions*, not knowing what Credit the *Popes* will bestow upon them hereafter; and therefore leaving them to their Chance, we have thought it expedient to return to the ancient *Canon-Law*, revived and approved not long since by *Gregory* the Thirteenth, where we find a new Ocean of Questions, Disputations, Quarrels, and Brabblements: For as it happen'd with the Civil-Law, that it no sooner was again renew'd and restor'd by *Lotharius*, but sundry great Doctors began to write many Books and Commentaries upon it, to explain it, and to discuss the Difficulties which did arise in it: So fell it out with the *Canon-Law*, the number being almost infinite of Glossographers, that made short Notes upon it, and of *Canonists*, who set forth large Discourses for the salving of Contradictions, and many other Absurdities. Amongst all which Lawyers, Doctors, Glossographers, and Canonists, assisted (as every Man's Fancy led him) with many Schoolmen and sundry Divines, such as they were, there did shortly after grow many great Controversies and endless Oppositions. The *Civilians* of *Italy* perceiving by the body of the *Civil Law*, how far the Empire was dejected from that Royal Estate and Majesty which once it enjoyed; and finding also that many of the best Reasons in their Judgments, which the Popes, the Canon-Law, the Glossographers, the Canonists, the Schoolmen and many more, had brought to prove that the Pope ought to have Jurisdiction over all the Churches in the World; (as, that Bees had a Captain; that Beasts a Leader; that One is fit to end Controversies;

Genebr.Chron.

that

Dominic. Soto de Jure, & Justit. lib. 4. Quæft.4.Artic. 2.Barth. Caſſanæus in Cat. Glor. Mundi, part.5. confid. 29. Navarr. in cap. Novit.

that a Monarchy is the beſt Form of Government, and that One muſt be over All to receive Appeals, to give Direction unto All, to puniſh all rebellious perſons, and many ſuch like) were fully as forcible, and ſtrong to prove, that there ought to be one Emperour over all the World; they did very ſtifly and refolutely infift upon that Point, and went ſo roundly to work in it, by force of the faid Reaſons, and with many other Arguments, that ſome of them would needs have it Herefie for any man to hold the contrary; alledging a Text for their purpoſe, where it is ſaid, *That in thoſe days there*

Luc. 2. 1.

came a Commandment from Auguſtus Cæſar, *that all the World ſhould be taxed.*

Barth.Caſſan. ibid.Ferd. Vaſquez. Controv. l. 1.c. 20,21.

Againſt thoſe *Italian Civilians Ultramontane*, the *Civilians* on this ſide the *Alpes, Frenchmen, Spaniards,* and of other Countries, oppoſed themſelves with all their force; not in any diſlike of the Honour due to the Emperours, but becauſe otherwiſe their Maſters, the Kings of *France*, of *Spain*, and of divers other Kingdoms, who had freed themſelves long before from the Empire, ſhould be brought again *de jure* at the leaſt, by the foreſaid Reaſons to be ſubject unto it: Whereupon in Confutation of them, and to ſtrengthen their own Aſſertion, they alledged, that one Bee was never the Captain over all Bees, nor one Crane the General of all Cranes, nor one Beaſt the Leader of all Beaſts; that it was againſt the Law of God, the Law of Nature, and the Law of Nations; that there was never any Monarchs ſo great, but there were in the World many Kings who were never ſubject unto them; that the place of Scripture is to be underſtood of all places in the World that were then under the *Romans*, and ought to be extended no further; That a Monarchy is then beſt, when it is contain'd within ſuch limits, as it may well be govern'd; that all Monarchies hitherto had ever their bounds, which were well known: That it is impoſſible for all men to fetch Juſtice from one place, or to receive

receive thence any benefit by their Appeals; and so after many other such Arguments, they do conclude, that to think that the Emperour ought to have the Government of all the World, is a vain, an absurd, and an untrue conceit.

Now we are to consider, how in all these troubled Disputations and Oppositions, the *Glossographers, Canonists*, School-men and Parasitical Divines, that were sworn to the Pope, behaved themselves. As soon as the Civil Law began to flourish, as being read by the Emperour's Commandment, in sundry Universities; *Gregory* the Ninth, began to smell what was like to come of it, and therefore did afterward forbid it to be read in *Paris*, being the especial Place then (as it seemeth) where it was most esteemed. But as touching the Point so controverted, when these Champions of the Popes saw how the Matter went, That either they must hold, that there ought to be but one Emperour over all the Kingdoms in the World, or else be forced to confess, that there ought not to be One Pope over all the Churches in the World (the same Reason being as pregnant for the one, as for the other) they joyned with the *Italian Civilians*, that there ought to be but one Emperour. Marry how? Forsooth remembring *Gregory* the Seventh, *Adrian* the Fourth, *Innocentius* the Third, and that great *Augustus Cæsar*, *Boniface* the Eighth, and divers other Popes, how Emperour-like they had demeaned themselves, and what great Authority they challenged; the said Pontifical Champions fell to this Issue, That the Pope being Christ's Vicar, who was *Lord of lords, and King of kings*, it must needs follow, that the Pope was likewise that One Emperour, who was to govern all the World, in Temporal Causes, as he did all the Churches in the World in Ecclesiastical Causes. And thereupon they reasoned in this sort: " Christ is Lord of all the World:
" but

Carion.Chron.

Genebr. Chronol.

Ferdin. Vasquez. ut suprà.
Barth. Cassan. ut suprà.

" but the Pope is Chrift's Vicar on Earth: therefore
" the Pope is Lord of all the World. Again; The
" Emperour is the Pope's Vicar, and his Succeffour, in
" all Temporal Caufes: therefore the Emperour is
" Lord of all the World; all Temporal Jurifdiction
" being habitually in the Pope; and from him derived
" to the Emperour. And many of the *Italian* Lawyers,
efpecially fuch as mixed their Studies with the Canon-
Law, were well enough content, that fo as the Emperour might be Lord of all, how, and whence he had
it, whether from God, or from the Pope, they ftood
indifferent. But for all this, the *French* and *Spanifh*
Lawyers ftuck to their tackling, and were peremptory,
That neither the Pope, nor the Emperour had any fuch
Univerfal Dominion over all the World. And divers
likewife of the faid *Italian* Doctours, that were not
too much addicted to the Canon-Law, were not afraid
to hold, and maintain, That the Empercur held as well
from God the Authority, which he had, as the Pope
did his Papacy. Howbeit fuch was the Clamour of
the *Canonifts*, of the *Gloffographers*, and of the *Schoolmen*, and *Divines*, that took their part in the Pope's
behalf (upon whom all their Preferment, Credit, and
Countenance did depend) as they would needs, by
force, carry the Bell away; though their Oppofites,
each of them, were very confident, that the common
Opinion fway'd with their fide; more ftanding for
them, than were againft them.

We have before briefly touched the chief Grounds and
Reafons, whereupon the *Civil Lawyers* (divided amongft
themfelves) did infift: and therefore, that we may
not feem partial, we thought it fit to hear the *Canonifts*
with their Adherents, whilft they tell us, That all the
World is the Pope's, at his difpofition; as well the
Emperour, as any other the meaneft Perfon whofoever:
" Becaufe (1.) that Chrift had all Power given him.
" (2.) That

" (2.) That the Pope blesseth the Emperour. (3.) Navarr.Relect.
" That the Bishops of *Rome* do anoint them. (4.) Notabil.
" That the Church Triumphant hath but one Prince.
" (5.) That *Innocentius* told the King of *France*, that
" he did not intend to abate his Jurisdiction; whereby
" it is collected, that, if he had pleased, he might have
" so done. (6.) That in the Vacancy of the Empire
" the Pope hath the Government of it. (7.) That
" the Pope translated the Empire from the *Grecians* to
" the *Germans*. (8.) That the Papacy exceedeth the
" Empire, as far as Gold doth Lead, or as Men do
" Beasts. (9.) That Pope *Nicholas* saith, Christ gave Stanisl. Orisho-
" to St. *Peter*, the Key-Carrier of Eternal Life, *Jura* vius in Chimæ-
" *terreni simul & cælestis Imperii*; The Authority both of
" *the Earthly, and of the Heavenly Empire*. (10.) That
" *Optimum optima decent*: but the Monarchical Go-
" vernment is best, and so fittest for the Pope. (11.)
" That no Man giveth that to another which he hath
" not himself: but the Pope giveth Licence to chuse
" the Emperour, and to govern in Temporal Causes.
" (12.) That as the Body is for the Soul, so Tempo-
" ral Government is for the Spiritual. (13.) That
" Reason teacheth us, when an Office is committed
" to any, that also is thought to be committed, with-
" out the which it cannot be executed: but except the
" Bishop of *Rome* may rule all the World, he cannot
" discharge the Office, that is committed unto him.
" And (14.) *lastly*, (to omit infinite such like Collecti-
" ons) this Argument is reserved after many other, by
" a great Clerk, that it might strike home, *viz.* be-
" cause it is defined, by *Boniface* the Eighth, that *No*
" *Man can be saved, except he be subject to the Bishop of*
" *Rome*. Which Argument is held so strong, as it
" carries with it divers other of little less Force than
" it self; as that St. *Peter* had a Sword, because Christ
" bad *him put up his sword*. (2.) *Ecce duo Gladii*, Be-
" hold

"*hold here are two Swords*: One Sword muſt be under "another: the Temporal under the Spiritual. *(3.)* "It is not agreeable to the general courſe of things, "that they ſhould have all equally their immediate be- "ing. *(4.)* The Spiritual Power ought to inſtitute "the Temporal. *(5.)* The *Spiritual Man judgeth all* "*things*: and therefore what Catholick can deny, that "the Biſhop of *Rome* hath both Swords, the One actu- "ally, the Other habitually, to be drawn at his Com- "mandment.

We have not quoted the ſeveral Authors, that are Parties unto the Particulars, which we have touched in this Chapter: becauſe twenty ſuch Margents would not contain them. Only we refer our ſelves, in that behalf, to theſe few, which we have noted and ſelected from the reſt: Unto which Number if we ſhall add *John* of *Paris*, *Bellarmin*, and *Covarruvias*, they altogether will furniſh a Man with divers ſorts of other Authors, ſuch as they are, who have diſputed theſe Points at large, and in that manner, as we are driven into a great admiration, that any Men of Underſtanding could be ſo ſottiſh, either to write, as they have done, or to give any Credit to ſuch ridiculous Janglings: or rather indeed, that ever Chriſtian Kings and Princes ſhould have endured ſuch Impoſtors, ſo long to ſeduce their Subjects, and preſumptuouſly to ſhake and diſhonour the Royal Authority, given them from God to have bridled ſuch Inſolency.

Marginal notes: Johan. de Pariſ. tract. de pot. Regiâ, & Papali. Bell. de ſum. Pont. l. 5. c. 1. Didac. Covarruv. 2. part. Relect. §. 9.

Placet eis.

Jo. Overall.

CAP.

CAP. XIII.

Notwithstanding that the Bishops of *Rome*, especially since *Gregory* the Seventh's time, have ruffled, and tyrannized, as before we have shewed; and that still they have been supported in all their wicked attempts, partly by stirring up Subjects to rebel against their Soveraigns, and partly by the *Canonists, Schoolmen, Monks, Friers,* Hirelings and Flatterers: Yet their Hypocrisy, Pride, Covetousness, and Ambition, were never so closely cover'd, and cloaked with St. *Peter's* name, and sundry other Falshoods, Wringings, and Wrestings, but that their nakedness in that behalf, with all their Deformities, were clearly discover'd by the wiser sort; and there were always some, that spared not, as there was occasion, for the discharging of their Consciences, to speak the truth. When the said *Gregory* did so proudly encounter with the Emperour *Henry* the Fourth, he was Condemn'd for a perjur'd Person, and depos'd from his place, by a Council held at *Worms*, in the year 1076. by all the Bishops of *Germany* almost, saving those of *Saxony*, who in his Quarrel were become Traytors to the Empire. And afterward also, in the Year 1080. the said *Gregory* was more roughly handled in another Council of thirty Bishops at *Brixia*; wherein he was declared to be a *perturber of the Christian Empire, a sower of Discord, a Protector of Perjury, a Murtherer, a Necromancer, one possess'd with a wicked Spirit, a Man altogether unworthy of the Papacy*; and *therefore to be deprived, and expelled.*

  Henry the Fifth, with his Council, did easily discern the packings both of *Paschal* the Second, and of his Predecessors; "When he complain'd of their thrusting

Abbas Usper-
genf.An. 1076.
Aventin. l. 5.

Urspergenf.
An. 1080.
Aventin. l. 5.

Aventin. l. 6.

"him

"him into Arms against his Father; and how, *Geni-*
"*tore oppreſſo, his Father being overborn*, they ſought
"likewiſe his ſuppreſſion and overthrow. He charged
"them with great Unthankfulneſs, in that, being
"made rich by the Emperours, they were never ſatiſ-
"fied; but under a Religious pretence of Eccleſiaſtical
"liberty, deſired ſtill more and more; and that by
"ſhaking off from their ſhoulders all duties and ſub-
"jection, they did affect the Empire it ſelf, and would
"not ceaſe until they had it ended. With this the

Ibidem.

Emperour's plainneſs, the ſaid *Paſchal* being incens'd, made certain unlawful Decrees againſt the ſaid Emperour: which Decrees the Divines of *Fraxinum* (who were accounted the moſt learned men in all *Germany*) did condemn and reverſe, as being contrary to the word of God. Upon the inſolent Speeches of *Adrian* the Fourth's Meſſenger, one, that was preſent, had ſlain

Ibidem.

the ſaid Meſſenger, if the Emperour had not ſtaid him. And two Archbiſhops thereupon did write to *Rome*, accuſing the Prieſts there of Pertinacy, Pride, Covetouſneſs, and Faction againſt the Emperour; ·requiring them to give *Adrian* their Pope ſome better Counſel.

Matth. Pariſ. in Hen. 3. Aventin. l. 7.

Frederick the Second, in one of his Letters to the Princes of Chriſtendom, in defence of himſelf againſt *Gregory* the Ninth, does likewiſe moſt notably deſcribe the ambitious aſpiring hearts of the Biſhops of that See; affirming, "That they ſought the overthrow of
"the Empire, and to bring all Men in ſervitude under
"them, to the end, that they themſelves might there-
"by be the more feared, and reverenced, than Al-

Munſter Coſmogr. l. 3. Aventin. l. 3.

"mighty God. But the Archbiſhop of *Juvavia*, now called *Saltzburg*, in an Oration, which he made in a Council of State, during the ſaid Emperour's Reign, exceedeth in this Argument; where he affirmeth, that thoſe Biſhops, *Libidine dominandi*, did trouble the whole World,

World, *audendo, fallendo, & bella ex bellis ferendo*. Also *Otho Regulus Boiorum*, the Prince of *Bavaria*, in the days of *Innocentius* the Fourth, told the Bishops, that joined with the Pope, that as they grew to their greatness by discord, so being overcome with desire of honour, in stirring up Wars, they were worse than *Turks*, or *Saracens*. Moreover in the days of *Honorius* the Fourth, the Bishop of *Tulle*, when the Pope would have set the Emperour in War against the *French*, and under that pretence, required by his Legate, of all the Clergy in *Germany*, *Non Decimas, sed Quartas*, not the Tenth, but the Fourth part of their Livings, moved the said Clergy, and many of the State, then present, that they should no longer submit themselves unto the *Romish* Vultures, who had very long tyrannized, and labour'd nothing more, than to thrust Princes into War, one against another: adding thereunto, that the Pope had arm'd the *Scythians*, *Arabians*, and *Turks*, against them; and that he verily thought, that the Pope loved them better than he did the *Germans*.

<small>Ibidem.</small>

<small>Ibidem.</small>

And what Men thought, when they durst speak of the Bishops of *Rome*, and his Priests, in the days of *Nicholas* the Fourth, it may appear, by the words of a Nobleman, one *Menardus*, Earl of *Tyrol* (as we conceive) when he said, *That he would never make himself a scorn to such effeminate Antichrists, and prodigious Eunuchs; who being indeed* (saith he) *our Servants, do fight for superiority, and would domineer over us, that are their Lords.* They are worse than *Turks*, *Saracens*, *Tartars*, and *Jews*; *and do more injury to Christian simplicity.* Dominationem arripiunt, they will by force over-rule all. In the time of *Ludovicus Bavarus* the Emperour, although three Popes successively opposed themselves against him, with all the mischievous practices that they could devise; yet many learned Men, both Divines and Civil Lawyers, did justify the Emperour's Proceedings, and condemn

<small>Avent:n. ut supra.</small>

<small>Marsil. Patavin.
Jo. Gandaven.
Luit. de Berbenburg.
Andr. Bishop of Fraxin.
Ulric. Hangenor.</small>

the

<small>Dante Aligerius.
Will. Ockam.
Bona Gratia.
Mich. Cæsenas.
Anton. Patavin.
Aventin. l. 7.</small>

the Popes. And some wrote Books to that effect, saying to the Emperour, *Tu nos pugnis, ense, ferro*, &c. *Do thou deliver us from the Pope's servitude by force*, &c. *Nos te lingua*, &c. *And we will revenge our quarrel, with our Tongues, our Pens, our Letters, our Stile, our Books, and words.* And thereupon accordingly (as their own Author saith) they proved by the testimony, both of Divine and humane Laws, *Joannem libidine dominandi insanire*, that John *the Pope was grown mad through his desire of Principality and Soveraignty.* Also the Empe-

<small>Ibidem.</small>

rour himself, about the year 1324. speaking in scorn of the said *John* the 22th saith, That *the Pope, in taking upon him to be both* Augustus *and* Pontifex, *shew'd himself therein to be* Monstrum biceps, *a Monster with two heads; and that it was apparent, by Divinity, and all Laws, that the Bishop of* Rome *had no interest to both these Dignities.* Many notable things are contain'd in divers of this Emperour's Letters and Decrees, as also in the said Orations and Writings, above here mention'd, which are very worthy to be perused, and made more known than they are: All of them labouring to suppress that Insolency of the Bishops of *Rome*, in challenging to themselves the Right of the Empire, and the Authority to confirm the same, as they thought good; making the Emperours thereby their Vicars, or Substitutes.

But it is most of all worthy the diligent Observation, That in these later times, when the grosness of Popery hath been more throughly looked into and scann'd; the *Jesuits* themselves are grown to be asham'd of the said most absurd, and ridiculous challenge. And there-

<small>Bell. de Rom. Pont. l. 5. c. 1.
——c. 2.
——c. 3.</small>

fore *Cardinal Bellarmin* hath written five Chapters against it, wherein he first distinguisheth them from Catholick Divines, who maintain'd that Opinion: and then setting down these three Propositions, as sure grounds of truth, viz. *Papam non esse Dominum totius Mundi;*

Mundi; That the Pope is not Lord of all the World: *Pa-* c. 4. *pam non esse Dominum totius mundi Christiani*; That the Pope is not Lord of all the Christian World: *Papam non habere ullam temporalem Jurisdictionem directe*; That the Pope hath no temporal Jurisdiction directly; he confuteth their Arguments, who are of another Judgment. Where c. 5. he shaketh off, very lightly, the chief places of Scripture, and some other Testimonies, whereupon the said Arguments are principally grounded; as that of *Two Swords*; and where Christ saith, *All power is given unto me, in Heaven and Earth*: And the Testimony likewise of Pope *Nicholas*, affirming that Christ committed to *Peter*, the Key-Carrier of Eternal Life, *terreni simul & cœlestis imperii Jura*, the Interest both of the Earthly and Heavenly Empire; which he casteth away, either as an Assertion, forged by *Gratian*, (the same being not found in the said Pope's Writings) or else to have another sense, this (as it is urged) being against the said Pope's direct Words, in one of his Epistles.

His first Proposition, "That the Pope is not Lord of c. 2. "all the World, he justifieth, in respect, (1.) That "Infidels are not his Sheep. (2.) That he cannot "judge Infidels. (3.) That Princes, Infidels, are true, "and supreme Princes of their Kingdoms; because Do-"minion is neither founded in Grace, nor Faith; as it "appeareth, because God approved the Kingdoms of "the Gentiles, both in the Old and New Testament. "And upon these said Reasons, he inferreth it to be a "ridiculous Conceit, for any Man to think, That God "gave to the Pope any Right over the Kingdoms of "the whole World; considering, that he never gave "unto him Ability to use any such Right. And for the confirmation of his second Proposition, "That the Pope c. 3. "is not Lord of all the Christian World; he proveth the same, by these Reasons. (1.) "Because if he had "any such Dominion, by the Law of God, the same
X x   "ought

" ought to appear, either in the Scriptures, or by some
" Apostolical Traditions: but it appeareth by neither:
" *Ergo*. And his second Reason is this; Christ neither
" did, nor doth take Kingdoms from any, to whom
" they do appertain; but doth rather establish them:
" therefore when the King becometh a Christian, he
" doth not lose his Terrene Kingdoms, which lawfully
" before he enjoyed; but he obtaineth new Right to
" the everlasting Kingdom: Otherwise (saith he) the
" benefit received by Christ should be hurtful to Kings,
" and Grace should destroy Nature. Also he confu-
" teth the ordinary Distinction amongst the *Schoolmen*,
" and *Canonists*, who affirm, That the Pope hath both
" Powers in himself, but doth commit the executi-
" on of the Civil Power unto others, and writeth thus:
" Whatsoever Emperours have, they have it from
" Christ: and therefore (saith he) the Bishop of *Rome*
" may either take from Kings and Emperours the exe-
" cution of their Authority, (as being himself the high-
" est King and Emperour) or he may not: If he may,
" then is he greater than Christ: if he may not; *Ergo*,
" he hath not in truth any Regal Power. And he concludeth this Point, with this Observation; " *As the Sun*
" *did not make, or institute the Moon, but God himself:*
" *so likewise the Empire, and the Pontifical Dignity are not*
" *One, neither doth the One absolutely depend upon the*
" *Other*.

Ibid. cap. 4. Lastly, To prove his third Proposition, " That the
" Pope hath no Temporal Jurisdiction directly, he reason-
eth in this sort.. " Christ, as he was Man, whilst he
" lived here upon Earth, neither took, nor would take
" any Temporal Dominion: but the Bishop of *Rome*
" is Christ's Vicar, and doth represent Christ unto us,
" *qualis erat, dùm hic inter homines viveret, as he was,*
" *whilst he lived here amongst Men:* therefore the Bishop
" of *Rome* hath no Temporal Dominion. Now before
he

he comes to the Proof of the firſt Propoſition of this Argument, and that he might make the Ground thereof more plain; he ſaith, (1.) "That Chriſt was al-
"ways, as he is the Son of God, the King and Lord
"of all Creatures, in the ſame ſort that the Father is.
"(2.) That his Kingdom is Eternal and Divine, and
"neither taketh away the Kingdoms of Men, nor can
"agree to the Biſhops of *Rome*. (3.) That Chriſt, as he
"was Man, was the Spiritual King of all Men, and
"had moſt ample Spiritual Power over all Men, as
"well faithful as Infidels. (4.) That this Spiritual
"Power of Chriſt, ſhall, after the Day of Judgment,
"be ſenſible and manifeſt. (5.) That the Glory of
"this Kingdom, did begin in our Head, Chriſt, when
"he aroſe from the dead.

Upon which Grounds he maketh theſe Inferences. (1.) "That the ſaid Spiritual Kingdom of Chriſt,
"(the Glory whereof began after His Reſurrection)
"is not a Temporal Kingdom; ſuch as are the King-
"doms of our Kings. (2.) That the ſaid Spiritual
"Kingdom of Chriſt over all Men, cannot be commu-
"nicated to the Biſhop of *Rome*, becauſe it pre-ſuppo-
"ſeth the Reſurrection. (3.) That Chriſt, as he was
"Man, if he had liſt, and had thought it expedient
"for him, could have taken upon him a Kingly Autho-
"rity, but would not: and therefore neither did re-
"ceive any ſuch Authority, neither had not only the
"Execution of any Dominion, or Kingdom, but not
"the Authority, or Power of any Kingdom Temporal. And ſo he cometh to the Proof of his ſaid Propoſition; ſaying, "That if Chriſt had any ſuch Temporal King-
"dom, He had it, either by hereditary Succeſſion, or
"by Election, or by the Law of War, or by the Eſpe-
"cial Gift of God: but He had it by none of theſe four
"ways; *Ergo*, He had no ſuch Dominion. For the Proof of all which Particulars, he taketh good Pains,

and then cometh to the Explication of these words in his second Proposition of the first Argument, concerning this point, *viz. That the Pope doth represent Christ unto us as he was, when he lived here amongst Men*; and saith, (1.) "We cannot attribute unto the Pope
"those Offices which Christ hath, either as he is God,
"or as he is an immortal and glorified Man; but those
"which he had, as he was a mortal Man. (2.) Nei-
"ther hath the Pope all the Power which Christ had,
"as he was a mortal Man. For he, because he was
"both God and Man, had a certain Power, which Men
"call *the Power of Excellency*, whereby he ruled both
"Faithful, and Infidels: But the Faithful only are
"committed to the Pope. (3.) Christ had Authority
"to institute Sacraments, and to work Miracles by his
"own Authority; which the Pope hath not. (4.)
"Christ had Power to absolve Men from their sins
"without the Sacrament, which the Pope cannot
"do.

With *Bellarmin* (that he may not bear this great burthen upon his own shoulders, and undergo alone the Envy thereof ensuing) an Army of Writers, both old and new, do concur. He hath himself set down the names of some: and for his better supportation, we have thought it fit to assist him with two more; *viz.* the Archbishop of *Compsa*, one *Ambrosius Catharinus*, and *Boëtius Epon*, a Count Palatin; whose Book *of Heroical, and Ecclesiastical Questions*, Printed at *Doway* 1588. a place wholly *Jesuited*, is greatly approved by *Tho. Stapleton*, our Countryman, and *Balthazar Seulin*, the Dean of *Amate*, a *Licentiate* of the Pope's Law, and the ordinary Visiter, or Allower of such Books as are thought meet to be published. " *Non desunt pleriq;*
Catharin. in " &c. There are many (saith *Catharinus*) who are not
Ep. ad Roman. " content with that, that is sufficient, *Ne dicam nimi-*
c. 12. " *um, that I may not say, It is too much*; Who either to
" flatter,

"flatter, or of too grofs fimplicity do affirm, that the
"temporal Dominion of the whole World, doth be-
"long of Right to the Bifhop of *Rome*, as being Chrift's
"chief Vicar. in Earth, in that Chrift faid, *All things*
"*are given to me of my Father.* *Verùm ridicula hæc pro-*
"*fecto, quæ neq; ipfimet Pontifices auderent afferere.* But
"affuredly thefe are ridiculous Joys: the Pópes themfelves
"dare not for fhame fo affirm. *Quòd autèm Papa fit Vi-*
"*carius Chrifti*, &c. For that the Pope is called *Chrift's*
"*Vicar*, what force hath it to perfwade us, that all the
"Kingdoms in the World are committed to be govern'd by
"him in temporal Caufes? Nay, faith he, *it rather in-*
"*duceth us to believe, that they are not committed unto*
"*him; quoniam Chriftus abjecit ea, & ut Homo erat, in*
"*Mundo non habuit:* becaufe he caft them from him; and
"as he was Man, had them not himfelf. And the faid
Boëtius Epon, having fet down the reafons, why fome [Heroic. qu. 5.]
have maintain'd the Pope's faid Univerfal Dominion in
temporal Caufes, and given a touch of the *Jews* Errour,
and of the Apoftles overfight in that behalf; he faith
thus, *Neq; nos forfitan Judæis multò vel meliores, vel mi-*
nùs inepti fumus, dum, &c. *And we perhaps are not either*
much better, or lefs foolifh than the Jews, whilft we do ri-
diculoufly mingle the temporal and Earthly Kingdom or Em-
pire, with the Kingdom Ecclefiaftical or Spiritual, by wreft-
ing to that purpofe the Teftimonies of the facred Scriptures,
which do nothing lefs, than make either Chrift, or Peter, *or*
the Pope, the temporal Monarch, either of the whole World,
or of the Chriftian World. *Digni profectò*, &c. *We are*
certainly worthy of this anfwer of Chrift; *Nefcitis, quid*
petatis, quidve difputetis; you know not what you ask, nor
what you difpute of.

And thus it appeareth, what Oppofition there hath
been, ever fince the days of *Gregory* the Seventh, a-
gainft the Infolency of the Bifhops of *Rome*, in challenging to themfelves fuch eminent and Soveraign Authority

[338]

<small>Henr. Quodl. 6. qu. 24. Jo. Driedo l. 2. de Lib. Christ. c. 2. Jo. de Turrecremata sum. l. 2. 113. & seq. Alb. Pighius Hierarch. Eccles. l. 5. Tho. VValdens. l. 2. Dr. Fido art. 3. cap. 76, 77, 78. Petrus de Palude de potest. Ecclesiastica. Cajetan. in Apol. c. 13. ad 6. Fr. Victoria de pot. Eccles. q. 2. Dominic. a Soto in 4. distinct. 25. q. 2. Art. 1.</small> thority temporal over all Kings and Emperours; and how in these later times, through the light of the Gospel, Men of any good parts or modesty (though otherwise our Adversaries) are driven for shame to acknowledge the truth; notwithstanding all the vain, and ridiculous Conceits, and Janglings, either of the said *Glossographers*, *Canonists*, or *Schoolmen*; or the false, proud, and insolent vauntings of the Popes themselves, from the said *Gregory* the Seventh, pretending themselves to be *Cæsars*, and *Emperours*. It is true, that *Bellarmin* laboureth afterward to advance the Pope's Authority in temporal Causes *indirectly*; thereby to bring them so far within the compass of the Pope's reach, as that he may depose them, if they hinder the good of the Church. But his dealing herein is very indirect (that we use his own word) and cannot salve his former Conclusions and Inferences: Whereby he, and the rest, have so wounded the Bishops of that See, and disclosed their Nakedness, as all their Adherents will never be able to cure them.

Placet eis.

Hæc omnia suprascripta ter lecta sunt in Domo inferiori Convocationis in frequenti Synodo Cleri, & unanimi Consensu comprobata. Ità testor,

Apr. 16.
1606.

Johannes Overall, Prolocutor.

FINIS.

www.ingramcontent.com/pod-product-compliance
Lightning Source LLC
Chambersburg PA
CBHW030317240426
43673CB00040B/1192